Praise for *The Best Argument for God*

"One finds many books on the market seeking to present arguments for the existence of God. However, Pat Flynn's book is supremely unique in that he is able to freshly introduce the necessary concepts surrounding theism in a ground-up approach while also taking the reader by the hand up the stairs toward the complex heights of classical theism. Flynn speaks from the perspective of someone who has lived and contemplated every corner of the atheistic worldview and can rationally speak to those who are the most astute in their naturalistic explanation of the world in such a way that shows empathy for their deepest intellectual concerns while marvelously showing the way toward the untenability of their conclusions. This is not done all in one bang. Rather, Flynn employs a cumulative process that, while comfortable to the reader for its systematic and easy-to-follow presentation, compresses a variety of angles, starting from the mind's thirst for explanation and reaching finally to perhaps the most difficult point in all theism-versus-naturalism debates: the problem of evil. In the end, the reader finds all the most compelling reasons for naturalism chopped down, leaving almost no breathing room. We are all very much indebted to Pat Flynn's years of thoughtful investigation into theism versus naturalism since it yielded for everyone a well-deserved title: *The Best Argument for God.*"

— **Erick Ybarra,** *author of* The Papacy

"Pat Flynn has written an informed and adventurous defense of classical theism. He deploys a traditional philosophical approach to God's existence yet with his own unique updates, flare, and wit. He shows an awareness of important objections from naturalists and provides strong rebuttals. At every turn, he introduces the reader to important philosophical concepts and provides excellent sources in the footnotes. Some philosophers prefer deductive arguments for God's existence and denigrate the strategy of worldview comparison. Others denigrate the deductive arguments and reverence the strategy of worldview comparison. Pat Flynn sets out to show that the best of both strategies leads us to classical theism. This is a must-read book if you're interested in some of the best philosophical support for the existence of God."

— **John DeRosa,** *author of* One Less God Than You,
host of the Classical Theism Podcast

"Pat Flynn is one of the most dynamic and creative thinkers today on theism and theistic apologetics, and *The Best Argument for God* is a prime example. In it, Flynn provides a new line of thought in proving God's existence. It is insightful, thorough, and very accessible. I highly recommend this book!"

— *Gary Michuta, author of* The Gospel Truth *and* Why Catholic Bibles Are Bigger

"Pat Flynn presents a powerful and innovative case for the existence of God. Flynn skillfully breaks new ground on classical Thomistic lines of inquiry. His presentation is impressively clear, and the analysis is profound. This book is a must-read for anyone interested in the latest and best work on the question of God's existence in an accessible style."

— *Joshua Rasmussen, Ph.D, associate professor of philosophy, Azusa Pacific University and author of* Necessary Existence, Who Are You Really, *and* How Reason Can Lead to God

"Patrick Flynn's *The Best Argument for God* is a gem of a book. Flynn has provided us with a text that is excellently suited to a broad readership and is especially good for classroom use. Flynn's method for addressing the question of classical theism (worldview comparison) is sophisticated and at times novel, yet he has presented his argument in a format that presupposes no prior training on the part of the reader. Moreover, the material he covers is an outgrowth of standard sources for philosophy-of-religion and natural-theology classes, and it will be read with reward by both students and their instructors. The text is not a neutral introduction but a sustained argument in defense of classical theism. Flynn, however, goes to great lengths to be charitable and to take on the very best argumentation to the contrary. Thus, *The Best Argument for God* will also be fruitfully read by those who are apt to deny classical theism. Flynn draws considerations from a sweeping range of philosophical topics — e.g., philosophy of mind, metaphysics, epistemology, moral theory, the problem of evil —so anyone looking for a primer on the very best contemporary thought in the analytic Thomist vein should see Flynn's work as a reliable access point to this field."

— *James D. Madden, Ph.D, professor of philosophy, Benedictine College and author of* Mind, Matter, and Nature: A Thomistic Proposal for the Philosophy of Mind *and* Thinking about Thinking: Mind and Meaning in an Era of Technological Nihilism

THE BEST ARGUMENT FOR GOD

PATRICK FLYNN

THE
BEST
ARGUMENT
FOR
GOD

SOPHIA INSTITUTE PRESS
Manchester, New Hampshire

Cover by LUCAS Art & Design, Jenison, MI

Cover image: *God Took Enoch* by Gerard Hoet

Sophia Institute Press

Box 5284, Manchester, NH 03108

1-800-888-9344

www.SophiaInstitute.com

Sophia Institute Press is a registered trademark of Sophia Institute.

paperback ISBN 978-1-64413-780-2

ebook ISBN 978-1-64413-781-9

Library of Congress Control Number: 2023943677

Acknowledgments

For their feedback on the contents of this book, I must especially thank Suan Sonna, Danny O'Malley, Joshua Rasmussen, Gaven Kerr, Jim Madden, Lydia McGrew, and Kevin Vost (RIP). I also owe an enormous debt of gratitude to Michael Torre, a friend and mentor, for his patient instruction on theological matters beyond my area of competence. Above all, I am incalculably grateful to my wife, Christine, for her constant help with this project and her beautiful presence. True cliché that I could have done none of this without her.

Contents

THE BEST ARGUMENT FOR GOD

Introduction: Setting the Stage

The Best Argument against God?

WHEN THE MEDIEVAL THEOLOGIAN Thomas Aquinas addressed the best arguments against God in his masterwork the *Summa Theologiae*, he listed only two. The first was the problem of evil, which I'm sure we've all heard. This argument asks the question, "How can God — who is perfectly good — exist alongside His contrary?" In other words, if evil exists, surely God cannot.

But there is another argument that Aquinas considers, which I believe is the best argument against God, even if it is not as common or as popular as the problem of evil: Is God really needed to explain the world, or are natural principles enough? In a nutshell, we can think of this argument against God as this:

If two theories explain just as much, believe the simpler.

Theism and atheism explain just as much;
atheism is simpler.

Therefore, believe atheism.

Is this true? *Is* atheism the simpler (equally good) explanation? The purpose of this book is not just to challenge what I consider to be the best argument against God but to positively *reverse it*. Ultimately, my claim is this:

Atheism can only explain some, but not all,
of what theism can explain, and it can only do
so when strapped with greater complexity.

So, believe theism.

While more complex, this argument is the best one for demonstrating, from a purely philosophical perspective, God's existence, and throughout this book, I will lay out the argument — including all the sub-arguments assumed therein — as simply as possible.

There is a lot for us to work through. Thinking about God is not easy; it never has been, and never will be. But I will do my best to keep this book as accessible as possible while taking on the biggest challenges that confront us. Sometimes, we will have to go deep. In these deeper waters, I will guide you through whatever obstacles we encounter, while encouraging you to grapple with the material. Good armchair thinking *is* a challenge, but it is a challenge that bears remarkable intellectual fruit. This is a book for people who like thinking hard about things.

THE FINER POINTS

See this? These "finer points" sidebars are provided to dig deeper into certain points or aspects of the larger philosophical debate. As the name suggests, these points will sometimes (but not always) be a bit more technical and could be skipped without missing anything crucial. Nevertheless, they're here for those wanting to better understand the many nuances nested within the God debate.

Before getting started, there are a few things I'd like to mention, by way of introduction and expectation management and all that. First, on the personal front. Philosophically and religiously, I used to maintain beliefs quite the opposite of what I maintain now. Not only did I *not* believe in God and was quite irreligious, but I thought there were good reasons to think God did not exist at all and all religion was false. I would have counted myself among the philosophical naturalists, and while I never had any serious grouse with religious believers, religious belief just did not seem like a reasonable position to hold.

For many reasons, I have changed my perspective on both matters substantially, and some of those reasons, particularly the more intellectual ones, are shared throughout this book.

I bring this up to say that I can relate. If you are a skeptic about belief in God, here is my promise to you: Your position throughout this book will be treated with respect and understanding. I have no mockery or scorn to heap upon those skeptical of belief in God — I used to be a skeptic myself. I will, of course, be arguing against that position, but such arguments, I hope, will be seen as cooperative investigations, composed largely of 1) trying to dispel false or misleading notions about God, and 2) showing how a proper philosophical search can lead to not just belief in God, but a more refined and sophisticated understanding of divinity.

What you might come to discover is this: The god you have been skeptical of is really just a lowercase-g "god" and not the real McCoy. In that sense, your skepticism has been justified. But you might also discover there is another, different way to think about God. Maybe you had not considered this approach before and, upon consideration, perhaps you will find theistic belief to be reasonable indeed. That has been my personal experience, anyway.

Let's talk now, briefly, about how this book is organized. It'll be helpful to have a roadmap, given the nature of the upcoming terrain and its inherent complexity.

The first two chapters of this book are stage setting. I have several things to say about the relation between philosophy, science, and God, and why the question of God is properly philosophical, not strictly scientific. I will also touch upon why philosophy itself matters and how far philosophy can get us in thinking about things, including fundamental things, like God. It's important stuff, so please don't skip it.

I'll also highlight several mistakes that get people off track or prevent them from considering God's existence as a philosophical question at all.

We'll then consider the primary argument for the existence of God, which itself is composed of many different arguments all fused together. This, as you might expect, is the meatiest and most substantial part of the book. But the presentation is largely narrative and conversational; I want it to feel as if we are sitting next to each other, perhaps at some coffee shop or pub, exploring ideas together, in a relaxed but nevertheless serious way. Don't think this makes the argument less than rigorous. The arguments presented are rigorous — quite rigorous, in fact. I'm just interested in doing my best to make it accessible and engaging because, like I said, there are some difficult ideas we are going to have to wrestle with, but even the challenge can be fun.

For those familiar with philosophical approaches to God, you will notice this book actually blends methodologies: a traditional metaphysical approach for inferring the existence of God alongside a more contemporary "worldview comparison" approach. The details of these different approaches will be discussed shortly, but for now, here's what you need to know:

We will begin our investigation with fundamental reality, asking, first off, whether there is a most fundamental reality. To accomplish this, we'll use a traditional philosophical method that will help us see what the "necessary conditions" are for anything to even exist at all, and this will form our Fundamental Theory of Everything (call this our "worldview hypothesis"), which is classical theism. We will pick up additional confirmation of our worldview hypothesis, showing, for example, how well the classical theistic theory explains very many broad features of the world, including our experiences with things such as order, stability, morality, reasoning and so on. The reason for combining approaches is not just to help bolster a person's confidence in the existence of God but to fill out our theistic world picture and hopefully come to better understand the relation between God and the world — ultimately, between God and ourselves.

Along the way, we will wrestle with many big questions, questions concerning why anything exists, why anything continues to exist, how beings with minds emerged, and why suffering and evil occur — not easy things to consider, but consider them we will.

Finally, an obvious disclaimer: Not everything on such a topic so broad and so deep can be covered in a single volume. There are always further questions to be explored and new and interesting objections to answer. For my part, I have done my best to include what I believe are the most important and challenging objections to classical theism (many of which are considered throughout the development of the primary argument, while others are treated separately in the appendix on objections), while indicating other interesting aspects of the debate in footnotes. I encourage the reader to allow this book to be not the end of their investigation, but the beginning, and I hope to make it an exceedingly strong start.

Explaining Terms and Exposing Common Mistakes

As the title suggests, this is a book about God. However, that does not mean this is a book about religion or prayer or mystical experience. Instead, this is a philosophy book.

And in the pages that follow, we're going to lay the foundations for our study. These foundations — including terminology, the differences between philosophy and science, and the different methods of philosophy — are all important to the arguments that I will be laying forth later in this book. So, let's spend some time together setting the stage as we explore our God Hypothesis.

As mentioned above, this is a philosophy book. Specifically, this is a book in the category of *philosophy of religion*. Unfortunately, that phrase can be misleading. Philosophers of religion are not just a bunch of religious people. In fact, some affirm the existence of God, some deny the existence of God, and some are quite unsure about the existence of God. Philosophers of religion are *system builders*, discerning as much about fundamental reality as possible and constructing or discovering a worldview from their endeavors.

Common Terms We'll Encounter along the Way

When we use the term **worldview**, we mean "large-scale theory of everything," or "Big Picture of Reality." And philosophers engage in *worldview comparison* to see which Big Picture makes the best sense of reality. Worldviews are systematic, attempting to explain the wide range of human experience, from causation to ethics to science and more, with the fewest fundamental principles. There are many different worldviews. This book considers two of them, classical theism and atheistic naturalism.

Theism is the worldview that God exists.
The most prominent theistic worldview is **classical theism**. *Hang with me during this paragraph. If you're unfamiliar with any of the terms that follow, I will*

explain and define all of them as we get into our argument later, trust me! Classical theism maintains that God is absolutely the first cause of all causable things, purely actual (without intrinsic passive potency, and therefore immutable), and has no nature or essence distinct from his act of existence. Upon further analysis, it turns out these commitments entail God is also "uniquely unique" (one and only one), eternal (not just everlasting, but always existing outside of time), necessarily existing (cannot *not* exist), omnipotent (capable of bringing about all logically possible realities), omniscient (understands all essences, possibilities, contingent truths, and necessary truths), and perfectly good (suffers from no privations).[1]

Again, don't worry about understanding the above commitments just yet. For now, we're just reporting the position. We'll explain it later.

Atheism is the worldview that holds that God does not exist.

The most prominent atheistic worldview is **naturalism**, which claims nature is self-sufficient.[2] Typically, this means that the naturalist would say "there are none but natural entities with none but natural causal powers."[3] And while it is difficult to say precisely what a natural entity or natural causal power is, naturalist philosopher Graham Oppy tells us that "natural causal entities and natural causal properties are those causal entities and causal properties recognized in ideal completed, true science."[4] Confused by those last few sentences? You're not alone; unfortunately, this leaves our understanding of naturalism a

---

[1] For classical theists, being itself is convertible with goodness and truth (among other things). This is the medieval notion of the transcendentals — i.e., that certain concepts can be added to being that express a mode of being not expressed by the term "being" itself. Truth, for example, is just being as intelligible, being as graspable by some intellect or other. Likewise, goodness is just being as desirable, or perfectible. For an articulation and defense of the transcendentals, see Gaven Kerr, "Goodness and Being, Transcendentals, and Participation" in *The New Cambridge Companion to Aquinas*, ed. Eleanor Stump and Thomas Joseph White (Cambridge, UK: Cambridge University Press, 2022).

[2] Importantly, while naturalism is the most prominent form of philosophical atheism, not all atheists are naturalists. However, all naturalists are atheists.

[3] Graham Oppy, *Atheism and Agnosticism* (Cambridge, UK: Cambridge University Press, 2018), 13.

[4] Graham Oppy and Kenneth Pearce, *Is There a God: A Debate* (London: Routledge, 2021), 103.

little vague, especially since most naturalists admit "ideal completed, true science" doesn't and probably can't exist.[5] But while the definitions are vague, what is common for the naturalist is this: *there is no God or anything like a god. Fundamental reality — whatever that turns out to be — is mindless and impersonal. Essentially, we just shouldn't go beyond science.*

Going further, atheistic philosopher Paul Draper tells us naturalism is "source physicalism," meaning that the fundamental layer of reality is mindless matter,[6] which entails that the physical world existed before the mental world and caused the mental world to exist.[7] We can think of this position as Mindless Naturalism — not to be polemical, but to distinguish this interesting theory preferred among most atheistic philosophers from the various vaguely New-Age ponderings about nature being suffused with mind or that nature is God or godlike. These folks would probably not consider themselves atheists, even if they did not consider themselves traditional theists either.

Ultimately, the question of this book is whether God exists. And for our purposes, the primary worldview competitors under consideration are classical theism and naturalism. While these worldviews are not exhaustive, much of what I will say in favor of classical theism will rule out other worldview options as well, since several of the reasons presented for believing in classical theism maintain that God is *the only possible condition* that can explain certain features of the world. Other reasons are more modest, suggesting that God explains certain features of the world better than naturalism while still leaving open the possibility of other worldviews to offer an equally adequate explanation.

---

[5]   For example: what is a natural entity? Well, it is something that science tells us about, says the naturalist. What does science tell us about? Natural entities, of course. If the reader finds this articulation somewhat unhelpful, they have my sympathies. Still, I believe there is enough content within the naturalistic paradigm for us to engage it in worldview comparison.

[6]   For a discussion and rebuttal of Draper's position, see Ted Poston, "The Intrinsic Probability of Grand Explanatory Theories" at Ted Poston (blog), August 20, 2020, at tedposton.org.

[7]   Obviously, not *all* naturalists would say they are committed to source physicalism and the like, but we cannot cover every possible worldview permutation that labors under the label of naturalism, whether it should or not. So, we go with what appears most common and theoretically interesting.

Some Preliminary Remarks about Philosophy, Science, and God

With our terminology now defined, I'd like to begin by clearing away common misconceptions related to both God and philosophy. After all, there are people just as skeptical of the project of philosophy as they are the idea of God. We have science, didn't you hear? Who needs philosophy anymore anyways?

Moreover, there are other people who think that even if philosophy can be a legitimate source of knowledge in some areas, they are skeptical that it can be a legitimate source of knowledge in far-reaching areas, like questions concerning ultimate reality.

So, let us discuss some of these issues, for the sake of seeing the indispensable role philosophy plays in each of our lives, whether we know it or not, including going beyond the reaches possible for science. First, let's take a minute to discuss what exactly *is* philosophy.

The purpose of philosophical investigation is to answer philosophical questions. Simple, yes? However, it is *critical* to understand that not all questions are philosophical questions. For example, *What happens when I mix chemical (x) with chemical (y)?* is a scientific question and should be answered in a controlled environment. What separates the scientist from the philosopher is special knowledge and special equipment. The scientist answers questions by engaging in technical research and using specific forms of experimentation, which frequently require training and technology that are not available to everybody.

Philosophers, on the other hand, think about the data of common experience that is available to everyone, always. There is no special technology required for the philosopher to do their work (cushy armchairs aside) because the only work for the philosopher to do is to think hard about the puzzles that arise from ordinary life. Philosophers don't run laboratory experiments; scientists do. Occasionally, philosophers may look through telescopes, but having a telescope is not required for doing philosophy.

This isn't to say philosophers work apart from experience. It's just that philosophers work from the most general (in fact, undeniable) experience, i.e., that things exist, change, are caused, and so on. Philosophers latch onto and subsequently analyze experiential features of the world that are so broad that they cannot be coherently called into question and must therefore be considered pre-scientific. Philosophers work with experiences the denial of which would make science itself impossible.

THE FINER POINTS

Take the occurrence of change. Certain Sophists (Zeno and Parmenides, for example) argued, absurdly, that change cannot be real because it would require something coming from nothing. This cannot be right; not only do we experience change, but we cannot doubt its occurrence. To do so would involve changing our mind (which involves moving through different stages of a philosophical argument—another instance of change). Hence, any possible doubt about change can only make conceptual sense on the assumption that change is real. The question, then, is not whether change occurs, but how it is possible—that is, what conditions are necessary to affirm—that change occurs. In response to the Sophists, Aristotle answered the question by drawing a distinction between actual and potential being. Change, according to Aristotle, ultimately involves "the reduction of potential being to actual being" (a process which requires something already actual to make happen), and therefore does not involve something coming from nothing.[8] Notice also that all scientific inquiry must presuppose that change occurs: for example, when measuring some activity scientific instruments change in their recordings but nevertheless remain the same instruments. To deny the reality of change would undermine something that is essential to science itself.

There is, for example, no special equipment available (or conceivable) that could answer the question, "What is the difference between existence and nonexistence?" There is only one way to answer that question and that is to think about it, long and hard. On the other hand, there *is* special equipment to answer the question of what the physical differences are between amoeba and paramecium. The latter is a scientific question, the former a philosophical one. And it is, of course, philosophy (including philosophy of science) that helps distinguish between the two.

[8] For a detailed defense of the reality of change (and an overview of the debate) see Edward Feser, *Aristotle's Revenge* (Germany: Editiones Scholasticae, 2019), 13–20.

Unfortunately, mistakes are often made by philosophers who inadvertently try to answer questions which belong in the domain of science and, what is far more common these days, by scientists trying to answer questions that belong in the domain of philosophy. When Neil DeGrasse Tyson, an astrophysicist and science popularizer, remarks that he is skeptical of God's existence because of the problem of evil, he is not answering that question as a scientist, but as a philosopher, however competent.[9] His philosophical opinion, therefore, is only as good as the philosophical argument he uses to support it, which I often see little of.

To be fair, it is not just scientists who make this mistake of confusing philosophical and scientific questions but even some of the greatest philosophers throughout the ages. When Aristotle thought about the nature of causation, he was asking a properly philosophical question. But when Aristotle speculated on the matter of celestial bodies, he ventured beyond the realm of philosophy and into questions that ought to have been left to scientific investigation — questions which were, in fact, better answered by later astronomers who had available the equipment to look. The former question — that is, about causation — requires no special equipment. There are no experiments (nor could there ever be) that reveal the nature of causation. All science presupposes causation, just as all science presupposes change, and can only hope to describe in mathematical terms the causal relationship between entities. It is the philosopher's business to work out what causation and change fundamentally are.[10]

Another useful way to understand philosophy is to glimpse at the questions philosophers ask. Consider the following questions from the branch of philosophy known as metaphysics, which is the study of being:

Are there different modes of existence? Does everything exist in the mind or do some things have existence outside the mind? Do only physical

9   See: "Neil DeGrasse Tyson on God," YouTube video, from CBS Sunday Morning, posted by CBS on 30 April 2017, www.www.youtube.com/watch?v=4x2ZrklQQYU.
10 For a nice philosophical treatment of the nature of causation, which should help the reader understand why this is, in fact, a question that only philosophy can answer, see Michael Rota, "Causation," Michael Rota (blog), August 2020, at mikerota.files.wordpress.com/2020/08/ch8_rota-proofs.pdf.

things exist? Does everything that exists change? Does everything that exists, exist necessarily, or contingently? Are there more possible things than actually existing things?

Then there are philosophical questions of ethics, such as:

What is the difference between right and wrong? Are right and wrong the same as good and bad? What is the nature of evil? Is it possible to pursue evil for evil's sake? Are things good because we choose them, or do we choose them because they are good? Where do moral obligations come from? Are there any objective (read: universally binding, culturally independent) moral laws? Are there circumstances where goods conflict? Can there ever be such a thing as a just war? Was bombing Nagasaki wrong? Is it okay to steal a loaf of bread to feed your starving family?

Some of these questions are basic; some more complex. All are questions that no scientist can answer, at least not in their role as scientist, because these are questions that no *science* can answer. Rather, each is a proper philosophical question and deserves a proper philosophical response. Conceptually, all these questions either come prior to, or extend beyond, the scientific mode of knowing. Notice that they are questions that only philosophy can answer, *if* they can be answered at all. If the scientist has an opinion about them, that opinion is a philosophical opinion. This is fine. Everybody is entitled to philosophical opinion just so long as they are aware that that is what it is (as opposed to some established scientific consensus) and that they must offer philosophical reasons to support it. Another unique aspect of philosophy is that it is the only intellectual discipline that can interrogate fully its own foundations — foundations of thought and knowledge and so on — leaving no assumptions as *mere* assumptions. Philosophers seek to understand everything from what *is*: existence (metaphysics), change (philosophy of nature), the structure of thought (logic), knowledge (epistemology), the good life (ethics), science (philosophy of science), and authority (political philosophy).

Conversely, science comes with numerous critical assumptions that science can neither justify nor explain. From logic to mathematics, from the reality of the external world to the principle that scientists should not fabricate data, all of these are positions science itself cannot establish, nor are they questions that science can answer in any noncircular way (since science must assume these realities for its legitimacy). They are questions that philosophers think about.

The point of highlighting these, which may be painfully obvious facts to many of us, is to hedge against two common confusions of our age. The first has already been stated, that God's existence is a scientific question. The second is that science is the only way of knowing anything about reality.

This brings us to a brief evaluation of the two rival views concerning the relationship between philosophy and science. This we must also get right. Otherwise, little else in this book is going to make sense.

One view is that whatever philosophy does, it does so on the outskirts and in a territory that is either uninteresting or will be overtaken by science in due course. On this view, philosophy lingers but contributes nothing significantly useful in our modern times and will most likely expire as science expands. This would be the posture taken by certain, but certainly not all, science popularizers known to make disparaging remarks about philosophy, including the late Stephen Hawking.[11]

This position is essentially *scientism*. It makes a claim — implicitly or explicitly, and either ontological or epistemological (or both) — that science is the be-all and end-all. Whatever exists is whatever science tells us exists, and whatever we know comes through the hypothetico-deductive method, which is the pattern of gathering data, forming a hypothesis, and then making predictions to either confirm or disconfirm one's theory through subsequent gathering of evidence.[12]

THE FINER POINTS

Ontology = the study of being. Epistemology = the study of knowledge. We'll say more about each later.

---

[11] See Stephen Hawking and Leonard Mlodinow, *The Grand Design* (New York: Bantam Books, 2012), for Hawking's opinion that philosophy is dead.

[12] For further overviews and critiques of scientism, see Andrew Ter Ern Loke, *God and Ultimate Origins* (London: Palgrave Macmillan, 2018), 2–13, and Edward Feser, *Scholastic Metaphysics* (Germany: Editiones Scholasticae, 2014), 6–25.

Another position — the better position, I think — says this: science and philosophy are as distinct, if not more distinct, from one another, as many of the social and physical sciences are distinct from one another, both in the questions they ask and the methods they use to arrive at their conclusions. What the physicist does is decidedly different from what the historian does, and their methods differ respectively. They are, however, both legitimate fields of inquiry that produce unique knowledge. One could draw similar distinctions between the biologist and the engineer, and so on.

This position maintains that the truths which philosophy can uncover — truths which can be held either with certainty or strong probability — are themselves *philosophical truths*. Some of these truths are *moral* truths. Whereas science can help us produce an atom bomb, only philosophy can tell us what conditions, if any, can justify dropping one. Some of these truths are *metaphysical* truths, like the structure of being itself. Some are truths about the *nature* and *kinds* of knowledge: what counts as knowledge, as opposed to mere opinion? None of these truths, if any such truths exist, are truths which science delivers to us. Science must presuppose these truths, just as science presupposes logic, which is a branch of philosophy, by the way. Again, for science to make sense, it must presuppose intellectual virtue, an external world (i.e., that everything isn't illusion), cognitive reliability, and many other things. Science cannot prove these assumptions. If they are investigated at all, they must be investigated philosophically, since philosophy is the only discipline with no foundations left unturned.

With respect to the first position of scientism, it must either resign a great number of important questions to the category of meaninglessness or else contend that they are essentially unanswerable. Worse, as many have pointed out, the position of scientism is either trivial or self-defeating. It is trivial since it includes, more or less, everything under the category of science, in which case there is no real conflict between science and philosophy, because philosophy will count as a science under this expansive view. Alternatively, it is self-defeating, since it wants to exclude philosophy as a legitimate avenue of human inquiry, thus restricting everything to the hypothetico-deductive method, thus positing that we can only know that which comes through the scientific method. *That*, of course, is not something we know through the scientific method. It's a decidedly philosophical claim. Hence anybody who asserts it has just betrayed their commitment to the second position in order to affirm the first.

When somebody says that science has disproven God, they are confused. Science is, strictly speaking, *etiological*. It seeks to describe *how* one physical process unfolds into another physical process. Philosophy, on the other hand, and especially metaphysics, is *ontological*. It seeks to understand *why* there are any physical processes (events, things) at all. God is not a physical entity, process, or event. Thus, it would be a mistake to think questions about God are questions that science can definitively answer. When the scientist says, "If science bumps into a bearded old man sitting on a cloud, *then* we'll know that God exists," he is betraying his philosophical ignorance — not just of the nature and relation of science and philosophy, but of the nature of God as well.[13]

Of course, this doesn't mean science has *nothing* to say about greater philosophical questions. The boundaries, as we'll see later, are not always so quick, convenient, or clear. For now, I simply hang a lantern on the matter and note that any discussion about science itself disproving God is committing a category error. It hinges upon the mistaken assumption that God is something to be discovered within the physical universe, rather than the necessary condition for the existence of any physical reality, full stop.

God, then, is a properly philosophical question. As such, it deserves a properly philosophical response. Science may play some supportive role, but no specialized knowledge or equipment will be required to evaluate the arguments in this book. When it comes to "doing philosophy," Mortimer Adler reminds us, "there are no special kinds of phenomena that you can observe, no documents that you can seek out and read, in order to find out what change is or why things change. All you can do is reflect upon the question. There is, in short, nothing to do but think."[14]

Philosophy is everybody's business, not just the specialist's, and as the saying goes, you cannot escape "doing" philosophy, only doing it well. That includes the philosophy of God.

13 "Tyson on God."
14 Mortimer Adler, *How to Read a Book* (New York: Touchstone, 1972), 277.

Mistakes to Be Avoided

I want to address what I believe are common errors concerning philosophical thinking about God, not just common errors concerning philosophy in general, so let me proceed through these quickly. Many of these may not apply to you; if so, feel free to skip them. But chances are they apply at least to someone you know. So, maybe don't skip them.

Mistake #1: God Is Not Something We Can Really Think About

Perhaps you have encountered the person who claims that God is not something that can be thought about, reasoned to, or philosophized over — that God is a matter of blind faith or religious imprisonment of the mind. That is to say, God is not susceptible to rational inquiry, and thus belief in God is a matter of will, not a matter of intellect. This attitude, of course, flies in the face of history's greatest philosophers, from Plato and Aristotle to Augustine and Aquinas to Leibniz and Kant, who all thought deeply about the existence of God. Even philosophers skeptical of the existence of God, such as David Hume or Friedrich Nietzsche, thought about the existence of God, even if only to arrive at positions opposite of this book. Ironically, to even conclude that God is not something that can be thought about requires God as something which can be thought about: i.e., even being thought about only as something which *cannot* be thought about is still something which can be thought about. If necessary, re-read that sentence.

There are different ways philosophers have thought about thinking about God. Given everything to come, it will be helpful to have an overview of these approaches — if only to disprove the notion that God's existence is something beyond the realm of rational inquiry. Thinking about God is serious business and has been done by the world's most serious thinkers.

So, we'll take a brief survey of the different philosophical approaches to God. As mentioned, I combine these different approaches throughout this book, so explaining the approaches in advance will better help you to see how the primary argument for God is organized and what some of its strengths and novelties are.

First, there is what we might call the *traditional philosophical approach to God*. Philosophers, including but not limited to Aristotle and St. Thomas Aquinas, thought God could be reasoned to from various very general phenomena,

THE BEST ARGUMENT FOR GOD

such as contingent, changing, or caused being — that is, a being that didn't need to exist, is alterable, and came into existence in time (this could be anything from a cloud, hot coffee, you and I, and so on). They maintained that God's existence firmly demonstrated *the only possible explanation* for why such phenomena occur. This approach to demonstrating God's existence is metaphysical (metaphysics is the study of being as such; though, technically, some arguments for God are rooted in the philosophy of nature, not metaphysics — see the footnote if that distinction interests you) and focuses on some exceedingly general aspect of reality, aspects of reality that are pre-scientific, and then searches out the necessary conditions for the existence and occurrence of the identified phenomena (contingency, change, becoming, etc.).[15] This ultimately winds up with God as understood as something transcending or escaping the categories demanding explanation (noncontingent, unchanging, uncaused). An example of this line of argumentation would be Aristotle's Unmoved Mover argument or Aquinas's First Way[16] — arguments which, unfortunately, are frequently misunderstood on both the popular and academic level.[17]

To give just a quick, concrete example, an argumentative sketch in the spirit of Aquinas's unchanged changer might go something like this: Change occurs (water goes from cold to hot, for example). Change itself is the actualization of potential. No potential can actualize itself. Thus, anything moving from potential to actual has an already actual cause. This line of causes — if there be such — cannot regress infinitely but must terminate in something purely actual in some respect.

Further, philosophical work is then done to interrogate the nature of this purely actual reality. Is it purely actual in one respect, or all respects?

---

[15] By pre-scientific, I don't mean "naïve," only that, as these phenomena are so general, science must presuppose them. They are not something any science could verify but rather must take for granted.

[16] Aristotle, *Physics*, VIII, 4–6, and Thomas Aquinas, *Summa Theologiae*, I, q. 2, a. 3. Again, "technically," Aristotle's argument launches from philosophy of nature, which is the study of being *as mobile (changing)*. Aquinas's, on the other hand, is properly metaphysical; they are not the same argument. This is just to get certain philosophers off my heels, mainly those who love to interject with "well, *technically…*"

[17] For a stern (and highly polemical) rebuke of popular and academic misunderstandings of many of these traditional arguments for God, see Edward Feser, *The Last Superstition* (South Bend, IN: St. Augustine's Press, 2010).

Could there be more than one such entity? And so on. Philosophers, Aquinas included, ultimately maintain there can be just one purely actual reality, which is immaterial, eternal, omnipotent, omniscient, and perfectly good — i.e., God. The purpose for now is not to examine the details of such argumentation (of which there are many), but only to give the reader the general flavor of their approach.

In short, metaphysical arguments for God — or cosmological arguments, as they are often called — typically begin by identifying some feature of reality that belongs to all natural beings. The cosmological reasoner then claims that 1) this feature requires a cause distinct from itself, 2) that the subjects possessing this feature cannot account for this feature, or 3) both. Next, they claim there must exist some cause distinct from the subject to explain the subject having the feature. Finally, they show that this cause must be different in kind from the natural subjects that possess the feature.

Put differently, cosmological arguments ultimately claim there must be some cause *categorically distinct* from the caused category under consideration — i.e., an unchanging thing to explain changing things, a noncomposite thing to explain composed things, a necessary thing to explain contingent things, and so on — and this will be true no matter how many things fall into that category (finite or infinite) and no matter how those things are arranged (linearly, in a circle, etc.).

And while it is not always the business of the cosmological argument to completely interrogate the nature of the uncaused (or unchanging, or noncomposite, or noncontingent) entity, many assert that that is what people mean by God. Of course, thinkers in the tradition often run conceptual analysis upon such a reality to unpack the traditional divine attributes of classical theism, as Aquinas did.[18]

So, that is one way of thinking about God: beginning with common phenomena, then engaging cause-effect reasoning to arrive at some necessary, transcendent, primary cause. Again, let us call that the traditional approach. And the important thing to note about the traditional approach is that it purports a *necessary limitation* concerning explanation and naturalism; that is, if these arguments work, they work by showing there is something, in principle,

---

[18]   For Aquinas's exposition of the divine attributes, see *ST*, I, q.3–13.

that only God as we understand Him can adequately explain. Atheists often criticize what is called the "god of the gaps" perspective. I'll have more to say on this soon, but for now, it's important to note that this traditional philosophical approach to God does not possibly run afoul of the god of the gaps error. The traditional approach cannot be accused of arguing from ignorance, since it proceeds (or so it is claimed) deductively from what we know — really, from what cannot be coherently denied. This is not to say any of these traditional arguments ultimately work (there may be a false premise somewhere involved), but it is to say their method is of a particular form that avoids this logical error.

Other philosophers, such as St. Anselm, thought one might reason to God just from the very idea of God.[19] Descartes thought something similar.[20] That is, from the very notion of God — as that of which nothing greater can be conceived — there is necessarily included the notion of necessary existence. Thus, once one properly understands what one means by "God," one can subsequently understand that God must exist. This approach, often called *the ontological argument*, has drawn enormous attention from philosophers down the centuries and is still hotly debated today.[21] It is not the approach defended in this book, though we will utilize certain aspects of the ontological argument later in conjunction with cosmological reasoning. (There is a way, as we'll see, of melding the two.)

In more recent times, philosophers have modified their intellectual approach to God, arguing for the existence of God as the best respective explanation, though perhaps not the only possible explanation, of various specific phenomena. Scientists often do this, coming to an explanation that best fits the problem they are studying.[22] Utilizing what is called "inference to the best explanation," this modern approach is more modest than the other approaches, though advocates claim it can still provide the inquirer with powerful assurance of God's existence, even without the absolute

[19] Anselm, *Proslogion*, 2.

[20] Rene Descartes, "Meditations on First Philosophy (1641)" in *Modern Philosophy: An Anthology of Primary Sources,* ed. Roger Ariew and Eric Watkins (Indianapolis, IN: Hackett, 2009), 51.

[21] Alvin Plantinga, *God, Freedom, and Evil* (Grand Rapids, MI: Eerdmans, 1989).

[22] An example of this approach is featured heavily throughout Richard Swinburne, *The Existence of God* (Oxford, UK: Oxford University Press, 2014).

certitude claimed by metaphysical demonstration. An example of this approach would be first to acknowledge some specific data point or phenomena — say, physical fine-tuning or irreducibly complex systems in biology — and then argue that the likelihood of encountering such phenomena is greater, often far greater, if God exists than if God does not exist.[23] Thus, these phenomena count as evidential weight, however considerable, in favor of the so-called God Hypothesis. Really, this is basic hypothesis testing, just on the grandest possible scale. Of course, the skeptic will want to claim evidential weight *against* the God Hypothesis, and traditionally they have pointed toward the problem of pain in an attempt to tip the scales back the other way, by suggesting that suffering, particularly horrendous suffering, is more likely to occur if God does not exist.

Which way the scales ultimately fall, at this point, is not our concern. I am simply attempting to highlight the various ways people have thought about God across time, so as to show that thinking about God is not only possible, but a serious matter engaged by serious thinkers. Thus, if one wants to insist that God's existence is not something that can be thought about, they are separating themselves in attitude from many of the world's finest intellects, theists and atheists alike. God's existence is certainly something that can be thought about, debated, and — as is the contention of this book — rationally affirmed.

So, I think it's fair to say that it is indeed a mistake to assume God cannot be thought about. The only question is whether somebody is thinking *well* about God.

Mistake #2: The God Hypothesis Can't Be Falsified, So It Isn't Worth Real Study

Another mistake people make is this. They'll say something like, "God cannot be a good hypothesis because God is not falsifiable." This is a mistake for two reasons. First, it's not clear that the criterion of falsifiability is the be-all and

[23] For a conversation around the former point, see Geraint Lewis and Luke Barnes, *A Fortunate Universe*, (Cambridge, UK: Cambridge University Press, 2016); for the latter point, see Michael Behe, *Darwin's Black Box* (New York: Free Press, 1998) and Behe, *Darwin Devolves* (New York: HarperOne, 2020).

end-all, either in science or philosophy. This is something philosophers themselves heavily debate.

But setting that issue aside, things can be falsified in various ways. One is through empirical observation. For example, we have falsified the theory that all swans are white by discovering a black swan. But another is through *conceptual analysis*. This one is best explained with an example: We know that round squares simply cannot exist (to be a square means to have four straight lines of equal length and four vertices; a square, by the very nature of what it is, can never be round), not because we have observed a round square, but because the concept is contradictory. We have falsified the idea of a round square not by empirical considerations but by our understanding of concepts. Relatedly, various philosophers have tried to show that God has been falsified either by way of conceptual analysis (for example, paradoxes concerning omnipotence, which we'll have opportunity to consider later) or in relation to certain facts of the world, say by the occurrence of suffering, with the claim being that such an occurrence is strictly incompatible with the existence of God. While such attempts are ultimately unsuccessful in my view, *that* such attempts are made tells us that thinkers have assumed that the notion of God *can* be falsified, or if not strictly falsified, then at least evidenced against to whatever degree, which is plenty to go on when trying to establish what the true position is.

This brings us back to the concern of "god of the gaps" reasoning. The person who claims arguments for the existence of God are "gap arguments" is suggesting that the theist is wantonly plugging holes in areas of knowledge, often scientific knowledge, that while as yet unfilled, can or will be in the future in an ordinary, natural way. Often, the objector will trot out examples of where this has happened previously, ranging from the comical (such as Zeus being the explanation for lightning) to the more serious (such as evolution apparently negating the requirement of a divine designer of biological life).

Out of the three methods we've discussed for reasoning about God, including effect-to-cause "metaphysical demonstration," the ontological argument of inferring God's existence from God's nature, and inference to the best explanation, the god of the gaps charge could only possibly apply to the third method. The first two, if they work at all, do not work probabilistically, since they are not utilizing inference to the best explanation. That is, the metaphysical approach is arguing that there is just one possible explanation for the phenomena under consideration, such that if that explanation (God) did not hold, then neither would the phenomena. Again, maybe these arguments are no good. Perhaps they suffer from a faulty premise. Nevertheless, formally speaking, these metaphysical effect-to-cause arguments cannot be dismissed as arguments from ignorance.

It's the same with the various ontological arguments. Because these arguments are made a priori, if they are sound, their conclusion must follow. Again, maybe these arguments are not sound — skeptics will almost always challenge a particular premise. Nevertheless, they too are not susceptible to the charge of being an argument from ignorance, and to assume otherwise is just to misunderstand the type of reasoning involved.

The third approach, which does utilize inference to the best explanation, must be more careful about plugging gaps. Nevertheless, the best proponents of this approach are quite aware of the god of the gaps fallacy, and amply support their arguments to avoid committing it. To provide just one example, Dr. Michael Behe argues that Darwin's mechanism of selection and mutation does not adequately explain irreducibly complex systems in biology. Behe explains at great length, utilizing the best contemporary science, why this is so.[24] Thus, his argument is one based in knowledge — the best contemporary scientific knowledge, or so Behe argues (the reader, of course, must evaluate this for himself) — not ignorance. From there, one simply engages in hypothesis testing, asking whether the phenomena under consideration — in this case, irreducibly complex systems in biology — are better expected to be seen in a theistic or atheistic universe, and assign confidence levels accordingly. Again, this is not an absolute demonstration, but a probabilistic inference, and there is nothing illegitimate about engaging in such a practice. While it is possible new evidence may come around to change our perspective, this approach is using the best evidence currently available and seeing which worldview hypothesis is better supported by it. That is decidedly not randomly plugging holes in our areas of knowledge with a supernatural agency. To suggest otherwise, again, is to misunderstand the method of reasoning at play.

---

[24] Behe, *Darwin's Black Box* and Behe, *Darwin Devolves*.

The point is whatever approach one takes to thinking about God, the god of the gaps charge is not a particularly serious one and, in fact, completely irrelevant with respect to the first two methods.

Mistake #3: The Burden of Proof Is Only and Always on the Theist

The next mistake is this: assuming the theist — and the theist alone — has the burden of proof. "Burden of proof" is courtroom terminology, and in this context it relates to who has the obligation to argue for their position and whose position should be the rational default. The burden of proof, if one can help it, should be avoided. Why? Because it is almost always more difficult to argue positively *for* something than to be skeptical about it. Hence the *burden* of proof.

Nevertheless, the burden of proof debate need not detain us long. As I see it, anybody making any claim whatsoever about the world, about what exists or doesn't exist or about what we can know or cannot know, probably has a rational obligation to defend that position. This means both the theist and atheist are under a burden of proof, certainly insofar as they are claiming their position is the correct one and assuming the other person should be convinced of it.

Nevertheless, the atheist may say only the theist has a burden of proof for several reasons. First, the theist believes in everything the atheist does, plus something more — namely, God. The atheist just believes in the world and not God. Because the godless position is simpler, one should default to that.

But this analysis is simplistic and if it proved anything, it would prove too much, particularly since the philosophical solipsist — that is, the person who believes only they exist and that everything else is a projection of their mind — probably believes in less stuff than anybody else. Yet nobody thinks solipsism should be the rational default simply because it has fewer commitments to the number of existing entities. Moreover, the solipsistic position, as a fundamental theory, affects how one sees the rest of the world: in their case, as projections of mind, not things really existing independently of the subject.

It is the same with theism and atheism. If one believes in God, this drastically alters how one sees the rest of the world. To draw out this point, let me skip ahead to a few considerations that will be argued for more substantially in subsequent chapters: for the theist, the rest of reality is ultimately grounded in God's power, always continually upheld in existence by the activity of the

Supreme Being. So, there are contingent entities — things which exist but need not have existed — and there is a necessary entity which grounds and explains all the contingent entities, and which is itself explained because of its special nature.

Atheists lack this grounding, and for them, there are only contingent entities, but now possibly of two sorts: caused or explained contingent entities and uncaused or unexplained contingent entities. The theist can avoid having uncaused or unexplained contingent entities in their worldview, since everything apart from God traces back to God's creative activity. Nothing for the theist floats around as a "brute" unexplained fact.

The atheist, of course, might themselves posit a necessary reality to explain various contingent realities, but unless it bears the traditional divine attributes, this reality would require (as we'll argue later) a deeper explanation, and would be incapable of finding one. Either way, this complicates the atheistic theory in ways the initial simplistic analysis failed to capture. The point is that the theist could say, upon more substantial analysis, that the atheist believes in certain things the theist does not (e.g., ungrounded or unexplained contingent or necessary beings) and that their worldview is not obviously simpler.

Trying another strategy, the atheist may then say that theism is extraordinary and for that reason has the burden of proof. The atheist just believes in ordinary things, the theist believes in God. Extraordinary claims, they say, require extraordinary evidence. Or something like that. But again, this argument is not a very good one. For atheism, *as a theory*, is pretty extraordinary itself. As we'll see, naturalism must either maintain that everything came from nothing or that stuff has just already been around in an everlasting manner. I grant that the notion of God is extraordinary, but the fundamental atheistic claims, however they are cashed out, seem no less extraordinary and in many respects far more difficult to believe. Ultimately, the problem with this burden of proof argument is that people are not thinking in terms of fundamental theories, or Big Pictures of Reality, but just about the stuff that exists according to each respective worldview. But when it comes to wider philosophical debates, we must distinguish *the data to be explained* from *the theory that explains the data*. Once we compare theism and atheism as explanatory rivals, I hardly see one as being more extraordinary than the other; if anything, I find atheism to be more extraordinary insofar as it lacks the explanatory comprehensiveness that theism does — again, a claim to be substantiated later.

However, there is an obvious way that theism is more ordinary, and that is with respect to belief. It is not contentious to say most people from ages past and still today believe in God. Belief in a supreme being or higher power is the predominant belief around the world; atheism, however, is really something of an aberration. Due to their incredibly small numbers in many countries, Pew Research groups atheists along with agnostics and religiously unaffiliated, bringing their total to 16 percent of the entire global population, and that number is on the decline.[25] While this does not prove that God exists, it may shift the "burden of proof" if it can be maintained that basic beliefs should be the starting point and that God is a basic belief. What are basic beliefs? Things like the belief that other people have minds, belief that the external world is world, memory beliefs, and so on.

By basic beliefs, we mean beliefs that are just occasioned in us, not beliefs we infer based upon other beliefs — beliefs that are so fundamental that we hardly think to question them, or think that people who do question them have not a philosophical problem, but a psychological problem.

And as it happens, many philosophers have argued that God is a *properly basic belief*— that is, not just a foundational belief, but also reasonable and consistent within a sensible worldview — and for this reason, it is reasonable to believe in God unless some powerful argument has been set against Him. If this account is correct, and here I am just reporting it, then it seems atheism, not theism, may have the burden of proof.[26] If it counts for anything, I believe this account is correct, but space does not permit an adequate defense now. So, I am simply content to show that the theist does not obviously have the burden of proof in this debate, and that minimally both theists and atheists have the burden of proof insofar as they are proposing some grand theory of everything. In such a case, may the best arguments win.

---

[25] "The Global Religious Landscape," Pew Research Center (December 2012) at https://www.pewresearch.org.

[26] For a defense of properly basic beliefs, see Alvin Plantinga, *Warrant and Proper Function* (Oxford, UK: Oxford University Press, 1993). For the defense that belief in God is properly basic, see Plantinga, *Warranted Christian Belief* (Oxford, UK: Oxford University Press, 2000).

Mistake #4: Thinking about God Isn't Important

Okay. Another (and for our purposes final) mistake that people make when thinking about God is thinking that thinking about God is not important. There are other concerns — concerns about how to pay one's mortgage, what movie to rent this evening, or what major one should declare at university. What does it matter if God exists? What difference does it make to anyone's life?

Here my reply will be brief. God's existence matters because God is a fundamental entity, which means that if God's existence is affirmed, then his existence fundamentally alters how we view ourselves and our place in creation. There are Big Questions all of us ask about life even as children. We ask who we are (identity), where we are from (origin), why we are here (meaning), how we are to behave (morality), and where we are going (destiny). These are natural questions, questions that just arise in us. Society, or even annoyed parents or teachers, can cause us to suppress these questions, but apart from that, they are questions all of us think about. They are good questions, perhaps the best and most important questions of all.

How one answers these questions of identity, origin, meaning, morality, and destiny is deeply dependent upon one's worldview. Classical theism, which affirms the existence God, is one worldview. Naturalism, which denies the existence of God, is another worldview. These worldviews are mutually exclusive. If one is true, the other is false.

Theists tend to answer life's Big Questions differently than atheists. The believer in God (or some kind of higher power) thinks we are here because God made us (though God may have used secondary causes, like evolution, to do so), that we are ourselves made in the image and likeness of God and unique within creation, that God has given us a moral blueprint to follow for our own flourishing and happiness, that we are here to ultimately become united with God once a state of moral perfection has been reached, and that this end awaits us after death. Death, then, is not necessarily the end, but rather a transition.

The typical atheistic response to these questions is reversed. Often, they say, "We are here by accident. Nothing intended us. We are not special but differ only in degree from other lifeforms like apes. Morality and meaning is something we invent rather than discover. At death comes oblivion. It is not a comma but a period."

Of course, there are atheists who are exceptions to these responses, just as there are theists who might deny an afterlife. But in the general run, this is how theists and atheists answer these Big Questions of Life, and only the most willfully obtuse would refuse to recognize that the existence of God strongly determines these responses, either in a highly negative (if not outright nihilistic) or else optimistic way.

My suggestion is that God's existence is not just interesting to contemplate in its own right, although this is certainly true, as it forces us to exit Plato's cave, think deeply about human experience, and make the critical reflective turn that just *is* philosophy. God's existence is important because it factors into a worldview which crucially determines, whether we are aware of it or not, how we think about ourselves, our purpose in life, what constitutes proper behavior (if anything), and our ultimate destination (if any).

This brings me to the final point of this section. All of us operate according to a particular worldview or philosophical paradigm. We all live according to certain commitments, such as what we believe is true, what we believe is valuable, and what is worth pursuing. Thus, it is not a question of whether someone *has* a worldview, Big Picture, or life philosophy — everyone does, if only implicitly. Really, the question is whether someone has the *correct* worldview, Big Picture, or life philosophy. Is one operating according to how reality actually is, or is one operating according to false assumptions and uncritically held beliefs?

Socrates is known for saying that the unexamined life is not worth living. My thought, following my friend Dr. Jim Madden, is that to engage in philosophy — especially philosophy of God, which concerns asking the most fundamental questions of all — is simply to refuse to live a sham existence. To take nothing for granted, to make a critical turn back upon our experience, attempting to discover, as best we can, the nature and necessary conditions of things, and then setting everything in an understanding relation to each other and the whole — *that* is philosophy. From there, perhaps using this philosophical framework, we can orient our lives so as to make something excellent of ourselves, as God intended.

PART ONE

How Come Anything?
The Stories Philosophers Tell

CHAPTER ONE

In the Beginning: On the Hunt for Ultimate Explanation

It is time to make the case for classical theism.

We'll begin by considering a perennial question, perhaps the biggest philosophical question that can be asked: "Why is there something rather than nothing?"

Let us look at the different stories philosophers have told in response.

You may have heard it said that philosophy begins in wonder. As for me, philosophy began in anxiety.

When I was around eight or nine years old, I would look outside my grandparents' window and wonder why the world was as it was. Why does any of this exist? Why are there houses across the street and why is there a birdbath in the yard and why am I, Pat Flynn, even actual? I would not only ask why anything existed but why anything continued to exist and didn't just blip out of existence randomly. This would often agitate me: what guarantees that *I* don't just blip out of existence two minutes from now? *Is* there any guarantee that I won't just blip out of existence two minutes from now? Talk about heightening my anxiety.

THE FINER POINTS

This may seem silly at first, but seriously think about it: Why does anything, including even yourself, continue to exist? Most find the notion of us just spontaneously snapping out of existence absurd,

> but why? What justifies our not being severely worried that, five
> minutes from now, everything could be blank? Nor would it help to
> say there is some law of nature that keeps us in existence. Because
> then we can ask: what keeps that law of nature in existence and
> operating?

While our experience of something existing, whether that be a neighbor's house or the neighbor himself, is common, we should not mistake the common for the unremarkable. It surely is remarkable — indeed, the most remarkable thing of all — that anything exists. It is no less remarkable that what exists continually does so, as far as we can tell, and that it continually exists in a remarkably orderly fashion. Things are not totally chaotic. All three of these observations, common as they are — that anything exists, that anything continues to exist, and that the continuing existing things exist in an orderly fashion — require explanation. Or seem to. Wouldn't it be nice if we could have one simple theory that could explain all these observations well?

Before moving forward, I should clarify what I'm stating. I was not particularly curious then (or now) about the proximate or physical cause of things. I knew well enough that I existed because a stork brought me into my parents' home, and that some construction workers built the houses across the street, and that some factory workers created the birdbath. I was instead more concerned about why anything, physical or otherwise, should exist and not nothing instead. And why anything, physical or otherwise, keeps on existing and doesn't just stop existing randomly. Years later I would come to learn what I was asking: I was asking a question of philosophy, a question that had been asked for ages. In effect, "how come anything?"

And in the history of philosophy, there have been different stories trying to account for why anything exists and not nothing instead, different attempts to answer the question "how come anything?" The answers essentially break into three groups:

1. There is something special in the world — something in an entirely different category — that demands or guarantees something exists. In other words, *there is some further story*. Call this the Further Story account.

2. There is not something special that demands something exists; instead there is just stuff of the same sort that goes back (or down) forever. In other words, *there is just more of the same story.* Call this the Same Story account.

3. Things just are; please stop asking why. In other words, *there is no story.* Call this the No Story account.

Each story has different renditions. Some who tell Further Story have different stories about what that further story is, but generally they share the feature that Further Story involves something special in nature, something "wholly other." Others say we can make sense of the collective story of our experience by just appealing to more of the same story, and by that, I mean stuff that is not remarkably different in any relevant sense. Others insist we should stop asking questions like these, that they are either confused or meaningless, or the result of prejudice or emotional longing, but not of reasoned intelligence. They insist there is no further story; sometimes things just are for no reason at all. Get over it. Move on.

I have read as many of these stories as possible, from the beautiful to the bizarre, and the type I find the most attractive and the most reasonable is the Further Story. And among the Further Story accounts, my favorite is the one where the something involved is not just special but completely perfect.[27]

There is much to unpack here, so let's begin. But first, a quick disclaimer: this story may sound a little too good to be true, at least at first. However, upon sustained reflection, I believe it ultimately becomes too reasonable to deny; it makes too much sense.

---

[27] We might think of an absolutely perfect being (as opposed to a relatively perfect being, like a perfect triangle) as something that is purely positive, such that whatever it exemplifies property-wise does not entail exemplifying anything negative or limited (for example, having a height demands having a limit or being bounded, and thus implies a lack or negative in some respect). Examples of purely positive properties include power, knowledge, goodness, existence, love, since none of these entail a bound. As Robert Koons states, "a perfect being would have essentially every possible power and would be disposed to know all actual truths and love all actual beings, since such dispositions entail no simply negative properties." Robert Koons, "God's Existence," in *Neo-Aristotelian Perspectives in Metaphysics*, ed. Daniel Novotny and Lukas Novak (Abingdon, UK: Routledge, 2016), 266.

Does Everything Need to Be Explained? *Can* Everything Be Explained?

Generally, we think things have an explanation for their existence or occurrence. Rarely, if ever, do we make exceptions to this explanatory rule of thumb. If we hear the song "Beat It," we want to know where it came from, which musician performed it, what stereo it is blasting from, and so on. If we see a snake in our basement, we want to know where it came from. We don't just think these things snapped into existence from nothing (though maybe they have; at this point I am not assuming otherwise); instead we seek an explanation of these facts — and by fact I mean some concrete state of affairs, like some buffalo giving birth or that Bob our neighbor is existing in his garage — and that explanation is often causal. We look for prior things or states that either demanded or made probable the existence of the song "Beat It" or the snake or Bob in his garage or a photon or what have you. And generally, we are pretty good at discovering these prior things or states. However, even in cases when prior things or state have not been identified, we assume we just haven't looked hard enough, long enough, or in the right places.

When we encounter what appears to be a murder victim, if we don't immediately find the explanation (the perpetrator), we typically don't say there isn't any explanation because not everything needs an explanation. Rather, we tend to say that there must be some sort of explanation for this; we just haven't found it yet.

Science assumes this "explain everything" principle as well — or if not exactly that, then perhaps something like "explain as much as possible," or "expect an explanation unless there is some good reason not to."

THE FINER POINTS

The Principle of Sufficient Reason—that is, minimally, the principle that whatever exists has an adequate explanation of its existence and whatever attributes it has—has a lot going for it, having recently been argued for on the basis of self-evidence, metaphysical necessity, inductive support, a priori intuition, the avoidance of chaos, the advertence of skepticism, its necessity for science, and

Explanations aren't always causal

more.[28] We cannot rehearse all the arguments in favor of PSR here, but we can focus on several that are of interest to our project, since a modest version of PSR is what lies behind most cosmological arguments for God.

So, in general, we journey through the world expecting there is an explanation for things that do not explain themselves, whether an extrinsic cause or principle of logic or whatever, and whether that something else is a single thing or a collection of things. Again, such explanations are often but not always causal. I, Pat Flynn, have a causal explanation: a stork. But we might ask what the explanation is for never finding a colorless frog that is green all over. I think we can agree that the correct answer is that there are no colorless frogs that are green all over because there cannot be. The notion is contradictory, and contradictions are impossible. That seems to me an adequate explanation, although it is not a causal explanation.

So, while all causes may serve as explanation (that is, something that removes mystery around a particular topic or thing), not all explanations need to be causes, in the sense of one concrete thing producing another concrete thing. Maybe, for example, there is something that can explain itself; if so, then we would have an example of something explanatory but not causal, since I don't think anything could ever cause itself (as in bring itself into existence from nothing).[29]

Let us turn once again to the question of why anything exists at all. People have asked this question for as long as we can remember. In fact, the question has been asked by some of the most brilliant minds in human history, including the co-discoverer of differential calculus. Like everything else, we expect that there should be some answer to this question, some explanation

---

[28] See Alexander R. Pruss, *The Principle of Sufficient Reason: A Reassessment*, (Cambridge, UK: Cambridge University Press, 2010). Joshua Rassmussen, *Is God the Best Explanation of Things?: A Dialogue* (London: Palgrave Macmillan, 2019), chapter 2. Edward Feser, *Five Proofs of the Existence of God* (San Francisco: Ignatius Press, 2017), 147–69.

[29] For something to cause itself to exist, after all, would first require that it exist to act as cause, which is absurd. By contrast, something might explain its own existence if it is necessary that it is existent somehow, that its nature is such that it could not *not* exist. In this sense, it would be uncaused, not self-caused.

to be found. Of course, if nothing existed, we would not be able to ask about it. But explaining how we are able to ask about why things exist (because of our existing) does not itself give an explanation of why things exist. We can only ask why something exists, if we exist. This is true, but trivial. It does not, however, explain why something, anything, exists.

The Further Story can provide an explanation. It goes like this: There is something that is, by nature, special. This something is the sort of thing that, unlike the song "Beat It" or electrons or capped landfills, *must* exist. Reality *must* include this something because this something somehow has a nature, or essence, that guarantees its existence. In other words, whereas everything we typically encounter (pop songs, particles, buffalo, etc.) did not need to be included in reality, because its existence is not guaranteed by the sort of thing that it is, this foundational special something in our Further Story is, in fact, necessary. Its nature does somehow guarantee its existence. There could not have been nothing. There must have been something.

THE FINER POINTS

Here is something fun to think about: the *totality* of reality, or *the complete collection of everything real.* Just consider everything that exists, collectively, in total. This consideration encompasses anything and everything that exists, whatever that may include. If—*if, if, if!*—something exists (people, unicorns, abstract objects, the past/future), it is within the totality of reality.[30] Conversely, if something doesn't exist, it is not within the totality of reality. Now, notice this. Even without knowing what all the things are included in our collection of everything, we *can* know this: there is no cause of the totality of reality. Because there is nothing beyond the totality of reality; that is, nothing beyond the complete collection of everything real. Which means there is nothing to act as cause of everything (all things considered collectively).

Although this may seem trivial, it is in fact a remarkable discovery of reason. It proves that not everything (collectively) can have a cause. So, while most things seem to be caused, we have just proved

---

[30] I leave open which of these has real existence, conceptual or possible existence, is no longer existing, or has yet to exist. This neutrality allows the cosmological argument to be run regardless of theories of time or the ontological status of abstract objects.

an exception. Reality in total is uncaused, and somehow stands on its own. There is no outside cause of reality in total because there cannot be. How is that possible?

Again, Further Story supplies an answer. Reality in total is uncaused because there is some aspect, some layer, some entity or collection of entities, that is itself uncaused and self-sufficient in its existence, that exists because it has to exist, cannot not exist.

So far, not much is being said about this special foundational something. Maybe it is one thing, maybe it is many things. All that is being said is that whatever this foundational thing is, one or many, it is special. In fact, it's remarkable.

Either way, the question of "how come anything?" is now clarified: what we are really asking is "why is there anything *contingent* at all?" The Further Story is telling us there are contingent things because there is at least one necessary thing, a thing so sturdy in existence it could not *not* exist, and this necessary thing somehow gave rise to contingent things. This helps to explain how reality in total is uncaused, though most everything we experience is caused.

At this point, there are many questions: How can contingent things arise from a necessary thing or things? How exactly is a necessary thing *necessary*? What could make something special in such a way that it had to exist no matter what? These are fundamental questions, and they deserve a fundamental answer. Soon enough, I will tell another story that tries to answer them, a further story within the Further Story.

Before we do, let us see how the Further Story compares to other stories, namely the story that Everything Is Just More of the Same Story and the story that There Is No Story.

Let's first consider the There Is No Story story. In this story, we should not expect or seek an explanation for everything. Some things might just *be*, and that's all there is to say. Maybe the universe just *is*, and while it may seem to make sense to ask why it is rather than isn't, there is really no reason to think anything provides an answer to that. The story is that there just is no story. There is no further page to turn to. Our story, the story of why there is *this* universe, *this* world (i.e., all physical reality), comes to an abrupt and unsatisfying end. And why would we think, apart from emotional prejudice, otherwise? Why would we expect that this story would have a satisfying end at all?

This story — or really, lack thereof — is indeed unsatisfactory. But I think it is worse than unsatisfactory; I think it is absurd.

For one thing, if anything can exist without some explanation as to why, then how do we discern which things have explanation and which do not? Surely, some things do have explanations as to why they exist. Where do we draw the lines of criteria as to which?

After all, if the universe is just every existing thing which either is a concrete *contingent* individual or individuated by concrete contingent individuals (like properties), then the universe itself is a concrete contingent thing. The universe is not like an elephant, which may be heavy even if everything that comprises it (at some level) is light; reasoning from part to whole in that instance would be fallacious. Instead, the universe is more like a wall, where if all the bricks are red, the wall is red, where part to whole reasoning is not fallacious. If everything within the universe is contingent, then the universe is contingent. Think about it: Does piling on more computers, even an infinite number of computers, to a single computer make the collection of computers any less contingent than the single computer we started with? Obviously not.

THE FINER POINTS

Skipping ahead a little, it also would not make sense to suggest the universe (seen as some composite whole composed of contingent things) is the necessary, self-sufficient reality. For the universe is made up of parts, and even if a higher mode of being could emerge from those parts, it nevertheless presupposes and depends upon them. The universe could not operate as a composite whole unless the parts already exist, and a necessary reality is something which exists entirely through itself and is not dependent upon anything else—including its parts. It is also incoherent to suggest that the universe is the necessary, fundamental reality that generates its own parts, since that would require the universe to be ontologically prior to those parts, so as to bring them into existence. But the universe cannot be at once the necessarily existing source of its non-necessary parts and yet dependent on them; that is absurd. So, while perhaps the necessary reality is something within the universe (we have not yet ruled that possibility out) insofar as the universe is partly composed of contingent things, it does not make sense to say the universe as a whole could be the necessary reality we're looking for.

If the universe needs no further explanation and there is no relevant difference between the universe and everything encompassed by the universe, then there is no reason why anything in the universe requires or has further explanation, in which case we can stop looking for explanation anywhere. So, if I say I think I have an explanation of a universe, and somebody tells me, "Hey, pal, we don't need it, because not everything needs an explanation," I can say the same about anything they think they have explained or want to explain.

They might say, "here is an explanation for this rabbit." To which I can respond, "Sorry, friend, but I do not accept. Not everything needs an explanation. Didn't you get the memo? It went out last Tuesday."

And even if some possible explanation is provided, even if presumably well evidenced, if I accept that not everything needs an explanation, then I can draw the line wherever I want on whether to accept explanation or not, whether at the level of the universe or a bunny rabbit or the evolution of human beings.[31] I can, for example, either accept the theory of evolution for how humans came about or just suppose humans popped into existence randomly, including with the misleading appearance of evolutionary lead up, and there is no reason to accept one over the other, if we are working under the

---

[31] Philosopher Bruce Gordon handily summarizes the epistemological consequences of denying the principle of sufficient reason (a common name for the explanatory principle being defended here):

First, why would knowledge elude us if we were to suppose some contingent states of affairs had no explanation? Briefly, if some states of affairs could lack explanation, the possibility of there being no explanation would become a competing "explanation" for anything that occurred. If something can lack an explanation, we are prevented from separating things that have an explanation from those that do not, for there is no basis to conclude that something having an explanation was not, in fact, something occurring for no reason at all. Since no objective probability is assignable when there's no explanation, there being no explanation becomes an inscrutable competitor to every proposed explanation, undermining our ability to decide whether anything has an explanation, scientific or otherwise. This means our current state of awareness might also lack explanation, irremediably severing our perceptions from reality. So denying that every contingent state of affairs has an explanation undermines scientific access to truth and opens the door to an irremediable universal skepticism. The principle of sufficient reason is thus a broad logical truth we know a priori; it's a precondition for knowledge and the intelligibility of the world.

Paul Copan, Christopher L. Reese, Michael Ruse, Alister E. McGrath, Bruce L. Gordon, *Three Views on Christianity and Science* (Grand Rapids, MI: Zondervan, 2021), 135.

assumption that not everything that seems to crucially require an explanation actually has one.[32] To avoid this absurdly skeptical scenario, we must admit that either everything has an explanation or, if something does not have an explanation, there must be some good principled reason why.[33]

Moreover, if we think we can know things, then this radical rejection of our commonsense principle that things that seem like they should have a further explanation actually do have one simply will not do. After all, we believe that we can and do know things, or at least are rationally justified in accepting certain claims, insofar as we have good reason to accept a belief *and* that this good reason *is the reason why* we accept the claim or proposition that we do. We believe we are rationally justified in holding certain beliefs only because we are linked up with the world in the right sort of causal way, and that our thoughts, beliefs, and so on are *not* just sprung into our mind from nothing, even if they come with the false appearance of being linked up in the right sort of way to reality. What I am saying is that denying the principle that things really do, unexceptionally, have explanation, we throw ourselves into a catastrophic, self-defeating skepticism, where nothing can be counted as knowledge, or any belief rationally justified, including — and this is important — the belief that things lack explanation.

Here is an analogy to drive home the point. If I read the newspaper and form the belief that the president was shot because that is what the newspaper tells me, that belief could only possibly count as knowledge if it is both true that the president was shot and that newspaper was reliably linked to the truth of the matter (for example, that the reporter witnessed the event and that caused him to write the article). But now imagine this: suppose I discover that

---

[32] Someone might say in the case of evolution we have reason to think there is further explanation for how human beings came about (whatever that is) and evolution is the best explanation. But of course, that is just what the cosmological reasoner is saying about any contingent thing or collection thereof: that there is reason to expect further explanation, and that a necessary being is the best available.

[33] Recently, philosophers Alexander Pruss and Robert Koons considered six theories of empirical knowledge, showing that on each account we cannot know we have empirical knowledge unless the principle of sufficient reason (effectively, that everything has an adequate explanation) is something we know *a priori*. Robert Koons and Alexander Pruss, "Skepticism and the Principle of Sufficient Reason," *Journal of Philosophical Studies*, 178, (2021): 1079–99.

the newspaper was created by my neighbor attempting to pull an elaborate practical joke. While it appeared to be legitimate, the newspaper was doctored, totally fake. Now, let's say it is actually true the president was shot and that the practical joke of my neighbor just happened to match up with this unfortunate fact of the world, unintentionally. Nevertheless, my belief would not count as knowledge, because it wasn't formed via a reliable process. Obviously, forming a belief on the basis of a practical joke, where the joker has no concern for the truth, is not connected to the truth about things in a reliable way. So, even if my belief were true and formed in what appeared to be a reasonable manner, because there was not a reliable basis upon which I formed by belief, my belief cannot count as knowledge.

Reliable connection, particularly to truth, matters when it comes to knowledge. Conversely, if our principle of explanation isn't true and things can just exist without explanation, particularly contingent things, then I must take seriously the possibility that this might be the case for all the "things" in my head. So instead of my beliefs being formed through causally reliable interactions with the world, they just spring into my head from nothing, totally disconnected from the truth of how things really are. At this point, however, knowledge (minimally of the world beyond my head, but perhaps even the world inside my own head) becomes impossible.[34] What's more, I cannot even write off this freakishly skeptical scenario as improbable, because objective probabilities concern things with regular and reliable casual connections, and here we are not thinking

[34]   Edward Feser pushes further the skeptical scenarios of denying our principle of explanation in a passage meriting full quotation:

But if PSR is false ... for all we know, what moves or causes us to assent to a claim might have absolutely nothing to do with the deliverances of our cognitive faculties, and our cognitive faculties themselves might in turn have the deliverances they do in a way that has nothing to do with truth or standards of logic. We might believe what we do for no reason whatsoever, and yet it might also falsely seem, once again for no reason whatsoever, that we do believe what we do on rational grounds. Now, this applies to any grounds we might have for doubting PSR as much as it does to any other conclusion we might draw. Hence, to doubt or deny PSR undercuts any grounds we could have for doubting or denying PSR. The rejection of PSR is therefore self-undermining. Even the critic of PSR willing to embrace perceptual skepticism and retreat into a redoubt of a priori knowledge will find no shelter there. To reject PSR is to undermine the possibility of any rational inquiry.

Five Proofs, 149–50.

about that. We are talking about things not causally connected to anything, that just *are* for no reason. This is bad news for those who think knowledge of the world is not only possible, but actual, at least of some things, in which case we should reject that things can just exist without any explanation (because it would undermine the conditions for knowledge), especially things which appear to cry out for further explanation — whether bunny rabbits, belief states, the song "Beat It," the universe, a particle, a fuzz ball, whatever. Science is gone too, obviously, if our principle of explanation isn't true, at least as something we can say is a genuine source of knowledge.

Another reason people might think everything has an explanation is simply because it makes good sense of our experience. Probably the best reason we don't see things just pop into existence randomly from nothing is because it is robustly true that things do have some adequate explanation, and so anything that could exist but does not have to exist — that is, anything contingent — must be caused by something else (otherwise it would lack adequate explanation). And if something lacks an extrinsic cause there must be something about its nature that makes sense of its existence.

If that principle that things have an explanation as to why they exist isn't true, it then becomes mysterious why things aren't blipping in and out existence chaotically all the time. For example, why Yngwie Malmsteen never appears right in front of me for no reason at all, shredding an amazing guitar solo, or why proton clouds never spring into existence from nothing. In other words, the world sure seems to behave as if our principle of explanation is true. For that reason, we have good reason to think that our principle of explanation is true. I have heard some philosophers say that the fact that the world is as orderly as it is would be a miracle if our principle of explanation were not true, and I agree. Relatedly, it seems that our principle of explanation is itself required to justify the practice of "inference to the best explanation" in scientific or philosophical contexts, especially when it comes establishing evidence for scientific laws or competing hypotheses. After all, if our principle of explanation were false, then who is to say things we think are explained by other phenomena are not just appearing from nothing while falsely appearing to be explained by other phenomena?

Inference to the best explanation (sometimes called abduction) involves inferring some theory is true or likely true because it is the most explanatory.

The practice is common to everyday experience, like inferring that my sprinkler turned on when I notice my grass is wet, but essential to science, for the obvious reason that many objects of science are not directly observable—particles, emergence of life throughout history, and so on; the list is expansive.

But for inference to the best explanation to be reliable, and by extension for science to be reliable, it seems our principle of explanation must be true, since inference to the best explanation requires one to believe things generally and genuinely have explanation. In other words, inference to the best explanation demands our commitment to the intelligibility of the world, which is just to say the Principle of Sufficient Reason (PSR, hereafter). In fact, atheist philosopher Thomas Nagel once suggested that the assumption that "the explanation that gives greater understanding is more likely to be true" is itself but a variant on the "traditional principle of sufficient reason."[35] And this Principle of Sufficient Reason is pretty much the principle of explanation we've been talking about.

I say "pretty much" because there are a few qualifications I would like to make, which I must now get into. These qualifications will cause us to journey into issues that may not seem immediately related to our overall project, but I insist that they do ultimately relate to our overall project, and for that reason they are worth discussing. You may even find them interesting to think about. Ultimately, I am going to defend our principle of explanation against prominent attacks.

But before doing so, let me sum up by saying that because we really *can* know things and because we could not reasonably hold to the skepticism that results from denying that things—particularly all contingent things—have an explanation, we must reject the There Is No Story account. We must cling to our intuition that reality is intelligible, that there really are correct answers to coherent questions, including why anything exists instead of not, especially if such things could not have existed. Maybe we have not found that answer yet, but we are definitely justified in believing it is there and in trying to figure it out.

Responding to Objections against PSR

Speaking broadly, our principle of explanation, the PSR, demands everything have an adequate explanation for its existence either through itself (via its own

---

[35] Thomas Nagel, *Mind & Cosmos: Why the Materialist Neo-Darwinian Conception of Nature is Almost Certainly False* (Oxford, UK: Oxford University Press, 2012), 17.

nature) or because of another (via some extrinsic cause). Many philosophers, and probably most people, think the PSR is deeply intuitive, if not self-evident. But not every philosopher accepts this principle, so if we are going to be thorough in our investigation of fundamental reality, we must consider reasons why people might reject the principle of explanation guiding our inquiry. And probably the strongest objections to the PSR are:

✣ Threats of necessitarianism ("modal fatalism")
✣ Purported counterexamples (from quantum mechanics, say)
✣ Concerns with the freedom of the will

In interesting ways, these objections are related, so we'll consider them in tandem.

For starters, some philosophers have claimed the PSR entails "modal collapse." This is a technical term, but in simple language it means that if the PSR is true, then the world is infected with necessity, and — contrary to commonsense — nothing is contingent.[36] Everything *had* to be just the way that it is. Everything is "necessitated." The reason this is a problem is most people probably find the suggestion that everything had to be exactly the way it is deeply counterintuitive. Saturn could have not had rings. Dogs might not have existed. Despite what my wife would say, chocolate is not an absolute necessity (metaphysically speaking).

In short, this alleged necessitarian consequence of the PSR typically involves a puzzle surrounding some big conjunction of contingent propositions. For example, take all contingently true propositions (that is, propositions which happen to be true but could have been false) and join them. Call that the "big contingent conjunctive fact" (or BCCF). If the PSR is true, then the BCCF requires an explanation. However, the critic maintains that the explanation cannot be necessary because whatever is explained by a necessary fact is itself necessary. Nor can it be contingent, because then the BCCF would explain itself, which is impossible because nothing contingent is self-explanatory. Thus, it seems the BCCF has no explanation and the PSR is false.

Here is what is wrong with that argument. First, it assumes propositions are themselves *things* requiring an explanation given the PSR, *and* it assumes

---

[36]   Peter van Inwagen, *An Essay on Free Will* (Oxford: Oxford University Press, 1986), 202–204.

that explanation is a matter of logical entailment.[37] Both commitments can be denied without much difficulty, though it is the latter that *must* be denied. Regarding the minor point, propositions are not like cats, dogs, or bicycles. Rather, as many philosophers maintain, propositions exist only in minds which abstract.[38] More specifically, they hold that propositions are *beings of reason* dependent upon concepts, and concepts themselves are dependent upon mental activity. Thus, it is preferable to endorse some version of the PSR that demands only concrete, rather than abstract, objects stand in need of explanation. From there, once the existence of concrete minds is explained — including the divine mind, if such a mind exists — propositions and other abstract objects simply come along for the explanatory ride. Here is how philosopher Edward Feser has put it:

> When we explain concrete objects and states of affairs the propositions describe and the minds (including the divine mind) which entertain the propositions, we have explained everything that needs to be explained. Propositions aren't some third kind of object over and above these, remaining to be explained after they have.[39]

Secondly, why assume that if q explains p, then q entails (necessitates) p? The threat of necessitarianism requires this assumption, which is almost certainly false. We think of explanation as that which removes mystery and makes the *explanandum* (the thing to be explained) intelligible, and one thing need not demand another thing to make it intelligible (remove mystery). Alexander Pruss provides the example of scientific and statistical explanations which are nonentailing:

---

[37] David Bentley Hart issues a related challenge against the fatalist argument: "The simplest problem lies in its failure to distinguish the logic of causality from the logic of propositional truth... a set, after all, is not a substance but only a purely notional abstraction, which merely delimits a certain collection of similar things in an altogether neutral way. It is indeed perfectly true that a substance cannot be the cause of some other substance upon which it is dependent... but the relation between a set and its contents is not one of causal dependency, and so it simply is not true that the explanation for a set of facts cannot be included among the items of that set." David Bentley Hart, *The Experience of God: Being, Consciousness, Bliss* (New Haven: Yale University Press), 337.

[38] Moderate and Scholastic realists, in particular.

[39] Feser, *Five Proofs*, 165.

This seems to say that something
D "explained" once it's at the simplest
or highest level?.
As in, just saying I want to run laun is
sufficient?.

Scientific causal explanations, in general, simply do not give conditions that entail the explanandum. This is obvious in the case of statistical explanations, since in these, the explanans gives laws of nature and states of affairs that do not entail the explanandum but either render the explanandum more probable than it would otherwise be, or at least are explanatorily relevant to the explanandum. Why did the cream spread throughout the coffee cup? Because it is very likely that random molecular motion would disperse cream in this way.[40]

David Oderberg makes a similar point, writing:

A sufficient explanation for my mowing the lawn might be that the lawn is long and needs mowing, but this might obtain without my mowing it. It might be thought that explanations of particular facts in terms of the laws of nature and initial conditions are not entailing, at least without (*per impossibile*) an infinitely long statement of all the conditions that do not obtain.[41]

Thirdly, any proponent of libertarian free will, which is nondeterministic, *must* maintain that an *explanans* need not entail the *explanandum*. What I'm saying is that people who accept free will should be quite happy with the way I'm presenting the principle of explanation. Now, without getting too far ahead of ourselves, if God creates the universe (or BCCF) by a free act, and God is a necessary being, then we have a way of explaining all contingent things through the action of a necessary being, and because that creative action is not necessary but free, that which it results in (the universe) is not necessary either. This is a nice result.

Interestingly enough, however, free will is sometimes *itself* used as an objection to the PSR in what's known as "the randomness objection," which states that if something is not determined, it is random, and vice versa. And if something is random, then it has no adequate explanation for why it occurred. So, on the one hand, free will is sometimes used to secure the PSR against the

---

[40] Alexander Pruss, "The Leibnizian cosmological argument," in *The Blackwell Companion to Natural Theology*, ed. William Lane Craig and J. P. Moreland (Hoboken: Wiley-Blackwell, 2012), 52.

[41] David Oderberg, "Principle of Sufficient Reason," at David Oderberg (blog), at davidoderberg.co.uk.

necessitarian threat, and, on the other hand, free will is sometimes used to object to the PSR as some contingent instance where explanation is lacking.

Can we solve the dilemma?

I say yes. The solution is that, firstly, there is a false dichotomy here; the terms *determined* and *random* are logical *contraries*. If something is determined, it is not random, and if something is random, it is not determined. True enough. However, it's not clear that these terms are logical *contradictories;* they do not obviously exhaust all options, where if something is not determined, it *must* necessarily be random, and vice versa. That this is a false dichotomy is itself supported, ironically, by another instance which critics of the PSR propose as a counterexample: quantum phenomena.

Although I believe that it is a mistake to hunt for free will in the realm of quantum mechanics, it should nevertheless be acknowledged that discoveries related to quantum mechanics have given us scenarios where things seem to be neither strictly determined nor entirely random. Rather, we have something of a "constrained indeterminism" or "adequate determinism," where objective probabilities are given — that is, explanations from the laws of quantum mechanics which remove mystery and make the *explanandum* intelligible even if not entailed. That is just what the proponent of the PSR is looking for.

Consider the following from John Haldane on this matter:

> There is a very natural and widely exercised way of thinking according to which a sufficient cause is a "cause enough" and a sufficient explanation an "explanation enough." In these terms the quantum events do have an explanation. For example, it may be a property of the experimental set-up that a certain percentage of emissions follow a given pattern. To observe this is not necessary to confine oneself to a statistical description. Indeed, I take it that the point of a realist interpretation is to attribute a natural propensity to the system. Propensities are explanatory even when they are non-deterministic. If I say that an event occurred because of a reactive tendency I have answered the question "why?" in a way that I have not if I say it just occurred.[42]

---

[42] J. J. C. Smart and J. J. Haldane, *Atheism and Theism* (Hoboken: Wiley-Blackwell, 2002),126.

And to quickly hedge a related objection, philosopher Robert Koons reminds us that, contrary to popular misrepresentation, nothing in quantum mechanics provides a counterexample to the PSR where something comes from literally nothing:

> According to the Copenhagen version of quantum mechanics, every transition of a system has casual antecedents: the preceding quantum wave state, in the case of Schrodinger evolution, or the preceding quantum wave state plus the observation, in the case of wave packet collapse.[43]

Returning now to freedom of choice, let me add this: Aristotelians and Thomists (those who follow the philosophical traditions of Aristotle and Thomas Aquinas) have traditionally marked the following distinction between behaviors of substances, especially among organisms: those that are caused from external forces, on the one hand, and those originated "from within" or by virtue of the substances' inherent controlling power, on the other hand.

This Aristotelian–Thomistic position allows for top-down as much as bottom-up causation. If true, then we can see how a possible third category emerges against the randomness objection. If there are substances with intellect and will, and these substances are, loosely speaking, able to "move from within," then they can engage in acts of *rational willing*, as the Scholastics called it, or *reasons-based action*. These substances can control their parts (including particles in their brain) instead of their parts controlling them. No science contradicts this, and much emerging science — particularly in quantum biology and neuroscience — seems to support it.[44]

The critical point is as follows: the Aristotelian–Thomistic approach is as top-down as it is bottom-up, which resolves much of the puzzle about free

[43] Robert C. Koons, *Realism Regained: An Exact Theory of Causation, Teleology, and the Mind* (Oxford: Oxford University Press, 2000), 114.

[44] See Peter Jedlicka, "Revisiting the Quantum Brain Hypothesis: Toward Quantum (Neuro)biology?," *Front Mol Neurosci* 10 (2017), at Pub Med, https://pubmed. ncbi.nlm.nih.gov/29163041/. See Andrea Lavazza, "Free Will and Neuroscience: From Explaining Freedom Away to New Ways of Operationalizing and Measuring It," Front Hum Neurosci 10 (2016) at Pub Med, https://pubmed.ncbi.nlm.nih. gov/27313524/.

will, since the puzzle is fundamentally about a lack of control. If something, including its parts, is controlled by prior conditions, including its parts, then even if those parts behave "randomly," free will is untenable. The Aristotelian–Thomistic alternative rejects that perspective and puts wholes (as opposed to parts) in control by arguing that substances are primary.[45]

Furthermore, under the Aristotelian–Thomistic view, the person is the cause of his actions, not his prior conditions or reasons under consideration, even if both can act as influences. A person *may* act because reasons *impressed* him, but the cause is not, even strictly speaking, his will, but the person himself — the entire agent. By *will*, we just mean his inherent power to act as cause in the relevant respect — that is, of being able to grant the dignity, the honor, of any finite reason ultimately being efficacious for action. The person makes the reasons *efficacious* — that is, determining. The reasons do not make efficacious (determine) the person. Suzi had the power to *choose* to play Billy Joel on the piano because of *reasons*; hence it is not "random," since to be random involves there being no rhyme or reason as to why something happened. She also had the power to *choose* not to play Billy Joel on the piano and, say, watch television instead, because of other reasons.

Now, if somebody asks what ultimately *caused* Suzi to favor one set of reasons over another, we must be careful to detect some subtle begging of the question against the proponent of libertarian freedom and Aristotelian substance causation. The *ability* to favor any finite reason, and to make it ultimately efficacious for action — more particularly the power to *end* deliberation, to make one consideration the *final* consideration — *is just what it means* to be an agent capable of rational willing. It is the ability to say, definitively, "I choose *this*."

---

[45] This does not, however, imply that wholes can cause all their parts to exist, so as to imply composite entities do not ultimately require an extrinsic cause to fund their unity. Rather, for the Aristotelian–Thomistic philosopher, free will is a matter of formal-to-final causation, where the substance, in choosing, can direct certain material parts. However, the individual human being is a metaphysical composite of form (principle of organization) and matter (principle of individuation), and something beyond the composite must ultimately account for the unity of these constituents, since each depends on the other in some significant respect to actually exist (matter depends upon form for its organization, form depends on matter for its being "tied down" to some particular time and place). This is a point we'll return to later.

So, there is nothing that *caused* Suzi to favor one set of reasons over another; it is precisely because Suzi herself is a *top-down* cause that a finite reason *was* chosen. In this sense, we have something that is, in a sense, self-explanatory — *in a sense*, because we still must explain the existence of that contingent, free-willing entity.[46] Either way, the PSR stands, and this approach fits well with our common acceptance of explanations like "she chose it of her own free will."[47]

Before returning to our original investigation, we should consider one other longstanding objection to the notion that contingent things have some adequate explanation. Finding its basis in philosopher David Hume, the objection goes something like this: What's wrong with supposing contingent things can't just exist, including come into existence, without a cause? This seems conceivable, the skeptic might say, as in no obvious absurdity or contradiction follows from the thought that this contingent catfish, say, exists without any cause. In such a case, how are we justified in holding PSR?

In response, we can point out that simply conceiving of a contingent thing while not also conceiving of its cause is no real indication that such a thing could actually exist without its cause.[48] For example, we can conceive of a man without also simultaneously conceiving of his exact height. Does this mean that such a man can exist without height? Surely not. Thus, it is not clear that *the absence of conceiving* a cause necessarily means conceiving of *that cause being absent.*[49]

Brian Davies offers another good point in reply:

[46] As Pruss explains, "that action A was freely chosen, or perhaps freely chosen for reason R, is 'almost' a self-explanatory claim, despite its contingency, with the only thing unexplained being why the agent existed and was free and perhaps impressed by R." Pruss, "Liebnizian," 54.

[47] Importantly, this proposal would challenge another assumption baked into modal fatalist objections against the PSR — namely, that no contingent fact could be self-explanatory, in any respect. Given models of libertarian agency like the one expressed above, one could take the free action of a contingent entity to be self-explanatory, though an extrinsic explanation would still be required for the *existence* of that rational agent.

[48] Imagining might be a better term in this context than conceiving, but I'll mention that technical dispute simply to leave it aside.

[49] For further responses to this objection and others by Hume, see Alexander Pruss and Joshua Rasmussen, *Necessary Existence* (Oxford, UK: Oxford University Press, 2018), 47–56. Also, Feser, *Five Proofs*, 41–42.

But how do you know that the thing in question has come into existence at the *time* and *place* you picture it as *beginning* to exist? You have to exclude the possibility that it previously existed elsewhere and, by some means or other, came to be where you picture it as beginning to exist. Yet how are you to do that without supposing a cause which justifies you in judging that the thing really came into existence, rather than just reappeared from somewhere?... In other words, to know that something began to exist seems already to know that it has been caused to begin to exist.[50]

In summary, it seems the advocate of the PSR can, without assuming any controverted theses (and certainly theses no less controversial than the positions challenging the PSR), overcome the threats of necessitarianism and the alleged counterexamples from quantum mechanics or libertarian freedom.

As Feser makes clear:

Nor will it do in any event for the critic merely to try to raise odd puzzles for some particular formulation of PSR. For one thing, there are, again, formulations of PSR which do not make the presuppositions that open the door to the puzzles. For another... there are arguments for the conclusion that some version of PSR is true, and indeed reason to think that even the critics of PSR must implicitly presuppose it.... Hence, the burden of proof is not on the proponent of PSR to show that it is true (though this is, as I have suggested, a burden which can be met), but rather on the critic of PSR to show how it can be coherently rejected.

With such challenges to the PSR out of the way, we have every reason to believe our explanatory principle is true, particularly in light of the catastrophic consequences of denying it.

While our discussion of the PSR may seem a bit tangential, the points concerning free will are going to come in handy in the next chapter as we think about how a necessary reality can produce a contingent reality. As you might expect, an act of free choice can do important explanatory work on this front.

---

[50] Brian Davies, *An Introduction to the Philosophy of Religion* (Oxford, UK: Oxford University Press, 2020), 53–54.

CHAPTER TWO

From PSR to God (or Near Enough)

LET US RETURN TO the last major point we were making before we diverted into defending the PSR, which is that our principle of explanation is supported by inference to the best explanation and the principle has the upshot of solidifying our intuition that inference to the best explanation is reliable.

Moreover, if inference to the best explanation is necessary for science, and if PSR is necessary for inference to the best explanation, then PSR is necessary for science. And if, as the Further Story implies, the affirmation of PSR leads ineluctably to God's existence, then there is an important connection, though perhaps not an immediately obvious one, between God and science. The implication is that one can have science *and* God, or neither.[51]

But we must resist getting ahead of ourselves. Let us once again zoom out to comparing the different stories (Further Story, No Story, and Same Story

---

[51] Christophe de Ray offers a powerful epistemological argument for theism by noting that inference to the best explanation (which science requires) demands that our intuition that the world is intelligible *actually tracks reality*. But as de Ray notes, there is no *possible* naturalistic origin story (as either shaped by biological evolution or cultural pressure or both) of that intuition in which it arises *because it is true*, which means the naturalist should either abandon the intelligibility intuition as reliable (that is, withhold trust in abductive reasoning and therefore science) or abandon naturalism. But for obvious reasons, including that the naturalist almost always wants to say science is a reliable source of knowledge, the naturalist cannot abandon the intelligibility intuition. Thus, they should abandon naturalism. Christophe de Ray, "A New Epistemological Case for Theism," *Religious Studies* (2020).

which we'll consider soon), since at this point I take it that the principle of explanation is secure, and that we are justified in asking, and subsequently demanding an answer, to the question "how come anything?"

In just a moment I will have another argument for why I think No Story is impossible, but for now let me present a different consideration first, which is this: simple principles are better — or so we think. However, the simplest principles may also have the unfortunate consequence of being false.

Here is a remarkable, refreshingly simple principle: Everything has a cause. How simple; there are no exceptions. However, this explanatory principle is not true, because it *cannot* be true. Not *everything* can have a cause, and the reason is actually quite simple. As mentioned earlier, there is nothing beyond everything (true by definition), hence there is nothing to act as cause of everything. So, that principle is too simple. Here is a better one: everything that *can* have a cause, *does* have a cause. This would include not just everything contingent, but anything that might be necessary yet cries out for deeper explanation.[52] The principle is simple and matches with experience, and the exception is not arbitrary, because it is obviously not contrived to exempt only something that could not possibly have a cause (if there is such a thing) as actually not having one. This explanatory principle would also, if true, set the conditions necessary for the possibility of knowledge. When applied to all of contingent reality, the principle results in at least one necessary reality, since we cannot explain why there is anything of the type contingent (without circularity) unless we transcend that category and accept something of the type necessary. Here is a little argument for that:

There is a cause (extrinsic *explanation*) *of all contingent things.*

The cause of all contingent things cannot itself be contingent.

So, there is at least one necessary thing.

[52] Things can be necessary in a sense yet still find a deeper explanation or cause. Crude example: imagine there is a necessary reality (something that exists because of its nature) that necessarily creates and sustains a Pop-Tart. That Pop-Tart would itself be necessary but still caused and explained by the more fundamental necessary reality. Moreover, there are certain mathematical truths that are necessary yet which find deeper explanation in axioms.

The first step in our argument is just a statement of the explanatory principle. The second step is an application of that principle, where the cause of all contingent things cannot itself be a contingent thing — otherwise we have circularity.[53] And if something is not contingent, then it is necessary. So, the application of our explanatory principle gives the result of some necessary being — at least one, maybe more — as the explanation of why there are any contingent things, like the song "Beat It," elephants, elementary particles, or Yngwie Malmsteen.

At this point, somebody might say that the necessary self-existent thing is just something within the universe (something natural, in other words) and, *at this point*, that may be correct. We have not investigated what this necessary thing or things is or are, if there are many of them. We are just letting reason run its course, and thus far reason is telling us that there must be something special in nature, something that must exist no matter what, in order to explain all the stuff that need not exist. Later, we will look at what sort of thing could be necessary in its existence and (spoiler alert) I will maintain it cannot be anything natural or physical; it cannot be anything within the universe unless we mean something rather quirky by "the universe." But at this point, we have not made that argument, so as far as we know, the Further Story is quite compatible with the idea of something within the universe being the necessary being we are looking for.

For now, we can say the Further Story is better than No Story, since it allows us to maintain the possibility of knowledge and rational justification (remember, these are necessary conditions for science), is not *ad hoc*, and

---

[53] Here we are looking for an explanation for a plurality of facts, where a plurality is just our way of referring to *some* facts taken *collectively*. This need not assume that pluralities form into a single composite whole. Either way, we seek explanations for pluralities (some flowers) just as well for individuals (this flower), even if the collection is infinite (ask yourself: would having an infinite collection of flowers make the plurality any less mystery than if there were only 110?). Importantly, however, one does not *need* to apply the PSR to a plurality to reach the result of at least one necessary being; one can just as well apply the PSR to a single contingent thing, then deny that any single contingent thing, collection of contingent things, or infinite regress of contingent things can provide an adequate explanation of that one single contingent thing (that is, why that one single contingent thing exists, *here and now*) and produce the result of at least one necessary being that way. For an example of this approach, see Feser, *Five Proofs*, Chapter 5.

runs off a simple explanatory principle. Again, I think more can be said against No Story, but I will wait until later to say it. With what we have just covered, let us now consider the story that everything is just more of the Same Story.

The story that there is just more of the Same Story goes like this: There is just stuff of the same sort (contingent) that just keeps going back (in time) or down (in levels of reality) or both indefinitely. So, each portion of reality either in time or along some layer is explained by something prior, but there is no bottom to it nor foundational layers composed of anything special. Things just keep going and going. The end.

I would like to say several things about Same Story.

Perhaps surprisingly, part of the Same Story is not incompatible with the Further Story. The story that there is something special (necessary and self-existent) is compatible with there being infinite regresses or stacks of contingent things, all of which are ultimately caused by (at least one) necessary thing. (Stock example: Imagine an infinite series of dominoes, each one toppled because of the one before it. However, the entire infinite series stands atop some foundational table. While there is an infinite series, there is still something holding that entire series up). So, maybe both are true. However, if one includes in their story of infinite regress the claim "and there is nothing more to the story," then these stories are obviously incompatible. Here, I should like to suggest why Further Story seems better than Same Story when understood in the more restricted sense. First, it seems that the person who wants to say "it's just more of the same" is seeking to offer an explanation. They are not saying there is no story and that's that; rather, they think just having more of the *same* story is adequate to explain everything that needs to be explained. Here, I disagree.

And so does Gottfried Wilhelm Leibniz, who gave the example of an infinite number of geometry books, stretching back forever, where each is copied from the one previous. In a sense, each geometry book is explained by the one that it was copied from. However, something crucial is left unexplained: why are there any geometry books at all, and why geometry and not biochemistry instead? This is why Same Story is not a good enough explanation. It leaves too much unexplained; namely, why is there any story at all (even if it goes on indefinitely) of a nature that need not be, and why is the story just the way it is and not some other way instead? Further Story can offer an explanation where Same Story cannot: Further Story can refer to a reality that can explain why there is any contingent story at all, and it can offer some good reasons as to why the contingent story is the type of story it is.

There is more that can be said against Same Story. Some philosophers, for example, have argued that no effect can be preceded by an infinite number of prior causes (or grounds); if that is correct, then the same story going on indefinitely cannot be true.[54] There must be a halting point and presumably that halting point would be something special in nature, if it must be able to explain everything resulting from it and yet cannot be something that itself demands a prior cause or explanation. I will not pursue the issue of infinite causal regresses aggressively here, because I think the more fundamental matter is that even if there could be an infinite causal regress (at least of a certain sort), for our purposes, it clearly would not provide the right sort of explanation we need to make sense of why there is any contingent story and not nothing instead.[55]

Here is perhaps the simplest way to think about it. We want an explanation for why there is anything of the *type* contingent, why there is any unfolding story of things that are but didn't have to be and not nothing instead. Same Story is inadequate because anything that is "more of the same story" already supposes there is a story of that sort or things of that type. To suggest that the Same Story can account for why there is any story of that type is assuming there is a story of that sort already around, and what sort of explanation is that supposed to be?

In our case, we want a story for why there is anything contingent, and we are told by Same Story that we can just look to some contingent thing or contingent things going on indefinitely for the reason why. But any contingent thing or infinite regress of contingent things presupposes (is causally posterior to the fact that there are) contingent things in the first place. And what assumes the thing to be explained obviously cannot explain that thing. Hence,

---

[54]   Alexander Pruss, *Infinity, Causation, and Paradox* (Oxford: Oxford University Press, 2018).

[55]   Shortly, we'll discuss a type of causal series that cannot regress infinitely.

the story of more of the same story is inadequate. There must be some further story; it cannot be more of the same story.

As we conclude our "how come anything?" preliminary discussion, I should like to highlight three further reasons why Further Story is the best available. Philosophical positions are often best established through a cumulative effort.

Number one: Things that are dependent or contingent in nature do not and cannot stack into something independent or necessary. If something has a nature that does not guarantee its existence, then simply putting more of these items together, no matter how they are arranged, whether in a line, or a circle, or a matrix, will not produce something that can exist on its own. To assume otherwise is like thinking if one just had enough white building blocks and enough time, they could eventually construct a purple tower. Reason tells us that the number of white blocks and the amount of time are irrelevant. One philosopher calls this a construction error, of failing to have the proper categories handy, since if *all* a person has is white blocks, one is never going to construct a purple tower.[56] This holds true for dependent things. If all is more of the Same Story, we have blocks that are contingent only; we have stuff that does not exist all on its own.

In fact, stacks or collections of contingent things would, in a sense, be even *more* contingent than just the individuals that comprise them, since if we have a stack or collection of (say) computers, that collection not only *depends* upon the existence of the individual computers, which need not exist, but their being stacked or collected together in just the way they are, which need not occur. "It is quite silly to pretend, then," says Edward Feser, "that when we get to the collection of ... all the contingent things there are, we might somehow suddenly have something that is not contingent."[57]

Putting more contingent things together, even an infinite number of them, doesn't offer the sort of explanation we're looking for, that how reality in total stands is independent of an extrinsic cause when nothing about the nature of anything in reality is capable of doing so. What's required is something noncontingent, or necessary, to terminate our hunt for ultimate intelligibility.

[56] Joshua Rasmussen, *How Reason Can Lead to God* (Westmont, IL: InterVarsity Press, 2019), 22–27.
[57] Feser, *Five Proofs*, 156.

Number two: There is a traditional line of thought, going back to at least Aquinas but arguably even before him, that offered a theory of contingency by way of things having really distinct internal principles of being. On the one hand, they have a principle of what-ness or *essence*, a principle that makes things to be *what* they are (for example, the essence of human or squirrel or water). On the other hand, they have a principle of is-ness or *existence*, a principle that makes things to be actively present in reality, as distinguishable from nothing. Aquinas held that things were contingent insofar as their essence is really distinct from (not identical to, and hence did not guarantee) their existence. This is a nice theory; it helps to make sense of why some things are not necessary in their existence. While it is necessary that any particular triangle has three sides, given that this is the essence of triangularity, it is not necessary that any particular triangle exists, because that is not the essence of a triangle nor any part of it.

But this theory has consequences. For if it is the case that there are things whose essence does not guarantee their existence, then we must try to make sense of how any of them acquire existence in the first place. How ever did existence "get into" things whose essence does not include, nor is identical to, their existence?[58] This sets up an explanatory hunt, which philosophers like Aquinas thought could

---

[58] "Get into" is indeed a crude way of putting it, because it may give the impression that there was something pre-existing its existence, which is absurd. There is no pre-existent item (essence) into which existence is then poured. Rather, we should think of an essence as the bound or limit of something's existence. Fido the pet dog, for example, is just the bound of Fido's existence. Fido is what maps the limits, ranges, or reaches of a particular instance of existence, ensuring such an instance pertains just to Fido and all his properties, and not Rover (the neighbor's dog) or some other dog instead.

As philosopher Barry Miller explains:

A peculiar thing about bounds is that, although they are real enough, they themselves are totally devoid of thickness: they are not to be mistaken for an enveloping film whether of butter or of any other material whatsoever. Despite their ontological poverty, however, they do have a genuine function, for they serve to distinguish every block from every other block. In that sense they can be said to individuate the blocks they bound.

Ultimately, "Fido exists" need not signify a pre-existing subject in which existence inheres; rather, "Fido exists" signifies, quite simply, a bounded instance of existence — namely, Fido. Barry Miller, *The Fullness of Being* (Notre Dame, IN: University of Notre Dame Press, 2002), 92.

only be terminated (in fact, had to be terminated if anything were to exist at all) in a being whose essence just *is* its existence, a being whose essence *did* guarantee its inclusion in reality. If we're going to make sense of beings that have existence in a "derivative" or "borrowed" sort of way, then this being had to have existence "built into" it. Aquinas's theory tells us that for however long contingent beings exist, whether they had a beginning in time or not, they exist only insofar as something extrinsic is imparting existence to them. Their existence is on lend. And if that is right, then it seems correct to say we must trace back or twist up to something whose existence is not on lend but inherent. And this thing's essence cannot just include existence but must be identical to existence, for any aspect of this thing that was not identical to its existence would be a caused thing, an aspect that must be brought into being and would not *be* the necessary being we're ultimately looking for. Aquinas therefore proposes a being that just *is* simple subsistent existence, a being of pure existence. For reasons we'll explore later, Aquinas thinks this being is God. But for now, it is worth noting some of the theoretical advantages of Aquinas's theory. For one, it helps make sense of how things are contingent; their what-ness does not demand their is-ness. For another, it helps make sense of how something could be necessary in itself; its what-ness does demand its is-ness, because in the necessary thing, they are not really distinct.

We should want to explain things as far as we can, and this offers a nice, albeit curious, result: There is something that *has* necessary existence because that something just is its existence.

Previously we asked what could be relevantly different to make something necessary in the first place. Aquinas's theory supplies an answer: the relevant difference is that its essence is not really distinct from its existence. It is a being of pure existence. Now, whether that ultimately makes any sense is something we'll have to consider later, but for now it surely offers a *principled difference* for how something could be necessary in its existence, and that is just the sort of thing we are looking for.

At this point, let me take something back. I said I would not pursue the issue of infinite regress aggressively because it was largely (if not entirely) irrelevant to the argument we're considering, but there is just one rather traditional point I would like to make that works against the possibility of an infinite regress of a certain sort. My point is this: if the causal regress we are considering is one where the members of the causal series do not possess the causal property inherently — that is, in virtue of what they are — but are deriving it from some extrinsic cause, then there is good reason to think a causal series of this sort is necessarily terminating, which is to say comes to a halt in some primary member that does have the causal property in virtue of what it is (i.e., has it in a "built-in" rather than "derivative" way).

There are some technical terms there, so let me explain what I mean in simpler language.

Here a stock illustration may be helpful. Imagine somebody wants to know why their bedroom is illuminated and somebody else tells them it's because of the moon, which is reflecting light. However, we know moons only *reflect* light; they do not *produce* light. Moons are borrowing or deriving the "causal property" of illumination. Thus, they are not ultimately responsible for its being in that causal network. At most, they can serve as a proximate cause, but what we are after is an ultimate case. Thus, even positing the existence of infinite moons, all reflecting light onto another (no matter how those moons are arranged), it will always remain utterly inexplicable how this moonlight came to be until we find the ultimate *source* of that light — namely a star.

The problem is this: If all the entities in our supposed causal chain are existentially dependent and thereby conditioned for their existence upon something else (and thus merely conditional of themselves), then nowhere in that chain will the actual conditions for the existence of any member be adequately satisfied. As Norris Clarke explains, "the search for the necessary fulfilling conditions will endlessly go on and in principle be impossible of completion. For in principle the necessary conditions can never be fulfilled.... But the original beings we started with do in fact actually exist here — which means that in fact all their necessary conditions must be already fulfilled."[59]

Now what we have been considering in investigation is the caused property of *the very existence* of things, and given that things are contingent, this means their existence is conditioned upon prior things, is caused to be in them by something else. Same Story is not saying No Story, remember; rather, Same Story just says we can get the full explanation we require from some infinite backward or downward

[59]   W. Norris Clarke, *Explorations in Metaphysics* (Notre Dame, IN: University of Notre Dame Press, 1994), 165.

chain of contingent things. But Clarke's earlier point, which itself is just a restatement of St. Thomas's insight that causal series that are *essentially ordered* are *necessarily terminating*, is that the proposal of an infinite chain in this context provides no adequate explanation at all. Said differently, if there were no primary member which possessed the causal property in virtue of what it is, there would be no effect or intermediary members in the series which had the property caused in them. We would have a series of borrowers (things to which existence is on lend), but never reaching back to anything with real money, as it were. And if contingent things do not possess existence in virtue of what they are, then no contingent thing could exist unless there were some necessary thing within that causal chain. An infinite chain of contingent things could not supply an adequate answer here.

THE FINER POINTS

Briefly stated, in an *essentially ordered* causal series of X → Y → Z, Y *borrows the power* (since it does not have that power *essentially*) from X to cause Z. The stock example of an essentially ordered series is the hand using the stick to push the stone, where the causal property within the series is *derivatively had* by the instrumental members. The implication is that if there is no first mover — that is, nothing with the in-built power to move (like the mental agent) — then there can be no motion, whereas in an accidentally ordered series X → Y → Z, Y *does not borrow* the power from X to cause Z. The stock example of an accidentally ordered series is Bob begetting Frank and then Frank begetting Harry. Frank can beget Harry after Bob is dead because Frank has the inbuilt power to do so. Aquinas famously maintained that while accidentally ordered series could stretch back infinitely, essentially ordered series could not. There has to be a primary member if that (essentially ordered) series is to exist at all.[60]

So, Aquinas argues, in order to put an end to all this, there must be something necessary, something whose essence just is its existence. This is required if we are to make sense of why anything (contingent) exists and not nothing instead.

[60] For a further defense of why essentially ordered causal series must terminate, see Gaven Kerr, "Essentially Ordered Series Reconsidered," *American Catholic Philosophical Quarterly* 86, no. 4 (2012), 541–55.

Number three: Our final consideration in favor of the Further Story is somewhat technical, but it relates to Aquinas's theory of things having an essence and existence element, not — and I should have made this clear sooner, but here it is now — as *separate* or *separable* parts of a being, but rather deeply intertwined and interpenetrating, yet nevertheless really distinct, "co-principles" or constituents.

THE FINER POINTS

Distinction amounts to a breaking of identity; when we acknowledge a distinction, we are noting some lack of identity between either things or parts or concepts or terms. Importantly, not all distinctions are *real*; that is, extra-linguistic or extra-conceptual (beyond how we talk or think about things). Some distinctions, rather, are just in the way we talk or think about things. For example, there is no real distinction between the morning star and the evening star.[61] There is, however, a real distinction between myself and my wife, and not just a real distinction but ontological separability—we can (and do) exist independently of each other *and* at different locations. That said, not all real distinctions entail ontological separability, since, as Gyula Klima explains:

"It is clearly possible to have distinct, yet necessarily co-occurring items in reality. For example, it is clear that the triangularity of any particular triangle (its having three angles) is not the same as its trilaterality (its having three sides), unless sides and angles are the same items. But it is also clear that one cannot have a particular triangularity without a particular trilaterality. So, we have two really distinct items here, which are nevertheless inseparable in reality."[62]

For philosophers like Aquinas, the distinction between essence and existence stems from what Aristotle says in his *Posterior Analytics*: that *what* a man is and *that* he is are different.[63] But how are they different? Those who affirm the real distinction suggest that the essence

---

[61] To reiterate, a real distinction is one that holds independently of how we think or talk about something: thus, it is not merely a verbal distinction (bachelor vs unmarried man) nor mental distinction (the glass being half full versus half empty), but a distinction that attains in things themselves.

[62] Gyula Klima, "Aquinas' Real Distinction and Its Role in a Causal Proof of God's Existence," at Symposium Thomisticum (2017).

[63] Important difference worth noting: The 'existence' that answers to the issue of whether a thing exists is not the 'existence' by which the essence is actuated. The

> element (the *what* determination) is really distinct from the existence element (*whether* determination) as regards its basis *in the thing itself,* not just in how we think or talk about the thing. While these elements may not be ontologically separable, they are nevertheless really distinct, where one is fundamentally irreducible to the other.

With this point, there is a consequence which takes a lot of concentration and patience to draw out, but bear with me, because it is quite significant. Here I can only tease the implication and invite the reader to think further on the matter whenever they have the time, like at bingo. So, when thinking of Aquinas's theory, we come to realize there is a certain priority concerning a thing's essence over its existence, insofar as a thing's existence is the existence *of that thing* and not of some other thing. Let us take Thumper the bunny rabbit, a pet bunny rabbit who belongs to our acquaintance. There he is stealing carrots. Naughty Thumber. Now, according to Aquinas, there is Thumper's essence (rabbit essence individuated in Thumper) and Thumper's existence. However, Thumper's existence requires Thumper's essence for its individuation; that is, Thumper's *existence* requires Thumper's *essence* to be the existence *of* Thumper and not some other being instead. Language hints at this: When we make the statement "Thumper exists," the predicate "exists" in this instance is meaningful *only* in relation to, or is dependent upon, Thumper. The logical analysis of language in this regard actually reveals the underlying structure of being — namely, there is priority (ontological, not necessarily temporal, in a certain respect)[64] to the Thumper element over the existence element, such that the existence element is crucially dependent upon the Thumper element for its individuation; that is, to be the existence of *this particular being.*[65] However, apart from Thumper's existence, Thumper

---

former is factual existence and correlates to the truth of a judgement, whereas the latter is the *actus essendi.*

[64] Of course, concerning Thumper's actuality, the existence element is prior. Nevertheless, the Thumper element is prior concerning individuality.

[65] Here I follow philosophers Michael Dummett and Barry Miller in maintaining that while a logical analysis of language may be a dusty mirror when it comes to reflecting the underlying structure of being (which is to say, predicates reflect properties, subjects reflect objects, etc.), it is the only mirror we have. This is to say that external reality can be apprehended (not constituted!) by the logical analysis of language. See Miller, *Fullness,* 67–68.

is literally nothing; thus, Thumper cannot do anything, including individuate or complete his existence.

Through such an analysis we seem to be approaching a contradiction: On the one hand, Thumper and his existence must be ontologically prior parts of existing Thumper. Yet upon analysis, it seems Thumper and his existence cannot be ontologically prior parts of existing Thumper. Why? Because Thumper has no capacities apart from his existence, including the capacity to be a part of existing Thumper via his ability to individuate his existence.

The Thumper part must come first, if we're going to "construct" (even just conceptually) existing Thumper. But it cannot come first, if Thumper is all there is to the story, since apart from his existence Thumper is nothing. But we know this paradox must be merely apparent, because Thumper is right there, stealing carrots. So, there must be some further story — there must be something *else* which supplies the capacity for Thumper to individuate or complete his existence. There must be, in other words, an extrinsic cause which funds the unity of these metaphysical constituents, which provides the capacity for Thumper to individuate or complete his existence (since Thumper, apart from his existence, is incapable of achieving this). Otherwise, Thumper appears to be a contradictory structure, something which must precede its existence before it exists, and that is absurd.

Again, the point is technical, and it does require assenting to the particular structure of being that Aquinas has in mind (that of affirming things are composed of an essence and existence element). Here I can only say there are very good reasons for thinking Aquinas's theory is correct, but unfortunately I cannot defend it in the limited space here.[66] This is just something to think

---

[66] A defense of Aquinas's wider metaphysical system can be found in W. Norris Clarke's *The One and the Many*. Clark does an able job showing how Aquinas's theory of being does real and important explanatory work in offering solutions across a wide range of perennial philosophical issues, form making sense of change, identity through time, the problem of the one and the many, and more. Moreover, one would have to accept that existence is a first-level property of concrete individuals and not just (as many modern analytic philosophers assume) a property of concepts only. See: W. Norris Clarke, *The One and The Many: A Contemporary Thomistic Metaphysics* (South Bend, IN: University of Notre Dame Press, 2001).

THE BEST ARGUMENT FOR GOD

about further, a bonus consideration that, if correct, adds further strong support to a conclusion we've already been driving at.[67] To make sense of why there is any contingent thing, we must ultimately get back to something that is not contingent but necessary, and presumably whose essence just *is* its existence — otherwise those contingent things could not exist, even for an instant. And if that's correct, then No Story and Same Story are not just improbable but impossible. Further Story must be true.

---

[67] It would, in fact, show both that No Story and Same Story are not just inferior theories but metaphysically impossible, insofar as the argument shows that Thumper cannot be a brute fact, existing apart from some extrinsic cause, else we encounter contradictory implications. Moreover, that the same analysis of Thumper applies to any contingent entity, so to avoid the contradictory implications one must ultimately arrive back at that which just is its existence.

And *That* Is What "Everyone" Calls God?

WE BEGAN BY CONTEMPLATING the question "how come anything?" We considered three rival stories trying to answer this question. No Story is absurd. Same Story is inadequate and absurd. What best answers the question of why there is any contingently existing thing is that there is something that does not exist contingently but necessarily. There is a story involving something special at the bottom level of reality. At this point, I should like to tell a further story about this story and discover a little more about it.

So far little has been said about what the Further Story includes as its primary character. We have only been able to reason our way toward something that does not exist contingently and (if we are going along with Aquinas) something whose essence is identical to its existence. But what is this thing? Is it more than one thing? What is it like? What *isn't* it like? We'll look at how we can answer these questions.

It must be noted that the foundational something that is the primary character of the Further Story has to be *relevantly different* from most things in our experience. If it were not relevantly different, then it would not be the right sort of thing that we could say is a necessary and truly fundamental reality. We never run into anything, so far as we can tell, that is concrete and necessarily existing — concrete in the sense that it has some real ability to affect things in the world. Real causal power, if you will. Everything we know of that is concrete is also contingent. It can fall into nonexistence.

Earlier I said there are reasons to think this special necessary something is God. Now it is time to see why philosophers have thought this. There are several strategies for moving from what exists necessarily toward the affirmation of the Divine. In the interest of making classical theism appear as the best further story about Further Story, I will highlight several of these strategies in a cumulative, though largely summary, fashion.

The first strategy is one of negating or clearing away certain features or attributes that we know necessitate, or at least strongly imply, contingency. Call these dependency-indicating features or attributes, insofar as they seem to be the types of features or attributes that naturally cry out for some further explanation. Because Further Story posits an element of reality that exists all on its own, then anything which implies something is not necessary in virtue of itself but dependent upon some further reality should thereafter be considered something that this fundamental reality is *not*. In "the tradition," this approach is known as *apophatic theology*, or the way of negation, a way of coming to learn something about fundamental reality (hereafter referenced as God) by clearing away certain things that God cannot be, so long as God is the ultimate fundamental explanation of things. Traditionally, philosophers thought various features of the world were strong, if not undeniable, markers of contingency or dependence upon prior conditions or causes, including change, compositeness, and finitude, just to list three. We will expand this list, but for now let us briefly examine each of these in turn.

I. Unchanging

Aristotle, and Thomas Aquinas following him, argued that if something is changing, then it is acquiring a new mode of being: it is moving from a state of potency to a state of actuality.[68]

---

[68] In short, potency, as relative nonbeing, has no powers, no causal capacity. Only something actual can do something. This seems like a perfectly safe principle. In fact, even in the case of animals, where they are apparently self-movers, Aristotle tells us the matter always comes down to one part moving another part — never does anything involve something moving itself from potency to actuality. Same with human free willing: the analysis of that consists first in the will being moved by some external object to will an end, the will thereby moves the intellect to consider means, and with means considered the will then wills them, and nowhere in such an analysis do we have anything that is potential and actual *in the same respect*.

The occurrence of change demands certain commitments for its affirmation, that is, for it to be intelligible: first, that every changing entity is
different at the end of change than at the beginning, but (and this is important!) it is nevertheless the same entity. For unless *something stays the same*,
we do not have change, but rather annihilation and replacement. To affirm
the reality of change we must accept two distinct modes of being, the "before" and the "after." Following Aristotle, we might call the here-and-now
present state *act* or *actuality*, and the aptitude or capacity to receive a different state *potency* or *potentiality*.

All change involves the reduction of a potential state to actual. In fact, all
causation involves the reduction of potency to act.[69] The pot, for example, is
potentially hot but actually cold. As I apply the flame, the pot transitions and
becomes actually hot (and the actual flame is the cause of the pot moving
from a state of potency to act concerning heat), but of course it is still the
same pot, only it has acquired a new mode of being. It has undergone a contingent modification.[70]

For Aquinas, all change requires a cause to introduce some new actuality
or state of being into the changing thing; therefore, change indicates contingency or of being a caused reality. Why? Because nothing can move itself from
a state of potential being to actual being in the same respect. Thus, something
else must cause it. Here is a brief argument from philosopher Gaven Kerr to
support this, drawing from Aquinas:

> Now the same thing cannot be both in act and in potency in the
> same respect; for then it would be actualizing its own potency in
> that respect; for example, the wood cannot be both actually hot and
> potentially hot, for in that case it would be both actually hot and
> actually cold, which is impossible.
>
> Moving on, the mover is actual with respect to the motion, in
> that it can bring about the motion, and the thing moved is in po-
> tency with respect to the motion, in that it undergoes the motion in

---

[69] While all change may signal an instance of causation, not all causation requires
change. For example, God bringing an entity into existence involves no change,
technically speaking, but it does involve the actualization of potency — namely, an
act of existence being imparted to a thing's *esse*, which relate as act to potency.
[70] In technical terms, acquired a metaphysical accident.

question. The mover then actualizes the potentiality of the thing moved. But if the same thing cannot be in both act and potency in the same respects, then the thing moved, which is in potency in respect of the motion, and the mover, which is in actuality with respect to the motion, cannot be the same. Consequently, the thing moved must be moved by another.[71]

To hedge a common objection, Aquinas and Kerr are not making the silly mistake of thinking that whatever actualizes some potency must itself be identical to what it brings about. For example, that only a chair could cause something else to be a chair is obviously false, even if it is true in many cases that things often produce their likeness, like fire producing fire. Rather, the point is modest: whatever introduces actuality into something must itself be actual and capable of bringing that actuality about. In short, whatever produces F must have an F-ness producing power, which means that something must itself be actual, since no merely potential thing can *actually do* anything.[72]

If we follow Aquinas in his metaphysical analysis of change, then we might think whatever explains all contingent things must itself be unchanging, since whatever changes is contingent in some significant respect — specifically in the sense of being dependent upon something else for its being as it transitions into a new state of actuality. If the necessary self-existent being is something which cannot be like that — that cannot be dependent for its being upon anything — then we have reason to think it is not the sort of thing that changes or even possibly could change, though it has the power to affect change (bestow actuality/being) in everything else. Potency, after all, is just an openness to being. Whatever is necessary and self-existent cannot be the sort of thing open to the causal influx of being from something beyond itself

---

[71] Gaven Kerr, *Collected Articles on the Existence of God* (Germany: Editiones Scholasticae, 2023), 159. I prefer using the term change or changed rather than move or moved since movement for Aristotle and Aquinas encompasses all the ways something could change (qualitatively, like changing in color, or quantitatively like changing in size) and was not restricted to local motion (change in spacetime location).

[72] As Kerr points out, "Aquinas offers an account of how perfections present in effects can pre-exist in their cause in a non-univocal, but virtual, sense and so causes, whilst not in act in the same way as their effects, are sufficiently in act to produce their effect." Moreover, something might not have an f-ness producing power on its own but might only when working alongside other contributing causes. Ibid, 166.

for the following reason: If some aspect of it came into being, it would be a caused reality, not necessarily self-existent, and thus not necessary or unchanging. This gives us reason to think this necessary being has no intrinsic passive potency.[73] It is immutable or unchanging. So, we have cleared away at least one attribute: mutability.

In summary, if something is changing, then it is being caused in its existence; it is receiving some new mode of being or actuality. However, the self-existent necessary reality is absolutely uncaused. Thus, we have reason to think it is absolutely unchanging.

Whatever is most fundamental does not change, at least intrinsically.[74]

II. Purely Actual

If causation involves the actualization of potency, and if our self-existent necessary reality has no intrinsic passive potency because it is necessarily self-existent and uncaused, then it is *purely* actual. However, one might wonder why our necessary reality must be purely actual in all respects rather than just purely actual in some respects. In other words, maybe our necessary reality causes things in some particular way but itself is caused in another way.

The answer to this question is found in thinking about the line of causality currently under consideration, which concerns the actuality of things. We are, of course, concerned with answering the question of how come anything actively exists (has actuality), so we are searching for something that is the cause of the actuality of things that are contingent. Thus, with respect to being the absolute cause of actuality, this necessary fundamental entity is uncaused

[73] Traditionally, thinkers like Aquinas maintained God could have active potency, which simply related to God's power to bring things about. However, the exercise of God's active potency did not require any real intrinsic change in God, merely the bringing about of some effect extrinsic to God with a relation of causal dependence to God.

[74] This leaves quite open the possibility of fundamental reality coming to change in *extrinsic* respects, including relational respects, which would be the case of it becoming creator of the world or coming to know the contents of the world it creates. Technically, these changes can be classified as "merely Cambridge" and do not require us positing an intrinsic change to fundamental reality or any change which demands the actualization of some intrinsic passive potency on behalf of fundamental reality. More on this in the appendix covering additional objections.

absolutely, since all other causal lines depend upon the causal property of actuality. Actuality is absolute. Thus, whatever accounts for the actuality of everything aside from itself is purely actual in the most robust respect. As Kerr explains:

> God is the source of all actuality for all things that are in motion, but whatever is in motion is in potency, in which case God is the source of actuality for all things that are in potency. As source of actuality for all things that are in potency, God himself can be in potency in no respect; for then he would not be the source of actuality for all things that are in potency. Hence, God must be pure actuality. If God as primary mover is pure act, then all things are subject to him and he is subject to nothing.[75]

Recall that motion just means change in this context. So, we are understanding God as that which actualizes the potency of all changing or contingent things *to exist*; that is, God is what causes them to have actual real presence in the world.

So far, we have cleared away any intrinsic passive potency concerning the self-existent necessary reality. We have arrived at a being that is purely actual. Still, one might wonder if we have gone too quickly, for could it not be the case that there are multiple beings that are purely actual? This relates to our next several points.

III. Uncomposed

Philosophers have argued that things with parts stand in potency to their parts. That is, they depend ontologically upon their parts existing and being arranged just so. This seems correct.

However, if our necessary reality were composed, then it would exist through its parts rather than through itself, contradicting its necessary nature. Moreover, because we are talking about fundamental reality, it would become fundamentally inexplicable why those parts exist and are arranged in just the way they are, since we cannot appeal to anything "underneath" to explain the compositeness of fundamental reality. We would ultimately require an explanation for the existence and arrangement of such parts, and

---

[75] Ibid, 171.

the whole composite object accounts for the existence and arrangement of its parts.[76] Why? Simply because if we say that the whole is the cause of its parts being unified in such a way, then the whole depends on the arrangement of the parts, and the arrangement of the parts depends on the whole. This suggestion is viciously circular, a metaphysical nonstarter.

For this reason, it really does not make sense to suggest the universe (seen as some composite whole composed of contingent things) is the necessary, self-sufficient reality. For the universe is made up of parts, and even if a higher mode of being could emerge from those parts, it nevertheless presupposes and depends upon them. The universe could not operate as a composite whole unless the parts already exist, and a necessary reality is something which exists entirely through itself and is not dependent upon anything else, including its parts. It is also incoherent to suggest that the universe is the necessary, fundamental reality that generates its own parts, since that would require the universe to be ontologically prior to those parts in order to bring them into existence. But the universe cannot be at once the necessarily existing source of its non-necessary parts while depending upon them; that is absurd.

Anyway, if all this is correct, then we have reason to think that whatever else exists necessarily and fundamentally is incomposite or uncomposed,

---

[76] Again, one might think animals are an apparent counterexample; don't they appear to be, in a sense, prior to their parts (for example, cells) or the cause thereof? Well, not so fast. First, there is obviously a difference between an animal and its parts considered independently; some obvious difference between a living animal and a heap of animal parts strewn around in some field. So, what accounts for this difference? If we say *nothing*, then we have things that are clearly distinct but nothing that makes them distinct, and that's absurd. If we say *something*, then I think we should go along with Aristotle and say the difference is one of form. The living animal has a metaphysical part, a substantial form, and this part accounts for the organization and functional interplay and even time-bound development of its other (including physical) parts. However, the formal metaphysical part is itself part of a larger metaphysical complex: following Aristotle, a matter-form complex. Form is what supplies the organizing principle, matter is what serves the principle of individuation. And now we can ask: how did these (metaphysical) parts come together? Because in one sense form depends upon matter (for individuation) and matter depends upon form (for organization), and the whole composite of the animal depends upon (stands in potency to) these parts coming together, and clearly cannot be the cause or explanation thereof without circularity. So, we are again — even in the case of animals, though it may take more analysis — pushed to look for some extrinsic cause.

physically and metaphysically. Rather, it is absolutely, ontologically simple. It is one, perhaps even *The* One (see next section). If that is correct, then another attribute is cleared from fundamental reality: complexity.[77]

Bonus: this point connects well with our necessary self-existent reality being *purely* actual (*metaphysically* noncomposite concerning potency and act, which is to say essence and existence).

IV. Pure Existence & Principally One

Aquinas argues that if something exists necessarily and serves as the cause of everything else whose essence is really distinct from its existence, this being will not only be a being of pure existence, but it will be principally one and primary. By "principally one and primary," we mean it is a matter of metaphysical necessity that this being is "uniquely unique" (cannot possibly be multiplied) and the primary or foundational cause of everything else that exists.[78] The

---

[77] There is here an obvious objection to be raised against the Christian doctrine of the Trinity. How does absolute divine simplicity "fit" with God being three Persons? The short answer is that persons are not parts of God, but subsisting relations, where each is identical with the divine essence though really distinct from one another (qua relations). Importantly, at least for Aquinas, we do not need to say there are no real distinctions in God, only that there are no real distinctions that amount to real composition. This objection will be discussed again in the appendix covering additional objections.

[78] Robert Koons summarizes another argument for divine uniqueness: "Is there one God or many? In *Summa Theologiae* Part 1, Question 11, article 3, Thomas offers three arguments for the oneness of God. The first argument appeals to God's simplicity. God is made to be God by His divine nature, and that divine nature also makes Him exist as a particular being. For there to be two gods, there would have to be two divine natures, each of the same species. But for two natures to exist with the same species, there would have to be something responsible for making each distinct from the other. So, for example, two men can be two by virtue of being combined with two packets of prime matter. Two packets of prime matter have no actual nature of their own, and so they can be fundamentally or primitively distinct. The divine nature is an actual nature (it is maximally actual), and so two divine natures cannot be fundamentally distinct. Since God is identical to His own nature, there cannot be two instances of the divine nature, just as there cannot be two instances of a single angelic species." Robert Koons, "Does the God of Classical Theism Exist?" in *Classical Theism: New Essays on the Metaphysics of God*, ed. Jonathan Fuqua and Robert Koons (New York: Routledge, 2023), 47.

latter follows from the former, for if there can only be one fundamental reality, then everything else which exists must trace back to it for its existence.

Here I will quote a summary of Aquinas's argument from philosopher Enric Gel to impart the general point. Concerning a being whose essence just is its existence, Gel puts the matter as follows:

> Such a thing could not be multipliable, because it could not be sub-jected to any differentiating feature, as a genus (animal) is multiplied in its species (human) by the addition of a specific difference (ratio-nality) or a species (human) in its individuals (Peter, Mary, and James) by the addition of matter. There is nothing outside pure being that could act, with respect to it, as a differentiating feature, as the specific difference rationality is outside the genus animal or as matter is outside form, because 'outside' pure being there is only non-being, and non-being is nothing. So pure being could not be differentiated, as pure being, into multiple instances of itself, such as pure being A, pure being B, pure being C, and so on. Hence, a purely actual reality that was pure being itself — and such is the classical theist's picture of God — would have to be unique, out of metaphysical necessity.[79]

In short, pure existence is simply what it is to be. And so, anything not encom-passed by pure existence is an impossibility of being, since there is nothing "outside" of being. Given this understanding, there can be nothing distinct from pure existence which stands to determine it in some way or another (cause it to be this way or that, here or there, etc.), which would have to be the case for its multiplication to be possible or actual. Hence, if there is a being of pure existence, there can be only one.

Moreover, if something just is its existence, then that something would be simple and subsistent (existing all on its own, not in or through something else). However, to have multiple instances of that which just is existence alone would require contradicting either its nature as simple or subsistent or both. Thus, if there is a being that just is its existence, it will be principally one and

---

[79] Enric Gel, "How Many and Why: A question for Graham Oppy that classical theism can answer," *Religious Studies* 58, no. 4 (2021), 846–56.

consequently primary. There could not be multiple instances. *If* there is one, which our argument tells us there is, there can *only be* one.[80]

This argument delivers another result: Anything that either is or could be multiplied is something whose essence is not its existence. And this would be true for anything of natural reality, for there are multiple rabbits, protons, pieces of cheese, and so forth. Thus, for all such things that are inherently multipliable, there is a real internal distinction between their essence and existence. They are contingent realities.

Again, the result of our self-existent necessary reality being pure existence connects well with the prior result of pure actuality, since actuality and existence are the same (existence is just what makes something actual, or actively present, in reality). Purely actual, purely existing, noncomposite; everything is so far coming together nicely.

Bonus consideration: If there were two necessary beings, there must be some difference between them excluding their necessary nature, which they have in common, otherwise they would be the same reality. If the difference is contingent, then said being is composite and requires a cause, which contradicts its necessary nature. If the differences are necessary to each, then each

---

[80] At this point, one might wonder whether this line of argumentation requires the principle of the identity of indiscernibles (IOI), which many philosophers take to be controversial. Fortunately, the core multiplicity argument Aquinas deploys does not require IOI, since it is simply claiming that given the nature of multiplication, something whose essence just is its existence could not be multiplied. This does not require us to say that if there were multiple "pure existences" they would be identical. Thus, controversy around IOI does not affect the multiplicity argument because the multiplicity argument does not require IOI.

We can further demonstrate this point as follows. Let us suppose there could be something whose essence just is its existence. This something would be simply "exists" (ontologically simple). But if there are two instances of "exists," there is some difference between them. Again, even assuming IOI is false such that these qualities or properties might be indistinguishable, nevertheless, trivially so, there is still a difference between these two instances. However, by the fact of there being two instances, this would imply that the *similarity* between the two instances be expressible in terms of qualities and properties, *and* that such expressions *are ontologically grounded*. But this contradicts the simplicity of pure existence, since to say that each instance *has* one or more quality or property *is just to say that it is ontologically complex*. This contradiction can be avoided only by affirming that pure existence is in principle restricted to one instance.

lacks some feature essential to its necessary nature that some other thing has on account of having a necessary nature, and so, is *not* necessary, and that is another contradiction. Either way, a contradiction results from trying to have more than one truly necessary being.[81] Thus, it seems we are constrained to only one truly necessary reality.

V. Omnipotent

We might want to think of omnipotence not as the unrestricted idea of being able to *do* anything but rather the ability to *produce* anything that is inherently producible. If we take omnipotence in the latter sense, which is how Aquinas thought of it, then we can attribute it to fundamental reality, since if there is just one fundamental reality and it is primary in the order of existential causality, then whatever exists can only exist insofar as this reality imparts existence to it. Thus, this reality can bring about all possibilities of being and is responsible for all possible beings which are actual. At this point, we are no longer clearing away attributes of fundamental reality but "filling in" attributes. This "filling in" is justified through the effect-to-cause reasoning utilized in our hunt for the best ultimate explanation of things.

VI. Omniscient

Omniscience is a little trickier to get at, but we should say at least something in its favor since we have claimed that fundamental reality is God — or at least a plausible case can be made to that effect — and virtually all theists maintain God is omniscient. However, like omnipotence, understandings of omniscience come in different forms. But again, the traditional approach is to move from effect to cause and then if something is revealed from that, great — *not* to start

---

[81] Specifically, when speaking of a necessary being (to differentiate from abstracta), we mean an entity that possibly causes something (i.e., is concrete) and exists through its nature (i.e., is uncaused). Further, when speaking of a truly necessary being, I mean to say this being is necessary through itself, rather than necessary through another. Medieval thinkers like Aquinas thought there may be multiple necessary beings, as in entities that always existed and never naturally corrupted (like material beings do) but were still causally dependent for their existence upon the activity of God, the one truly necessary being (and hence his definition of a necessary being differs from mine, but the accounts do not fundamentally conflict).

with some stipulative definition or understanding ahead of time. So, here is how certain philosophers of days long past reasoned to God's omniscience.

We live in a world full of patterns. Being is patterned in certain ways. There is being patterned as a horse, being patterned as a starfish, being patterned as planets, as electrons, and so on. These patterns are often called forms. Now, following the tradition, forms can be contained in reality in one of two ways. First, in a material way, such as when some chunk of matter contains the form of cat and hence just is *this individual cat*.[82] Another chunk of matter may also contain the form of cat and hence is *that individual cat*. Matter was seen as the principle of individuation for philosophers, or that in virtue of which something was *this particular cat*, whereas form was the principle of organization, or that in virtue of which something was a cat instead of a dog or whatever else.

But for our purposes, there is another way forms can be contained, and that is in an intentional way. Think now of an architect containing the form of a house in his mind and how the form contained intentionally in the mind of the architect serves as the exemplar cause of the house. Now, if one thinks we should explain as much as we can, it seems that the patterns or forms of this world require explanation, and we already have reason to think there is some unique fundamental reality. So how does it (fundamental reality) explain the forms or patterns of being we see in the world?

Fundamental reality does not contain these patterns materially, since to contain a form materially just is to be that form — say, to be a cat. But God is quite obviously not a cat, since cats are composite and mutable beings and we have argued God is none of those things. What's more, many forms are mutually incompatible, so God could not be all these forms at once. But there is another option: these forms could be contained in fundamental reality in an intentional way. In fact, this seems to be how they must be contained if we are to make sense of how they have come into existence at all. And this seems like a rather nice explanation, implying that God has or perhaps just is an intellect of sorts.

Of course, considering everything else we've already learned about God, he would be an intellect of a rather amazing sort. Nonetheless, our reasoning leads us to affirm that God is the ultimate container of all forms, but God can only be the

---

[82] For those interested in technical details, essence and form are not quite the same thing. For material things, an essence includes both form and (non-designated) matter.

ultimate container of all forms if they are contained in an intentional way, which means *in the mind of* God.

Omniscience follows once we put the above considerations together with God as primary cause. God knows what is happening in the world (for example, that I am typing this page) simply because God is causing it to be (he is granting existence to forms). God's knowledge of everything that exists is not observational (one of sitting back and looking at what's going on in the world) but executive (one of making it happen; a supreme sort of "know-how"). There is nothing that God does not know about the world, as anything that is in the world *is* only because of God's causal activity, for which the forms in the mind of God provide the proverbial blueprint. Omniscience follows from omnipotence in combination with God being an immaterial knower and intentional causer.[83]

That, I believe, is enough to allow us to say that God is omniscient and, by consequence, that God is intellect.[84]

However, another reason for attributing intelligence to the first cause is the dynamic interrelatedness of beings in our universe. Various beings, even very basic entities, such as electrons, are by nature ordered toward interaction with other beings, and thereby made intelligible by their relation to other entities like protons. The natures of things are often, if not always, defined by their relation to other things and intelligible only insofar as they are interactive with other entities in regular, predictable ways. As Norris Clarke tells us, "In such an interlocking dynamic system the active nature of each component is defined by its relation to the others, and so presupposes the others for the intelligibility of its own powers of interacting with them."[85]

---

[83] For a defense of God's knowledge and God being identical to His act of understanding, see Maurice Holloway, *An Introduction to Natural Theology* (New York: Appleton-Century-Crofts, 1959), Chapter 9.

[84] Though of course the considerations of simplicity should really just have us say God is "thinking" just as God is "existing" and, indeed, strangely, that there is no real difference between "thinking" and "existing" in God. One underappreciated attempt within modern philosophy showing the coherence of this account is Barry Miller's Thought and Existence. Barry Miller, "Thought and Existence," *The New Scholasticism* 48, no. 4 (1974), 424–37.

[85] Clarke, *One*, 224.

The existence of electrons presupposes the existence of protons and vice versa — or so it seems. The parts, thus, can only be understood and put in operation in relation to the whole. But what sort of cause can adequately explain the unity and dynamic interrelatedness of the universe and its constituents? The answer must be something capable of holding, or simply being, an immense idea. For holding entities in *relational unity*, while maintaining their inherent distinctness, is basically the definition of an idea, and that is just what our universe is: a unity of various, often incredibly complex, relations. It is then a short, if not obvious, step to affirm an intellectual first cause.

Clarke iterates the point as follows:

> Another reason why such a cause of the unified activity of the system as a whole must be intelligent is this: It must correlate the parts with each other before they actually exist and go into action, since they cannot engage in reciprocal action with each other unless they are already oriented from within, in the dynamic properties of their natures, toward such distinctive correlated action. But not-yet-existent agents cannot be correlated with each other except by an agent that can make the not-yet-existent present, and this can only be done by an agent possessing conscious intelligence, which can plan ahead through the medium of ideas. In a word, only an intelligence can order means to a future end.[86]

VII. Immaterial and Eternal

That God is not material is indicated from God not being composite (since all material beings are composite insofar as they have spatially extended parts) and mutable (since all material beings are subject to change). That God is eternal is also indicated from God not being composite (since things moving through time acquire new phases, or parts, of life) and immutable (if time just is the measure of change and God is unchanging, then God is not in time). By eternal, we do not just mean God is everlasting. After all, something can be everlasting in time. What we are saying is God does last forever in virtue of being a self-existent necessary being, but not in time. God is timeless.

[86] Ibid., 225.

VIII. Qualitatively Unlimited (Absolutely Infinite)

Philosopher Josh Rasmussen once pointed out that all limits seem to require further explanation insofar as those limits appear arbitrary.[87] For example, when talking about ontological limits, we may be talking about the shape or configuration of something, being located at some spacetime point, having some limited degree of power (the ability to produce 10^{73} electrons and no more), or number of parts, and so forth. Limits always invite "why" questions: why *these limits* and not some other? Why are the boundaries *here* rather than *there*?

In other words, it seems that anything with arbitrary limits (a cutoff without explanation) is a dependent reality pointing toward an extrinsic cause to make sense of those limits.

Rasmussen summarizes the arbitrary limits thesis as follows:

> Mere differences in limits are categorially uniform, where a difference with respect to dependence is not categorially uniform. To illustrate, consider a four-gram pile of sugar. This amount of sugar is dependent; four grams of sugar will not appear from nothing. The same is true for forty grams. A mere change in the amount is completely irrelevant. It is no easier for a four-gram pile of sugar to appear from nothing than a forty-gram pile of sugar. The uniformity of limits makes sense of why: limits, all limits, are uniform with respect to their dependence on outside explanations.[88]

So, Rasmussen argues, all arbitrary limits have an extrinsic explanation.[89] This means that there can be no relevant exception to what is causable if that entity is limited in some arbitrary respect.[90] His consideration is not only consistent

[87] See Joshua Rasmussen's Argument from Limits in Joshua Rasmussen, *Is God the Best Explanation of Things?* (London: Palgrave MacMillan, 2019).
[88] Joshua Rasmussen, *How Reason Can Lead to God: A Philosopher's Bridge to Faith* (Downers Grove, IL: InterVarsity Press, 2019), 71.
[89] Rasmussen develops his modal continuity principle further in Joshua Rasmussen, "Continuity as a Guide to Possibility," *Australasian Journal of Philosophy* 92, no. 3 (2014), 525–38.
[90] Rasmussen considers potential counterexamples, such as mathematical limits, like why a triangle has only a limited number of sides. Rasmussen's response is that these limits are explained in terms of more basic mathematical principles and definitions, and that the entire mathematical landscape is in total infinite and unlimited, though

with the principle that things, all things, have an explanation, but supports and clarifies it. It would further entail that all natural realities are causable. Why? Because anything natural is always arbitrarily limited in some respect, either in shape, location, power, number of parts (physical or metaphysical), and so on. Rasmussen's argument from arbitrary limits provides reason to adopt an explanatory principle strong enough that all limits must be explained ultimately by that which is qualitatively unlimited.

By happy coincidence, the notion of a qualitatively unlimited reality fits well with traditional understandings of God as purely actual, subsistent existence. After all, if we think things exist in virtue of having some act of existence (an act of existence = that in virtue of which something is actively present in reality, distinguishable from nothing) conjoined to some restricted or limiting essence, then anything that just is pure existence will lack the metaphysical "part" that is restricting or limiting and will just be entirely unrestricted or unbounded existence. In other words, it is an unlimited and absolutely infinite being. Whatever properties this entity has, it has them fully and infinitely. If it has power, it has unlimited power; if it has knowledge, it has unlimited knowledge. In fact, we can quickly make a case for both. After all, power is the ability to produce things, and we already know this fundamental entity has some power, since it is the cause of everything that exists. If what it has, it has unlimitedly, we then infer it has unlimited power (omnipotence). Moreover, it is not implausible to suggest that knowledge is a power (the power to know, after all), and so from unlimited power comes knowledge, and since that knowledge would itself be unlimited, we infer omniscience. Once again, this is a nice result, since it confirms what can be attributed to fundamental reality from different routes.

Let us approach this from another angle. Pure existence can have no limit. Why? Because a limit implies some possible thing beyond the limit, but nothing can be beyond existence.[91] Beyond existence is literally nothing. But a limit is something that must receive existence, and thus restricts existence to some mode: existence as limited to a horse-y mode or a banana-y mode or what have you. So, existence *itself* can neither have nor be a limit; it must be intrinsically

---

itself still something capable of finding a deeper explanation: namely, in the mind of God. Rasmussen, *How Reason*, 72.

[91] Koons, "Does the God of Classical Theism Exist," 46–47.

unlimited. The consequence is that anything that is just pure existence would be absolutely infinite, in the sense that it would possess every possible pure perfection, meaning any attribute, such as power, knowledge, love, and so on, that does not itself automatically imply limitation.[92] Once again, this implication seems to support the divine attributes (omnipotence, omniscience, goodness, etc.), which various philosophers have "fetched" by other means. This is once again a nice result. Whenever different paths converge upon what appears to be the same conclusion, it should raise one's confidence in that conclusion.[93]

IX. Perfectly Good

Most theists believe that God is perfectly good. Can our argument help to infer this attribute as well? Yes, especially if we assume a little more Thomistic background.[94]

Aquinas is well known for holding to the doctrine of the transcendentals, which maintains that being and goodness (among other things, such as truth) are convertible, that is, different in sense but the same in reference. Simply stated, goodness just is being under the aspect of desirability. Thus, goodness is everywhere that being is, because goodness is no thing over and above being.

As Gaven Kerr puts it, "Like truth, goodness does not add anything to being, but designates a relation. Whereas truth signifies the relation of being to an intellect, goodness signifies the relation of being to the will. In other words, the goodness of being is being considered as desirable; and this tracks with the traditional Aristotelian definition of the good as that which all desire."[95]

Kerr continues:

> Something is perfect when it is complete in itself. Accordingly, when something is lacking in some respect, it is perfected (in that respect) when it receives what it lacks. When such a thing receives what it lacks and is thereby perfected, what it received is good for it. All this

---

[92] That is, being *fully* (or wholly) good, powerful, knowledgeable, etc., does not entail limits with respect to goodness, power, knowledge, and so on.

[93] That is, because one might think we have successfully replicated a result or found multiple independent attestation or both.

[94] For a recent defense of these assumptions, see David Oderberg, *The Metaphysics of Good and Evil* (London: Routledge, 2021).

[95] Kerr, "Goodness and Being," 94.

THE BEST ARGUMENT FOR GOD

is to say that when a thing is perfected it is actualized in a certain re-spect. Now, nothing is actual unless it exists, and nothing exists unless it has *esse*.... *Esse* is the principle of being, without which there is nothing; and since *esse* is the perfection of all perfections, all being is good. Therefore, wherever being is found, goodness if found, with goodness representing the desirability of being.[96]

With this background in place, God's goodness follows from God being purely actual/pure existence, or pure *esse*, following Kerr, which is the traditional Thomistic term for "act of existence."

In case the implication is not immediately evident: given the convertibil-ity between being and goodness, God, in virtue of being pure being, is just pure goodness. Because there are no unactualized potencies in God, there is no higher or further perfection for God to attain.

At this point, we are not saying God is perfectly good in the sense of being a supremely excellent gentleman or lady — that is, good in the way a human moral exemplar is good, like Mother Teresa — because God, Incarna-tion aside, is not human, which means that God does not have acquired vir-tues or vices or even moral obligations, since all this would entail complexity in God. This is not to say God could do evil or sin. Sin, ultimately, is falling short of full activity, and God is fully actual. (Further, it is impossible for God to sin, since sin signals a privation or imperfection.)[97] We are simply saying that, whatever else God is, God is the most perfect thing of that sort. And the sort of thing God *is* is the most perfect sort of thing possible, though we should caution ourselves in assuming our attribution of goodness to God maps directly with our understanding of moral goodness as we apply it to human beings.

---

[96] Ibid, 96.
[97] And for what should now be obvious reasons, God's inability to sin is not in tension with God's omnipotence, since God's omnipotence refers to God's ability to make or produce whatever is inherently producible; it does not mean God can *do* literally anything, like swim in a pool of mashed potatoes.

CHAPTER FOUR

How Everything Can Be Explained with God (Including God)

WE HAVE SO FAR argued that the contingency of our world is best explained by a story that posits something extremely special at the foundation of reality — one, immutable, eternal, purely actual, and so on.

However, at this point, one might nevertheless ask what explains this special something. The answer has already been made clear: this special something must somehow be able to explain itself without causing itself. For we would be little better off in our quest for ultimate intelligibility if this fundamental reality, God, were just as mysterious concerning its existence as if we were to posit a pinecone at the basement of reality, with all its arbitrary limits and features inviting further explanation. We cannot, in other words, allow God to be a brute fact, as the pinecone would quite obviously be a brute fact, for then we would have slid back from Further Story into No Story, which we have already determined is untenable.

Properly understood, God is not a brute fact, but an *autonomous fact*, where if we could grasp the essence of God, we would "see" clearly and automatically God's necessary existence, just as we can "see" by grasping the nature of mountains that they automatically include peaks. (Notice: to ask *why* mountains include peaks is to show that one has not understood what a mountain or a peak is). Of course, we cannot grasp God's essence from our perspective, but if we have independent reasons for thinking God exists, and especially for thinking God's essence just is a pure act of existence, existing through itself — which, from everything just considered, we certainly do — this provides motivation to ascribe characteristics to God that are often associated with the ontological argument.

For those unfamiliar, the ontological argument claims that we can move from the idea of God to the affirmation of God as actually existing simply by thinking about God's nature. The argument is fascinating (though controversial) and has seen numerous iterations, stretching back to St. Anselm of Canterbury. It has recently seen something of a revival by philosophers, such as Alvin Plantinga, who have provided formulations relying on the contemporary logic of possibility.[98] For now, these details need not concern us. The primary thing to note is the argument claims that there is something about God's essence that guarantees God's existence.

To summarize, the claim of the ontological argument is that in God the concept of essence and existence are innately inseparable, since existence belongs to the essence of God. And since, according to one proponent of the ontological argument, French philosopher René Descartes, whatever is clearly and distinctly perceived to belong to a thing really does belong to a thing (such as there being peaks wherever there are mountains), so too does existence really belong to God.[99] Hence, God really does exist.

Unsurprisingly, many philosophers argue that these attempts to demonstrate God's existence are a failure, conflating the conceptual with the actual, whereas others have not only defended their soundness, but see them as being self-evident. The range of opinion on ontological arguments is immense, with brilliant thinkers on every side of the debate. St. Thomas, for example, rejected such *a priori* attempts to demonstrate the existence of God,[100] whereas contemporary philosophers — like Plantinga, as mentioned — have revived the tradition of ontological arguments, with new variations cropping up even to this day.[101]

---

[98] A nice overview of ontological arguments can be found in David Beck, *Does God Exist? A History of Answers to the Question* (Westmont, IL: InterVarsity Press, 2021).

[99] Roger Ariew and Eric Watkins (eds), *Modern Philosophy: An Anthology of Primary Sources* (Indianapolis, IN: Hackett, 2009), 59.

[100] Thomas Aquinas, *Summa Theologiae*, I, q. 2, a. 2.

[101] Alvin Plantinga, *God, Freedom, and Evil* (Grand Rapids, MI: Eerdmans, 1989), Part II, Section 7.

Again, such debates need not detain us. What we are interested in is not whether there is an independently sound ontological argument, but whether there is motivation for believing that God, as the ontological argument understands Him, exists. If so, then it becomes clear that God is not a brute fact, but an autonomous fact whose essence carries the explanation for God's existence, even if we are not in a position to grasp the essence of God.

For clarification, let us reiterate an important point: to satisfy our principle of explanation (PSR), we need a worldview that can reduce the number of brute facts to zero. If the suggestions above, including the link between the cosmological and ontological argument, are correct, then only theism can do this. To see how theism succeeds in reducing brute facts to zero, let us borrow from philosopher Kenneth Pearce.[102]

How to Reduce Brute Facts to Zero

Step 1: To satisfy the PSR, show that explanations may ultimately terminate in a single autonomous fact (i.e., a fact about which it makes no sense to ask "why?").

Step 2: Show that real definitions (i.e., statements of essences) are good candidates for autonomous facts. For example, it makes no sense to ask *why* a bachelor is an unmarried male. That is just what a bachelor *is*!

Step 3: Show that if we could grasp God's essence, we could just *see* a priori God's necessary existence and God's freedom. Hence, Aquinas's claim that God's existence is self-evident *to God* (who grasps His own essence) but not to us (who are incapable of grasping God's essence). In other words, Step 3 is arguing that there is a sound ontological argument, and that "God exists" would be part of the real definition of God (i.e., an autonomous fact).

Step 4: Argue that the cosmological argument provides independent ground for believing there is indeed a sound ontological argument and that God has the features described therein.

---

[102] See Pearce, Kenneth L. "Foundational Grounding and the Argument from Contingency," *Oxford Studies in Philosophy of Religion* 8 (2017).

Let us look at each of these four steps.

An autonomous fact differs from a brute fact in the following sense: a brute fact is not just that for which we do not see the reason for its existence (i.e., a mysterious fact), but that for which there is no reason for its existence at all. It still makes sense to ask why this (allegedly) brute fact exists; it is just that there is no answer to the question. Brute facts are just there, and that's all! There is no intelligible explanation to be found. As we have stated, brute facts are a denial of the PSR; ultimately, they are a rejection of the explanatory principle that we claimed cannot be coherently rejected.

However, according to classical theism, God's existence is not brute. As philosophers like Leibniz and Aquinas held, God carries the reason for His existence intrinsically in Himself. Whereas everything else, which is qualitatively finite and has arbitrary limits, points beyond itself to an extrinsic cause for an intelligible answer to the question of its existence, God's explanation is "internal" and has to do with his "special" self-subsistent nature, which we have been detailing to some extent above. In other words, God is what can ultimately satisfy the PSR, which says anything that exists has a reason for its existence, either due to some external cause or its internal principle(s). Minimally, whatever is has *that whereby it is* (i.e., an act of existence), either through itself or from another.

This invites the question of whether there is something about the definition of God — that is, something about God's nature — such that if we could grasp it, we could see that it would make no sense to ask why God exists. If so, this would make "God" an autonomous fact that could provide an extremely satisfying terminus to our explanatory framework. The PSR would be satisfied, brute facts eliminated, and we would have a foundational theory with enormous predictive and explanatory success (more on that in a minute).

To reiterate, an autonomous fact is something for which it does not make sense to ask "why." As Pearce explains:

> The most obvious candidates are the various sorts of definitions. Thus although the fact that the English word 'bachelor' means an unmarried male admits of a historical/etymological explanation, the fact that bachelors are unmarried males needs no explanation. If there are such things as Aristotelian 'real definitions' — definitions not of words but of things — then these are likewise good candidates for

autonomous facts. Real definitions would be statements of essences, and they would not require further explanation.[103]

Pearce continues:

> After we have posited God in order to explain History, we see that our explanation can bottom out in autonomous facts, and therefore give us a maximally satisfying explanatory structure, only if the real definition of God has certain features. This gives us reason to hypothesize that the real definition of God does have these features, i.e., that there is a sound ontological argument. Because we do not have independent grounds for believing the premises of this ontological argument, we cannot use it to establish the existence of God. This does not, however, prevent us from using it to explain God's existence and, indeed, God's necessary existence.[104]

So, the contingent universe is explained by God's creative act. God's creative act is explained by God's reasons and God's freedom. God's reasons and God's freedom are explained by God's existence and God having those reasons and freedom. God's existence and God having those reasons and freedom are explained by God's real definition, which is an autonomous (as opposed to brute) fact. The PSR is secure, as are the conditions for knowledge and rational belief. Everything is intelligible.

We have covered a lot of ground. Before we move onto the next section, let me summarize the major points made thus far:

✣ We began our philosophical hunt for God by asking why anything exists at all.
✣ We then defended an explanatory principle which caused us to posit the existence of at least one necessary being to make sense of the existence of any contingent being.
✣ We then considered many different reasons for thinking that the necessary being is God as traditionally understood — pure existence, simple, eternal, omnipotent, omniscient, and perfectly good.
✣ Finally, we explained how God can provide a principled explanatory terminus, not leaving anything crucially requiring explanation unexplained.

[103] Ibid.
[104] Ibid.

> For this reason, God, and God alone, is not just the best, but the only actually adequate explanation for why any (contingent) thing exists.

While more would have to be said to identify this entity as the God of any religion (Christianity, Judaism, Islam, what have you), enough has been said to have establish it as God understood broadly by classical theists.

What we have argued so far most aligns with the traditional philosophical approach to God, what philosophers have called "metaphysical demonstration." If the considerations above are good ones, then something significant has come into view: We have encountered an insurmountable explanatory limitation for naturalism. That is, we have identified features of the world that can only *in principle* be explained by a special sort of thing — a thing which we have argued bears attributes most would readily admit signal divinity. If this is correct, then the best argument against God has been defeated, for naturalism cannot explain as much as theism, and complicating the naturalistic theory would be of no help, for *only* God can explain why anything exists and not nothing instead.

Summary

We have argued that the contingency of the world demands necessity as its ultimate explanation and that something can be necessary (in the sense our explanation requires) only if it does not have contingency-implying features or attributes. In other words, it is a being whose essence just *is* its existence, is absolutely simple, immutable, and unbounded. Perfection *is* at bottom — or so we argued — because it *has* to be. And that is what God is, a being of pure positivity, unrestricted along all inherent attributes that do not themselves entail limitation: Power, knowledge, goodness, and so forth. Nothing could exist without a perfect foundation to reality. Something does exist. Ergo...

However, we are not going to rest our case entirely on the previous considerations alone. There are more points to be made in favor of theism and against naturalism. The large remainder of this book will take these considerations into view and mark a transition from the traditional approach to thinking about God to the more contemporary approach of worldview comparison, striving to answer the question: does classical theism or does naturalism offer the better large-scale theory of everything?

PART TWO

Shifting Methodology
Explanation, Simplicity, and God

CHAPTER FIVE

Explanation (It's Not Too Complicated) and Simplicity (It's Complicated)

WE ARE ABOUT READY to shift methodology. So far, we have used the traditional approach to argue for the existence of God as the necessary condition for the very existence of contingent things, and to gain clarity around the theistic hypothesis, by spelling out just what God is — i.e., purely actual, eternal, omnipotent, simple, and so forth.

Earlier I mentioned that this traditional approach can be further supported with the contemporary approach of worldview comparison, where different Big Pictures of Reality are pitted against each other as competitive, large-scale explanatory theories. That is, we can gain further confirmation of the classical theistic perspective by seeing how well it explains (or predicts) other broad features of the world — physical fine-tuning, an objective moral landscape, consciousness, and so on — not equally well explained by naturalism. As we shall see, classical theism accomplishes this with greater theoretical simplicity, or so the remainder of this book will argue.

When it comes to worldview comparison, we overall prefer theories which can explain more of the data with fewer fundamental commitments. The most important criterion for theory selection is, of course, explanatory comprehensiveness. How well does a theory explain, or anticipate or make sense of, some explanatory target or set of targets? After explanatory comprehensiveness comes the consideration of simplicity. That is, if we believe two theories are explanatorily on par, we prefer the simpler theory, since we believe — for reasons we'll explain shortly — more complex theories have more ways they could go wrong, and thus turn out to be false. Simpler theories, then, are more likely to be true, other things being equal.

THE FINER POINTS

While there are other criteria often used to evaluate between theories (such as explanatory scope and fit with background knowledge), when it comes to worldview debates, philosophers have argued these criteria drop out, because of how comprehensive these theories are supposed to be. In such a case, the evaluation of worldviews comes down to their respective explanatory power and simplicity.[105]

When it comes to evaluating the explanatory power of rival theories — in our case, classical theism against naturalism — we'll be engaging basic hypothesis-testing between worldview competitors.

In effect, we'll be using a widely endorsed principle known as the *likelihood principle*, which states:

Some data (D) counts as evidence favoring one hypothesis (H1) over another hypothesis (H2), just in case that D is more likely on the assumption that H1 is true than it is on the assumption that H2 is true.

For example, in our context, we might want to ask:

What is the likelihood of beings like us given the existence of God versus what is the likelihood of beings like us given naturalism?

If it can be argued that D is more likely to occur given H1 than H2, then D counts as evidence for H1. Again, this is a basic form of probabilistic reasoning, though a few clarifications are in order.

Firstly, precise numerical values need not be assignable to make a reasonable assessment of the situation. Consider the following example: You are

---

[105] Richard Swinburne, "God as the Simplest Explanation of the Universe," *European Journal of Philosophy of Religion* 2 (2010), 1–24.

wandering in the woods and stumble upon what appears to be an abandoned cabin.[106] You infer the cabin is abandoned because it exhibits features that you believe are more likely to occur if that is the case — front door falling off, mildew creeping up the sides, and so on. However, you peer into the cabin and discover something interesting: a cup of hot tea steeping on a nice wooden table. Immediately, you abandon the "this cabin is abandoned" hypothesis and adopt the "this cabin is occupied" hypothesis. Why? Because you know that one is far more likely to discover a cup of hot steeping tea in an occupied cabin than an abandoned one. Even if it were logically possible to account for the cup of hot steeping tea apart from an active tenant (some extremely unlikely confluence of natural accidents, perhaps), what we are concerned with is probability, not mere possibility.

Also, notice this. It might itself be quite unlikely that you discover a cup of steeping tea when walking into any given occupied cabin. What are the chances of that? 0.5 percent, maybe? Who knows. But it probably isn't high. Nevertheless, *it's the ratio that matters* — that is, the fact that even if discovering a cup of steeping tea might be unlikely given an occupied cabin, it is far, far lower given an abandoned cabin, and *that* is what pushes you to endorse the hypothesis that the cabin is occupied. Of course, all this is happening automatically for any person whose reasoning equipment is functioning properly. My point is just to highlight that this form of reasoning can be made more rigorous and is often deployed by philosophers and scientists to either confirm or disconfirm respective hypotheses.

In our case, maybe you might not think it would be all that likely that God would create beings like us — maybe you think there is a 1 percent chance of God doing so. I think this is an incorrect assessment, but setting that aside, the more relevant question is how that compares to the likelihood of beings like us emerging if naturalism (principle of indifference) is true. Maybe you think it is far lower — say, .000000000001 percent chance. If so, then it doesn't matter if you think it's unlikely God would create beings like us. Since you think it is far more unlikely beings like us would emerge if naturalism is true, the fact

---

[106] Borrowed from philosopher Tim McGrew.

we are here would thereby be evidence in favor of God's existence. In this respect, God is the better explanation.

Again, I should emphasize how commonsensical this approach is. For example, we reject the idea that there was a monkey at a typewriter if what comes out is a sentence reading, "This sentence was not written by a monkey at a typewriter." Why? Because we feel it is far more likely that a coherent sentence like that will emerge if there is not a monkey at the typewriter but rather a more intelligent agent. A more intelligent agent is the better explanation insofar as it better predicts or anticipates the production of a coherent sentence and is more likely to result in a coherent sentence than a monkey randomly smashing keys. Really, we are just taking this everyday form of probabilistic reasoning and applying it at large.

We almost have everything in place we need to begin asking whether theism is a better explanation, an equal explanation, or a worse explanation of certain worldly features than naturalism. There is, however, one final thing we should consider before we begin making such evaluations, and that is the respective simplicity of classical theism and metaphysical naturalism.

This might seem like another detour, but it isn't. To fully appreciate the power of classical theism as a Big Picture Theory of Everything, we must understand the *two* most important aspects of theory comparison. Explanatory comprehensiveness is one, simplicity is another. After that, we can begin to see which theory explains the most (explanatory targets) with the least (fundamental commitments). And that one ought to be declared the winner.

Simplicity – It's Complicated.

Determining which theory is a better explanation of some phenomena is not, at least in principle, terribly complicated. It ultimately comes down to whether some phenomenon is better expected (more likely to occur) given some theory in comparison to another. However, determining which theory is simpler is, quite ironically, complicated.

Nevertheless, because the claim to simplicity significantly factors in the naturalist's argument against God, further remarks now seem appropriate. (Organizational remark: I decided to put the chapter concerning simplicity following the sections on cosmological reasoning, for the cosmological arguments help to explicate the theistic picture in ways relevant for evaluating its simplicity as a large-scale theory of everything.)

Again, to the extent that the cosmological argument successfully picks out an *in principle* explanatory difficulty for naturalism, appeals to simplicity may appear quite irrelevant. Nevertheless, it can be instructive to set that conclusion aside and entertain, for the sake of argument, considerations of simplicity with respect to theism and naturalism, especially since a strong case can be made that theism is, in fact, a simpler theory overall.

What's more, perhaps not everyone will think the considerations concerning theism and explanation are as decisive as I take them to be, and so, for them, considerations of simplicity may become increasingly relevant. If so — that is, if it happens that deciding between these paradigms does come down to simplicity — then I should minimally like to make the case that this consideration alone should not cause someone to endorse naturalism and, if anything, it *should* cause someone to endorse theism.

Finally, considerations of simplicity will be important to the section following this one, where we will take a deeper look at what else theism better explains than naturalism *unless* naturalism complicates itself quite considerably (hence it'll be helpful to understand why such additional complication is a "bad thing" as far as theoretical competition is concerned).

With all that in mind, let's continue.

As I said, debates concerning simplicity are complicated. I will do my best to bring out the relevant considerations, suggesting that theism is not, in the relevant aspects, obviously more complicated as a worldview than even the simplest form of naturalism. Actually, theism is almost certainly a simpler theory overall, and the very notion of simplicity being a guide to truth is better situated within a theistic worldview. Hence, if someone thinks simplicity *actually is* a guide to truth, this may itself be some evidence for God's existence.

Most of us assume simplicity is a guide to truth, even if not an exclusive nor infallible one. Even in everyday circumstances, we intuitively select simpler theories over more complicated ones. For example, I prefer "it rained" as a theory to explain why my driveway is wet to "twenty children came by in the middle of the night and dumped buckets of water on it."

A theory, for what it's worth, is just a means for making sense of, or coming into cognitive contact with, the world; it's a narrative we fashion around relevant data. And we have criteria for selecting theories (explanatory comprehensiveness, simplicity, etc.) because we want to increase the odds of arriving at the theory that most closely tracks with reality.

One reason we think simplicity should be a principle in theory selection is that data, both in everyday and scientific endeavors, *underdetermines*. That is to say, data is often compatible with an exceptionally large number of theories, which means we need other criteria to help us choose the best (most likely to be true) theory. Scientific laws, for example, often go far beyond the evidence.

Generally, we reject what appear to be ugly, convoluted hypotheses and prefer what appears to be the simplest theory expressible in the simplest way.

Curve fitting is another example. We can draw curves however we want, yet we tend to draw the simplest curve that accommodates the data set. As it happens, when more data is gathered, simpler curves typically make more accurate predictions concerning those data points. Fortuitous? Fitting? Either way, in practice, the simplest alternatives (so far as we can tell, they are simpler) are preferred, with the important qualification that other things are equal (explanatory comprehensiveness). Why?

The link between simplicity and truth concerns probability, or so it appears. In short, theories with more basic components or "moving parts" seem to have more opportunities to "go wrong." We intuit this when considering the "twenty children with buckets of water" theory. There's just a lot of basic components that need to coordinate in a relatively improbable way.

Or think of grand-scale conspiracy theories. The reason we don't believe these conspiracy theories is not because they fail to explain the relevant data. In fact, most are designed for exactly that. Rather, it's because they often seem to have too many "moving parts," so many ways things could fail to come together. Just think of all the coordination between parties and the cover-up involved — of all the things that must go right for the conspiracy theory to be true that seem very improbable. Conspiratorial thinking — and its relation to naturalism — is something we'll revisit in a subsequent chapter. For now, we can say this: we assume simplicity is a guide to truth. Simpler theories seem like more probable theories.

It's tempting to say naturalism leaves us somewhat in the dark about this. After all, what about *naturalism* should cause us to think that simpler theories are more likely to be true than gerrymandered theories? As Alvin Plantinga explains, "Naturalism gives us no reason at all to expect the world to conform to our preferences of simplicity. From that perspective, surely, the world could just as well have been such that unlovely, miserably complex theories are more likely to be true."[107]

The naturalist, fairly enough, could appeal to what's already been said: Simpler theories are more probable. True, but that is not something specifically tied to naturalism. Besides, what has been said concerning simplicity and probability does not *guarantee* that the simplest theories will be true. It could have been the case that many more ugly, convoluted theories turned out correct. But this is typically not what we see, at least concerning most scientific theories and our everyday experience.

Theism, on the other hand, predicts simplicity as a guide to truth for other reasons. First, classical theists maintain that God Himself is ontologically simple. Also, as Plantinga reminds us, theists argue that humans are made in God's image (i.e., having intellect and will), and thus it is reasonable to think our intellectual preferences broadly resemble His. If correct, then it is reasonable to expect creation will itself reflect those preferences, which it certainly seems to. Plantinga writes, "We are so constituted that our intellectual success requires that the world be relevantly simple; the world is in fact relevantly simple. This fit is only to be expected on theism, but is a piece of enormous cosmic serendipity on naturalism."

The point is modest. Rather than arguing that theism is itself a simpler theory (stay tuned, that's coming), Plantinga is just saying that our very notion of simplicity as a guide to truth — and simplicity actually being a guide to truth makes better sense if God exists than if God does not exist — is itself *some* evidence of God's existence. I think that's probably right, though *far* from decisive. Thus, I note it merely in passing.

But let's get back to the criteria of simplicity for purposes of theory selection.

---

[107] Alvin Plantinga, *Where the Conflict Really Lies*, 298.

The current literature expresses two major understandings of simplicity.[108] The first is *theoretical simplicity*, the second is *ontological simplicity*. Plainly put, theoretical simplicity concerns the number and conciseness of the theory's basic principles (the fewer and less complicated *fundamental* principles, the better), whereas ontological simplicity pertains to the basic things and kinds of things that a worldview says exists.

Ontological simplicity itself is often broken into two understandings: *quantitative* (number of existing individual things) and *qualitative* (number of *kinds* of things). I will further explain these understandings of simplicity as we work through our analysis of whether theism or naturalism is simpler in each respect.

THE FINER POINTS

Which of these understandings of simplicity is the right one, or more important? It is difficult to say, and some philosophers are skeptical this can be adjudicated. As Bradly Monton warns us:

"Philosophers are sometimes too willing to take these relatively uncontroversial judgments from physics and wildly extrapolate them into controversial judgments in philosophy. For example, consider ontological parsimony (parsimony of objects) versus ideological parsimony (parsimony of concepts). Is it ontological or ideological parsimony that matters for simplicity? While some philosophers attempt to provide an objective answer to this question, I am skeptical. Maybe God has an opinion, but absent God's judgment, I maintain that it's just a matter of personal preference."[109]

---

[108] Joshua Rasmussen and Kevin Vallier (eds), *A New Theist Response to the New Atheists* (UK: Routledge, 2021), 65.

[109] Jerry Walls and Trent Dougherty (eds), *Two Dozen (or So) Arguments for the Existence of God* (Oxford: Oxford University Press, 2018), 185. I should note that other philosophers are even more skeptical of whether simplicity is a reliable guide to truth. Michael Huemer, for example, argues that in the absence of evidence, simple and complex theories are really on a par, and, moreover, that when it comes to philosophical (rather than scientific) application, the idea of a simpler theory being more probably true typically does not apply. Perhaps Huemer is correct about this. If so, then perhaps that makes the project of this book easier, because the naturalist will have lost what is perhaps her strongest *apparent* advantage (having a simpler theory and by extension having a more probably true theory). I cannot settle this larger dispute about simplicity here, but suggest the interested reader read Huemer's account. Michael Huemer, *Understanding Knowledge* (Independently published, 2022), 256–65.

While I share a certain skeptical sympathy with Monton, we'll persist in our analysis since, given the understandings of simplicity we have, it can still be shown that theism comes out on top. Plus, I don't think these understandings are necessarily unrelated or at odds, since the simplicity of a theory can reflect the simplicity of the underlying reality (or realities), which I think is obviously the case when considering classical theism against competing worldview paradigms.

Looking at the first understanding of simplicity, theism seems to fare better than naturalism, since the God Hypothesis can be expressed rather simply concerning its most basic principle. For example, the Anselmian tradition says God is "the greatest conceivable being."[110] Plantinga prefers "Maximal Greatness."[111] Aquinas uses *ipsum esse subsistens*, or subsistent being itself.[112] It is tough to see how naturalism could be as simple in this respect, since as a theory it must posit a fundamental principle (or collection of principles) limited in various respects, inevitably requiring more information to explain. For example: the existence of a number of natural laws, the parameters of those laws, and perhaps even the existence of each and every particle.[113]

However, we can definitively say this: For the naturalist to posit a fundamental theory, it must compete with or exclude God. For that to happen,

[110] One may wish to state it differently, of course, but regardless, the major traditions of understanding God all have quite simple expressions — i.e., "maximally perfect being," or what have you.

[111] Granted, it's not immediately obvious what the notion of, say, maximal greatness entails, but once one works out what is entailed by an absolutely perfect being (for example, being omnipotent or unconditionally loving), these discoveries (or "properties" if you like) are not complicating additions to the theistic theory but discoveries nested within it.

[112] Hopefully, as I've shown in the section on cosmological reasoning, these different understandings or descriptions of God are not just compatible but harmonious.

[113] Trent Dougherty makes two other important points as well. Given Humeanism about laws, which most naturalists are committed to, it's hard to see how there might not be trillions upon trillions of fundamental brute facts for the naturalistic — obviously, that would be an enormously complicated theory. Moreover, it is difficult to see how each of the more than 1080 fundamental particles would not be a bottom level brute fact on naturalism; again, quite complicated! For further discussion on these points, see T. Dougherty, *The Problem of Animal Pain* (London: Palgrave MacMillan, 2014), 41, nn. 11–13.

it must be a fundamental theory that is fundamentally imperfect. It must be bounded in certain respects. It must have arbitrary limits, either with respect to power or position or knowledge or all the above. This complicates the naturalistic theory, as Joshua Rasmussen tells us, since each arbitrary limit requires additional information to describe, reducing the internal likeliness of the theory under consideration. To illustrate, Rasmussen asks us to consider the following rival theories:

> A foundation which has (1) a mass of 2^{41} grams, (2) the shape of a sphere, and (3) the capacity to produce exactly 2&88 particles.
>
> VS.
>
> A foundation which has (1) no mass, (2) no shape, and (3) the capacity to produce any number of particles.[114]

As Rasmussen points out, the latter has fewer basic attributes and is simpler to describe, making a foundation without arbitrary limits, bounds, or cutoffs internally more likely. Rasmussen's illustration maps onto the relevant differences between the naturalistic and theistic hypotheses, between the necessary boundedness of any physical reality and the necessary unboundedness of God.

Notice this as well: the bounds or limits that the naturalist posits at the foundation are necessarily *brute* — that is, necessarily unexplained and unexplainable within a naturalistic framework. Because they are at the foundation, there is nothing deeper that could explain why *those* limits are just this way and not some other way instead, despite seeming to be something that should have a deeper explanation.

Theism doesn't have this problem, since theism can explain all limited entities by the one, simple, qualitatively unlimited entity: God. This preserves an important intuition of ours, one articulated in the previous section, namely, that all limits — especially all arbitrary limits — have some deeper explanation, since it presumably makes perfect sense to ask, *why those limits and not some other limits?* At some point, naturalism must come to some set of arbitrary limits which remain unexplained. Theism does not.

---

[114] Rasmussen, *How Reason*, 69.

Of course, this understanding of simplicity itself encounters the complication of how one determines just what principles are fundamental to one's theory. The best we can say here is that some commitment is fundamental, if that something has no further explanation according to that theory. If that is right, the following quick point can then be made: theism has either the least basic principles or no more basic principles than the simplest possible form of naturalism. God is obviously *the* basic principle for the classical theist. Theists often argue even other necessary truths can ultimately find deeper explanation via the existence of God, including mathematical and moral truths.[115] It is difficult to see how the naturalist could say something similar, and thus they will probably have to leave these necessary truths, if they affirm them at all, brute and unexplained, increasing their number of basic principles, and thus becoming a more complicated theory than theism. Perhaps infinitely more complicated since the range of such necessary truths are themselves infinite.[116]

Here's another thing to consider. Even if it turned out to be the case that theism posits "one extra thing," if it happens that that one extra thing can unify and explain everything "above it," then this is not an increase in complexity but simplicity in the relevant theoretical respect, assuming we have achieved

---

[115] By way of quick example, the theist could argue that mathematical properties are properties of concrete being (not denizens of some independently existing abstract realm, as Platonists maintain), with *being itself* being the logical source of the intentional being which are mathematical entities. All of this, ultimately, can be traced back to, and grounded in, the existence and nature of God, who is subsistent being itself, and who, in understanding Himself perfectly, would grasp the entire mathematical landscape in a single, simple, intuitive insight. This would not only provide a deeper explanation of mathematical truths but also of their obviously necessary nature, as grounded in the necessary structure of being itself. Similar things, of course, have been and could be said about logic and morality.

[116] Kenny Pearce emphasizes this point in exchange with naturalist Graham Oppy:
Graham admits a lot of necessary truths to his worldview — not just all of logic and mathematics, but also all of ethics and aesthetics, as well as the laws of nature and boundary conditions of the universe. The view that none of these things can be explained is intrinsically implausible and flatly inconsistent with the way mathematical and ethical reasoning is actually conducted. Further, this feature of Graham's worldview involves a massive (in fact, infinite) multiplication of primitives, and therefore it comes at a heavy cost with respect to the criteria of worldview comparison. Many worldviews — including many theistic worldviews — are able to avoid these costs.
Pearce, *Is There a God*, 185.

greater unity and explanation (whereas unity was previously lacking or a deeper explanation or both) through a simpler, fundamental theory.

As Kenny Pearce emphasizes:

> According to the naturalist, there is only one kind of fundamental stuff, physical stuff. God, however, is not physical, so the theist has fundamental physical stuff plus God, which is extra complexity. This, however, is a mistake. According to the version of classical theism I've developed, the physical is grounded in God, who is the only truly fundamental entity. So at the most fundamental level, this view not only has only one kind of thing, it has only one individual thing, namely, God. If the naturalist objects that I have introduced a new layer in the grounding hierarchy, this is quite correct, but when we introduce a more fundamental layer of reality that unifies and explains the layers to which we were already committed, this is not an increase in complexity. As a result, it is actually not clear that the naturalist has any advantage in simplicity at all.[117]

Turning now to ontological simplicity, certain naturalists will insist that their theory is "leaner" in this respect. For example, they might say the theist believes in everything the naturalist does (say, the physical universe), plus at least one more entity (God). On the surface, this seems plausible. After all, the person claiming both A & B is claiming something more — and something probabilistically less likely, considered abstractly — than the person who claims just A. But this is only on the surface. As philosopher Tim McGrew points out, the naturalist is not just claiming A and *being agnostic about the additional commitments* to which the theist holds but is *actively denying them*. So really, the naturalist is claiming A *and NOT-B*. And as McGrew notes, "There is no simple and straightforward ordering of these two positions with respect to simplicity, just as there is no general inequality that holds between P(A&B) and P(A&NOT-B)."[118] In other

---

[117] Ibid, 65.

[118] Paul Gould and Richard Davis (eds), *Four Views on Christianity and Philosophy* (Grand Rapids, MI: Zondervan 2016), 56. Relatedly, philosopher Michael Huemer explains "The following is also a theorem of probability: As long as $P(B/A) \neq 0$, $P(A \& \text{not-}B)$ is strictly less than $P(A)$. Therefore, if you can explain all your evidence by citing A, you should not go on to deny B in addition, since that lowers the probability of your theory." See Huemer, *Understanding*, 260.

words, there are no general rules of probability theory that tell us A & NOT-B is any simpler than A & B. So, the superficial analysis just doesn't work.

However, even the initial suggestion isn't quite right, since it is almost certainly false that the theist believes in *exactly* what the naturalist does, plus at least God. Or even if the number is the same, the kinds or categories almost certainly differ. As stated before, one's fundamental theory often determines how one conceives of everything above it. Upon substantial analysis, it seems the naturalist would have to be committed to certain things or certain kinds of things the theist is not. For example, the theist is not committed to any ultimately *uncaused* contingent entities or any ultimately *unexplained* necessary entities or truths (say, moral facts), since God can fundamentally ground all other contingent and necessary realities, and ultimately explain his own existence, as we explored with the cosmological argument and will explore further later. Since naturalism excludes theism, it looks as if the naturalist will be committed to either uncaused contingent things, unexplained necessities, or both. In this sense, the theist is committed to fewer categories — just caused contingent entities and explained necessary entities or truths — and these may be simpler overall once a more substantial analysis is engaged. Again, specifics matter.

THE FINER POINTS

Because specifics matter so much, this further complicates the analysis of this chapter. For example, different commitments will emerge depending on how naturalists analyze and attempt to explain different features of reality. Some of their accounts, admittedly, will be simpler than the traditional theistic one in certain respects (even if not overall, or on the fundamental level), but I suggest that this can almost only ever happen when offering an explanation that ultimately is not a good one. For example, if the naturalist wants to explain consciousness as simply neural processing ("the mind is what the brain does," to put it colloquially), probably they are committed to less than the theist or other theorists who—rightfully, in my estimation—see these reductive attempts as wholly inadequate.[119] Here, a quick point:

---

[119] For detailed critiques of naturalistic philosophies of mind, though varied in what they believe the ultimately correct account is (substance dualism vs hylomorphism, for example), see: Alvin Plantinga, "Against Materialism," *Faith and Philosophy* 23, no. 1 (2006), 3–32; Jim Madden, *Mind, Matter, and Nature* (Washington, DC: The

because we cannot replace our concept of consciousness with a concept of neural processing (a conceptual grasp of the latter offers no conceptual grasp of the former), this itself gives strong reason to think that this account of what consciousness *is* is false. After all, not every (any?) description of some consciousness phenomena or state is a description of what may be its underlying physical correlate. Describe any physical happenings from a third-person scientific perspective all you want; this gives us no understanding of "what it is like" to experience, say, pain, or the color blue, or the taste of chocolate.

In short, the impossibility of conceptual or explanatory reduction is a plausible indicator of the failure of ontological reduction in that respect. Said differently, if the claim is that some X (in our case, consciousness) just *is* Y (neural processing), then we should expect that talk of X should itself be replaceable (without loss of content) with talk of Y, which is not the case when it comes to not just the above example but *any* materialist understanding of consciousness or mind. In this instance and others, what might be gained with respect to simplicity is more than offset with respect to explanatory failure. Again, we see the primary theme of this book: Naturalism is simpler only insofar as it is explanatorily inadequate.

To reiterate a point that is once again relevant: a theory with fewer existing entities may ultimately be more complicated because the entity it omits in comparison to its rival theory is explanatorily powerful and unifying; thus, to keep up in the explanatory race the remaining components of the current theory *themselves become basic*, and must be wired together in quite improbable ways to keep up. Again, what might appear simpler on the surface is more complicated under the hood.

This, I suggest, is what naturalism is like.

For naturalism to keep up in the explanatory race, it must often adopt adjunct hypotheses that negatively complicate the naturalistic project overall and frequently introduce more into the naturalistic hypothesis, which itself fails to find adequate explanation. Progress, in this sense, for the naturalist, is like politics: replacing one problem with another. An example of this would be attempting to solve the explanatory difficulty of physical fine-tuning by

Catholic University of America Press, 2013); Richard Swinburne, *Are We Bodies or Souls?* (Oxford: Oxford University Press, 2023).

positing a multiverse, which itself appears to require fine-tuning to be theoretically feasible (more on that later). Not only that, but by dropping God out of the picture, things that were previously explained or explainable by God, such as the number and parameters of laws of nature, now become basic, seemingly scattered components of the naturalistic theory, making naturalism *fundamentally* more complicated *and* less explanatorily powerful *even if* naturalism has one less existing thing.

In other words, for naturalism to beef up its explanatory power in one area, it complicates itself and loses explanatory comprehensiveness overall. In this sense, it becomes worse than many grand-scale conspiracy theories. This is a point we will substantiate in subsequent chapters as we explore the explanatory details and ultimate poverty of naturalism in relation to various worldly features, whether morality or physical fine-tuning.

On this score, philosopher Richard Swinburne argues for the simplicity advantage that theism has over naturalism, since the fundamental fact of theism is one substance with just one property — or as other philosophers argue, zero properties held in the simplest way, which is with zero limitation.[120] In short, theism has an exceptionally simple fundamental structure, of the sort we are broadly familiar with and utilizing a familiar type of explanation, which is creative with respect to goodness (more on that in just a minute). Naturalism, on the other hand, will be inevitably strapped with greater complexity at bottom and committed to an impressive number of unexplained brute facts: contingent (and perhaps necessary) entities, number of laws, parameters of laws, and whatever else. Just how to count the piling complexities of naturalism is itself a complexity, but however

---

[120] Swinburne argues that property is omnipotence, from which the other divine attributes are entailed. Joshua Sijuwade, though following Swinburne in many respects, departs from him on this score, and argues that while God should be construed as an "omnipotence trope" and that the other divine attributes are derivable from this analysis, they do not follow by way of entailment but are related to God and each other by way of numerical identity. Sijuwade's analysis is more consistent with the tradition of classical theism and divine simplicity, but the differences between Swinburne and Sijuwade need not be settled for this section of the book, since either construal renders theism obviously simpler than the simplest form of naturalism. Joshua Sijuwade, "Grounding and the Existence of God," *Metaphysica* (2021).

attempts are made to resolve that difficulty, it seems almost inevitable that naturalism turns out to be a far more complicated affair than theism is.

Going further, Swinburne argues that even the simplest conceivable form of naturalism (here, he's being generous by not just considering theories of naturalism naturalists actually hold) will not, in principle, be able to match the simplicity of theism. He writes:

> Physical cosmology *could* postulate one unextended substance, a particle, as that from which all else evolved (or on which all else depended, if the universe did not have a beginning). It would need to be a physical object of a certain kind in having certain properties, powers, and liabilities. The normal kind of physical substance would have powers of particular mathematical quantities (such as the attractive and repulsive powers of mass and charge) and liabilities to exercise them under certain physical conditions. These would need to be fairly specific powers and liabilities (some mathematically precise mass and charge for example) if they were to make it probable that it would bring about a universe with substances of few kinds with the same simple powers and liabilities as each other, of a human-body producing kind; and this specificity would make the hypothesis of the existence of such a substance more complicated than the hypothesis of theism.[121]

It thus appears that theism has considerable advantages concerning simplicity, no matter how we try to analyze it. Theoretically, theism has a very simple basic principle.[122] Ontologically, theism has just one utterly simple existing thing and probably no more kinds or categories of things than naturalism has overall, if not fewer. By lacking the deeper unifying principle afforded by theism, naturalism, if it is going to keep up in the explanatory race, incurs disqualifying complexity costs.

To bring this point a little further into view, consider the following (admittedly silly) example. Suppose someone brings in a stack of turtles to explain the stability of the earth but when asked what explains that stack of

---

[121] Swinburne, "Simplest Explanation." Emphasis mine.
[122] Simple to state, even if not simple to comprehend. But that's okay. The same can be true of many scientific or mathematical theories.

turtles suggests the final turtle *necessarily exists* (or is *necessarily stable* or both). This proposal not only introduces greater complexity but expands, rather than contracts, mystery. After all, we only had the earth to explain before, now we have the earth and *all these darn turtles*, plus *another necessary turtle* (that doesn't explain its own necessity). Before there was just the question concerning the earth's stability; then came the turtle stack with presumably either one brute contingent turtle at the bottom or an infinitely extended stack of turtles itself existing without further explanation. Later, there are still contingent turtles, but now at least one necessary turtle that is nevertheless brute — i.e., can't explain its own necessity. The point? If the additional postulation of a necessary turtle seems not only inadequate but an increase in complexity, I claim that that is the sort of situation naturalism is in with its inability to explain various necessities, especially necessary beings, not just truths. What's more, if you think the invoking of necessity in this situation is arbitrary and ultimately fails to explain the relevant target, my sympathies are with you. Again, I suggest that this is akin to what naturalism is up to.

The example above, however artificial, relates to the point philosopher Enric Gel has raised concerning two important questions that classical theism can answer that naturalism cannot: how many fundamental entities are there, and why.[123] As we've seen with the section on cosmological reasoning, the classical theist can provide a principled answer to the question of how many fundamental entities there are and why (i.e., one, because there can only be one being whose essence is its existence).

For what it's worth, holding out for "future physics" won't help the naturalist, either, certainly not against those who insist the question of fundamentality is a metaphysical question. In other words, without begging the question in favor of physicalism, it doesn't seem like physics could be capable, in principle, of telling us the number of initial fundamental realities or why they're necessary or both.

---

[123] Enric Gel, "How Many and Why: A question for Graham Oppy that classical theism can answer," *Religious Studies* (2021), 1–11. For a defense against criticism of his project, see Enric Gel, "'There Can Only Be One': A response to Joseph C. Schmid," *Religious Studies* (21 November 2022) at https://www.cambridge.org/core/journals/religious-studies.

Granted, many naturalists *do* answer the question of how many fundamental entities there are. Unsurprisingly from the theistic perspective, they answer that question often very differently from one another. Other proposals are vaguer and, as we've seen, suggest something like a first necessary initial state of physical reality, and through a model of indeterministic causation, there comes everything else. Okay, but the question remains: how many fundamental *entities*, we can ask, and why? There does not seem to be any way to even guess how many items comprise said initial state. The problem isn't that naturalists don't give answers to this question; the problem is the question seems, given naturalism, unanswerable apart from arbitrary decree. Worse still, apart from picking an arbitrary number of initial items, there seems to be no reason to explain why that number would be necessary, assuming it is — that it had to be, say, 47, instead of 2, or 10,008. Again, classical theism avoids these difficulties entirely, given the simplest answer to perhaps the most important theoretical question. This is a significant advantage for classical theism concerning not just simplicity but explanatory comprehensiveness.[124]

There are objections, of course. Isn't God a new *kind* of thing, for example? Perhaps. But even if that was so, the admission of this new kind of thing seems more than paid for by how it explains and unifies both itself and everything above it, and does little to set back theism in simplicity, compared to naturalism and the various other kinds of things the naturalist is committed to absent God. However, theistic philosophers contest this notion, since God is ultimately a personal agent or mind, and these are things we're already committed to and familiar with. The retort will be that God is quite unlike personal agents or minds we're familiar with, minimally in being unembodied or immaterial, which requires analogy or "stretching concepts," something the naturalist may

---

[124] One might wonder if a timeless zero-dimensional point could work for the naturalist here as a fundamental entity. It seems not, for two reasons. If, qua point, this entity has location, then it is difficult to see how it would not, in principle, be multipliable — that is, as having one at this location and another at that location. If there are no other locations to occupy at sometime within this universe, that is a contingent limitation, not an in principle one, according to the naturalistic hypothesis. One could imagine a multiverse scenario here. Additionally, to exclude theism (to not be God), this entity must be limited in some respect, which invites the further (ultimately unanswerable question) for the naturalist: how many limits (with respect to power, position, etc.), and why.

avoid. And here the theistic response is that 1) it appears the skeptic may be assuming a material version of mind — which is up for debate, if not definitely false — and 2) the notion of a disembodied being seems less relevant than the similarity concerning agency, and 3) it's not clear naturalists *can* avoid stretch concepts, since science itself makes use of them (think about the notion of waves in theoretical physics; clearly that is stretching a concept and employing analogy). And so, the conversation continues as complexities mount. For my part, I'm confident that even if God did count as a new kind of thing, and even if our positing of God incurs additional ideological costs concerning the "stretching of concepts" (analogical predication), the overall simplicity considerations still significantly and overwhelmingly favor theism.[125]

For now, all this has been largely abstract. Soon, we will turn toward specific examples, where I will illustrate how naturalism can only (and only sometimes) keep in the explanatory race by adopting greater complexity.

But to do that, we first must ask what we can expect of God.

---

[125] However, Kenneth Pearce offers an account for how analogy may not incur additional complexity costs (Oppy and Pearce, *Is There a God*, 212–17). Going further, Joshua Sijuwade maintains analogy is not required at all and that theism wins across the board concerning all matters of simplicity. (Joshua Sijuwade, "Modal Metaphysics and the Existence of God," *Metaphysica* 1 (2022), 1–70). However, since I don't believe anything significant, for our purposes, hinges on whether Pearce or Sijuwade are correct on the matter of analogy, I leave further investigation to the interested reader.

CHAPTER SIX

Love Is More Fundamental than Molecules

THE QUESTION NOW IS this: Can we understand enough about God to make predictions about the types of things God would do, or more specifically the type of world God would create, or even if God would create a world at all? After all, if we're going to claim God is a better explanation of certain phenomena, we must be able to say that the phenomena are better expected *if* God exists than if He does not, and this means we must be able to generate certain, however broad, expectations of God.

Cosmological reasoning has us affirm that God — a being of pure positivity, pure love — in fact *did* create this world (including all molecules), since this world exists, and that God is the only adequate explanation of it. But we are trying to get at something deeper. We are trying to see *why* God created this world. To get an answer to this question, if such an answer is forthcoming, we must try to move from the nature of the cause, which means we must try to understand something about the nature of the cause. In this case, that cause is God.

I accept the familiar point that "divine psychology" is difficult, and that we should not expect to know exactly all the things God would or would not do. If God exists, His ways are not our ways, obviously enough. So it is not entirely surprising that certain philosophers over the centuries have claimed that God's ways are impenetrably mysterious and that we should just "let God be God."

While we can't know everything about God or fully comprehend His essence, at least in this life, I think we can know enough about God, either through cosmological reasoning and other philosophical observations at large or both, that we *can* generate broad degrees of expectation about the general types of things God might do or create.[126] So, while we may not be able to predict exactly every little thing God might do (like that God would create *this* or *that* specific person), I think we can render general actions (that God would create personal beings of some sort) relatively unsurprising if God exists. And that is where we are headed now.

To put the matter simply, if we can argue that God might have reason to create beings like us and also that we would not expect beings like us to emerge if naturalism is true, then the fact that we discover beings like us (because, you know, here we are) would be evidence in favor of God's existence. Obviously, there are details to be filled in, but that is the general thrust of the matter. This is an important step in our project as we explore several independent, interesting, and important philosophical topics, from morality to mind to suffering. While we cannot cover every aspect of this otherwise enormous discussion, my hope is that we can provide a generally accurate overview of the territory and make the case that classical theism makes the best sense of the widest range of our experience with the fewest basic theoretical principles — confirmation as far as worldview theory comparison is concerned.

Just What Can We Expect from God?

Before we examine the features of the world that I believe we should expect a worldview to explain, we should begin by trying to tease out some of the expectations of classical theism. If we posit the existence of God, what should we expect to follow?

After all, why should God want to create anything, let alone a world like ours? The simple and ultimately correct answer, I believe, is because it is good, and God would understand this and be motivated by it. Creativity with respect to goodness is a familiar and commonly accepted form of explanation.

---

[126] For philosophers: that is, expectations about types even if not tokens.

Interestingly, an increasing number of philosophers already think the explanation for why things exist is *because* it is good for them to exist, a position known as *axiarchism*. While there is something correct about this view, it doesn't go far enough. The fact that it is good for things to exist, or at least a certain organization of things to exist, does not explain *why* they exist. The goodness of something does not itself provide an explanation for the capacity for that something to be brought about. It seems we need something rather more concrete to offer the adequate explanation, even if it is true that it is good that things exist. God complements (completes) the axiarchist view and fills it in. In being a supremely good concrete reality, God has the power to bring other things into reality, and the reason for His doing so is just what is claimed by axiarchism: goodness.

As most theists believe God created this world because it is good, it is from this perspective that we can begin to generate expectations about God's action.

Cosmological reasoning leads us to the understanding that God is an absolutely simple and supremely good intellectual entity, and so God necessarily understands and loves the fullness of being, which is Himself. God's act and object of love are identical, just as God's act and object of knowledge are identical. However, if God is the fullness of being and fullness of goodness, then presumably, in terms of any intrinsic perfection, God lacks nothing. God doesn't just *have* the fullness of goodness, God *is* the fullness of goodness. Thus, it might seem there is nothing further for God to love or desire. So why would God create anything at all? Would that not imply that God is, in some sense, lacking or incomplete?

Norris Clarke offers the commonsense response that "there are two ways of loving one's own goodness: one is to enjoy it; the other is to share it with others, to communicate it freely to others out of sheer gratuitous generosity. This, and this alone, could be God's motive for creation of beings outside himself, not to obtain some finite good from them, even glory."[127]

Given God's nature, God is motivated by goodness and love, thus providing grounds for assuming that God would want to share or diffuse His

---

[127] Clark, *The One*, 267.

goodness by bringing other things into reality and allowing them to partici-pate in being.[128]

Moreover, if God is going to create, then we should expect a wide range of beings to result, not just a few. The good is naturally self-diffusive — that is, naturally seeks to share and communicate itself, as philosophers throughout the tradition have argued — and God in understanding Himself as the fullness of existence would understand all the ways anything could participate in existence and be motivated to bring about an impressive array of existing things, so long as they could be coherently ordered. God would not just put everything into being all at once chaotically. That would be irrational, which would imply a de-fect and would be inconsistent with the nature of God. The existence of God then anticipates the Great Chain of Being in ordered fashion — that is, a world of beings hierarchically ordered and interacting with each other in a coherent system; in other words, a universe. Aquinas writes:

> For He brought things into being in order that His goodness might be communicated to creatures, and be represented by them; and because His goodness could not be adequately represented by one creature alone, He produced many and diverse creatures, that what was want-ing to one in the representation of the divine goodness might be sup-plied by another. For goodness, which in God is simple and uniform, in creatures is manifold and divided; and hence the whole universe together participates in the divine goodness more perfectly, and repre-sents it better than any single creature whatever.[129]

Aquinas's position is a classic one: As argued as far back as Plato, for God to communicate His goodness more fully, God will create not just a multiplicity of

---

[128] In fact, there is a traditional philosophical principle — known as the diffusiveness principle — which holds that a good being will probably or inevitably communicate itself somehow, including by making other good things. Moreover, that goodness, by its very nature, is self-diffusive or self-communicative. While this principle has fallen a little out of fashion, I believe it is a genuine insight into the nature of being and has been ably defended in contemporary times by philosophers like Norman Kretzmann and Norris Clarke. See Norman Kretzmann, *The Metaphysics of The-ism* (Oxford: Clarendon Press, 1997), 223–25. Also, Norris Clarke, *Exploration in Metaphysics* (Notre Dame, IN: University of Notre Dame Press, 1995), 212–17.
[129] *ST*, I, q. 47, a. 1.

creatures but a hierarchy of being, determined by the grades of essential power each entity possesses; the traditional classifications include rational > sentient > vegetative. That such a hierarchy of being according to essential powers exists and is an actual hierarchy is obvious and implicitly admitted even among those who profess no belief in God, as they favor, in terms of what they find valuable, worth protecting, or just not eating, intelligent animals over nonintelligent animals, animals over plants, plants over minerals, and so forth.

There is more. Obviously, while it is very good to bring other things into existence, the very best thing God could share with other beings is Himself, His own inner life, intimacy with the Godhead. If this is possible — that is, friendships love and communion with God, and there is no reason to think that it isn't — God would make this the *ultimate* aim of creation; that is, He would seek to unite all of creation with Himself, because there is nothing better God could share than His own inner life. Existence is great, but existence *and* relationship with God is better. There's a restriction. Only spiritual entities, beings with intellect and will, can commune with God, because only spiritual entities can self-consciously choose to love (or not to love) God. Beings absent intellect and will are stuck in unconscious darkness; they cannot, by themselves, attain friendship's love with God. Can God unite with the remainder of creation that lacks intellect and will? Perhaps He can, by bringing about beings not just with intellect and will, but *material* beings with intellect and will.

Here is where things become interesting.

While even an omnipotent God cannot cause a rock to love Him, because rocks are incapable of such action, perhaps God *could* create a being that was a microcosm within the macrocosm, a being with both a material and spiritual element. Then, by inviting that being — a being with material sense and immaterial intellect — into union with Himself, God would be pulling all of creation along for the ride.

Such a being could then serve as mediator, a fusion of the material and the immaterial. And that is precisely what human beings are, or at least what they have often been seen to be.

God created human beings as the acme of creation, the microcosm within the macrocosm, the pinnacle. For the creative aim of God was not just to create but to unite creation to Himself and this meant bringing be-ings like us about, because unlike angels, who are purely spiritual, we are spiritual *and* material.

Norris Clarke drives the point home beautifully:

> We are microcosms: our bodies contain in us all levels of matter from the lowest atoms — blown out from exploding stars in the early stages of the universe's journey — to the highest animal life; these are part of us, part of our very being. We also reach up through our spiritual intellects and wills into the whole realm of the spirit — the 'lowest of spirits,' St. Thomas calls us — able, with God's help, to know, love, and be personally united to the supreme Source of all being. Thus we can take up the whole material world into our human consciousness, using both sense and intellect, bring it into the light of self-consciousness in us, and offer it back to the Source whence it came with acknowledge, gratitude, love for this gift. Thus we can take the whole material world with us as part of our journey Home to the Source, and so fulfill the implicit longing of this subrational world to find its way back Home and not be left in the darkness of unconsciousness.[130]

This point is so important because it is so correct and reframes our worldview completely: God's primary motive is love, pure and simple, and it is through this motive that He shares His goodness and ultimately shares Himself with beings like us. Anything else God aims at is, and must be, secondary to this chief impulse. Much bad philosophy (and far worse theology) has resulted from a failure to properly appreciate the nature and goodness of God, which anticipates a universe like ours, with beings like us, generated from an unre-stricted principle of love, which God just *is*. Love is what makes it all happen. Cliché as that may sound, according to this story, it — all of it — is true.

While the above conclusions may seem a little "woo" to some, I am so far operating from an entirely traditional set of philosophical principles, concern-ing the nature of God, goodness, and love. Nothing I have set forth marks a radical departure from what many other philosophers and theologians, of various traditions, have said previously, whether working from the armchair,

[130] Clarke, *The One*, 306.

divine revelation, or both. So, I believe I am on rather solid ground to say that, if classical theism is true, we have reason to think God would create a world like ours and know why He would do so.

Obviously, I cannot chase down all the details of this proposed account, but from an understanding of goodness and the motivations provided thereby, we can generate some positive probability about the general things God might do, including the general things God might create.[131] All this can be discovered by contemplating the very nature of the fullness of being and goodness itself, the simple pure act subsisting at the root of all reality. We are not in the dark (at least if we are attentive to the metaphysics of the matter, and the history of philosophical thought on this subject) about the types of things God might do. We really can have reasonable expectations concerning God even while acknowledging that God's essence remains beyond our ability to fully comprehend.

That, anyway, should be enough to get us started. I will fill in further aspects of the classical theistic story as we go along, related to what we think God might do and why, as it becomes relevant when considering different features of the world requiring explanation. For the most part the answer will be this: Because this thing is either good (like human beings), or it is a necessary condition for something that is good (like some particular physics), and because God has the power to do it. Being omnipotent, the question of God's power is not a problem. So, really, we should only have to recognize the goodness of something, or that something's being a necessary condition for something that is good, to see that God might be motivated to bring it about, and thus to judge that, if God exists, that something is not entirely surprising, perhaps even just what we would expect. And then we must ask whether we should expect such a thing to be equally as likely to exist or occur if God does not exist and if metaphysical naturalism is true.

[131] Some may recognize this story as one found within historical Christianity, which maintains that the Incarnation would have happened even if the Fall did not occur, because God's aim is ultimately to bring creation into union with Himself. But since the Fall did happen, the Incarnation was able to serve a redemptive role and, moreover, bring about other greater goods only possible against a backdrop of negative states (a theme we'll explore in the section on evil). As the reader might suspect, I am fond of this view.

THE FINER POINTS

I want to stress a point of considerable significance, often missed by those not familiar with these debates. It has typically *not* been thought, by either theist or naturalist, that God doesn't "predict" enough or that God is lacking in explanatory power concerning the many different features of the world, or that many of the features of the world, whether its order or beauty of what have you, are better expected if God exists than not. The problem is many thinkers believe God predicts *too much*: that if God existed, then our world would be much better than it actually is. And that, as everybody knows, is the problem of evil, about which we'll have much to say later.

The point I would like to emphasize now is that the problem of evil *assumes* that we can know enough about God to form some general expectation of the sorts of things God might create or refrain from creating. If we were entirely in the dark on this matter, there would be little to no basis to raise the problem of evil. Unluckily, those who are overly skeptical lose traction on both sides for their respective position in this debate. Sometimes theists want to address the problem of evil by raising their skepticism about what God would or would not do or create to such a degree that we are left entirely in the dark, but once that position is taken, how can that theist reasonably say God would be a good explanation of other things, including beings like us? Conversely, naturalists might assert a similar skepticism to dodge having to affirm God as the best explanation of different things, but in doing so, they lose whatever grip they might have had for arguing against God from the obvious imperfections of this world. I think both sides are unduly and unjustifiably skeptical, and I dismiss them as such. We can, through various means, know enough about God to expect certain things from Him. And then, we can begin to assess whether reality meets those expectations or not, to either confirm or disconfirm God as our fundamental theory. For the theist, this means that the problem of evil must be confronted. And so, when the time comes, we shall confront it.

PART THREE

Worldview Comparison
Which Theory Takes the Explanatory Cake?

CHAPTER SEVEN

The Conspiracy of Naturalism

SIMPLICITY IS A GUIDE to truth. And simplicity is best judged by one's onto-logical commitments, those theories that can explain the data with fewer entities and are thus more likely to be true. The most relevant ontological commitments are fundamental entities or basic principles.

The previous section attempted to argue that theism enjoys greater sim-plicity than naturalism overall in the most relevant respects. This chapter aims to be more specific, showing that naturalism must frequently adopt vastly greater complexity to keep up in the explanatory race with theism, which only further decreases the believability of the naturalistic hypothesis entirely apart from the considerations given by cosmological reasoning.

There is no alternative but to investigate specifics of naturalistic theory at this point; that is, to highlight certain features of the world requiring explana-tion and see how naturalists have attempted to explain them. Obviously, without having this book balloon in terms of its own ontological commit-ments, I cannot work through all the explanatory targets, let alone evaluate all the naturalistic attempts at explaining them. Rather, we will work through some of the explanatory targets and look at what I believe are the best natural-istic attempts at explanation. In doing so, my aim is to give the firm impres-sion of a trend that is general and inevitable for the naturalist: to keep up with theism, naturalism must become increasingly — in fact, enormously — com-plex. And even then, it still doesn't keep up.

THE BEST ARGUMENT FOR GOD

This section will promote my point in broad outline, articulating the general problem naturalism faces when trying to explain as much as theism. Afterward, we will look specifically at comparative theistic and naturalistic proposed explanations of things (order, consciousness, etc.).

We begin with an illustration.

Suppose someone told you their alternate theory of history, where they believe the same things as you, minus the existence of Abraham Lincoln. You might become curious to learn how their theory explains certain events, in particular those events formerly explained by what you thought was a man born in a log cabin in Kentucky, who grew up on the frontier in Indiana, eventually became a lawyer, and so forth. You might ask what about everyone who witnessed the Gettysburg Address, or the assassination at Ford's Theatre. Clearly, the absence of Abraham Lincoln doesn't explain this data by itself. Explanatory holes must be filled if this alternate version of history is to be seriously considered.

This is where our friend with his alternate theory of history tells us how Abraham Lincoln was an imposter, someone the government concocted to push through a particular agenda, with all the appearances of a humble and honest man. *He wasn't who you thought he was.* However, because this imposter didn't ultimately go along with their conspiratorial agenda (perhaps his conscience finally got the better of him?), they had him assassinated. Or something along those lines. As we know, the problem isn't that conspiracy theories don't explain the data. In fact, conspiracies are often difficult to refute precisely because they *are* designed with the data in mind, however contrived those explanations may be.

The problem, ultimately, is twofold. One, the conspiratorial hypothesis itself seems less likely to be true, given all the basic components or moving parts this theory has: deception, coordination, cover-up, and so on. Two, there are other data this alternative hypothesis doesn't appear to account for, at least not initially: what about Lincoln's mother who died of milk sickness, and his sister, and everyone else who knew Honest Abe long before he was a potential political candidate? Surely, the theorist could turn a story to explain these data points as well. But in doing so, the theory will almost certainly pick up "adjunct hypotheses" that are themselves improbable and not independently evidenced, further complicating the conspiracy overall, continuing to drop its likelihood of being true. At some point, the conspiracy theorist might have to go beyond government coordination and cover-up, adding suggestions that influence from extraterrestrial aliens was at play. Who knows? If you've ever talked to any committed conspiracy theorist, you know things can get interesting very quickly.[132]

As stated previously, we prefer less complicated theories because those theories are thought to have fewer "moving parts," as it were, and thus fewer ways things could go wrong and disprove the theory. Conspiracy theories are often good examples of narratives we find unbelievable — not, typically, because they lack explanatory power, but because of their inherent complexity and consequent improbability.

Naturalism is like this.

Recall that naturalism is governed by a principle of indifference; *that*, at bottom, is the fundamental root of everything, whereas theism holds to the principle of perfection or pure actuality. The problem is that indifference isn't especially predictive; it doesn't seem to anticipate the data of our world well or literally at all. What would we expect from some entity or collection of entities that is neither benevolent nor malevolent nor intentional nor personal nor anything of the sort? The answer, if we're being honest, is not much.

Thus, where things that were easily and simply explained by the existence of God (minimally, why any concrete thing exists instead of not, though with further conceptual analysis we see God predicts beings like us, and by extension a universe like ours), we are now left with gaping holes.[133] My suggestion is that, to the extent naturalism can wrap around the relevant data, it must necessarily complicate itself, quite like a grand metaphysical conspiracy theory.

For naturalism to keep up in the explanatory race, it must often adopt adjunct hypotheses, which not only further complicate the naturalistic project but

---

[132] Again, I emphasize conspiracies of a "grand-scale" simply because conspiracies of a much lesser sort happen all the time: conspiracies to murder, rob banks, assassinate people in power, and so on. Thus, not all conspiracies are false, nor even that complex or improbable. Some, we know, are historically true. Where conspiracies become unbelievable is when they are concocted on a much larger scale and must introduce an incredible number of moving parts with so many ways they could fail to coordinate, which is to say, so many ways things could go wrong.

[133] See Swinburne's *Existence of God* for this unpacking.

often bring more into the naturalistic hypothesis that fails to find adequate explanation. By dropping God out of the picture, things that were previously explained or explainable by God (say, the number and parameters of laws of nature) now become basic components of the naturalistic theory, making naturalism fundamentally more complicated *and* less explanatorily powerful *even if* naturalism has "one less existing thing."

THE FINER POINTS

Moreover, for naturalism to make accurate predictions concerning our universe, it must specify (complicate) its theory more and more. For example, just having a naturalistic theory that *there are physical laws* does not, by itself, cause us to expect *these* physical laws. The latter is a far more specific and complicated specification, and while that specification may, in a sense, allow naturalism to explain the physical laws (obviously a theory that just says "there are these physical laws" anticipates there being "these physical laws"!), the complexity cost it incurs would be quite considerable, if not totally disqualifying compared to theism, *plus* it would leave those specific laws unexplained and unexplainable—they would be brute. Nor would suggesting such laws are necessary help, because having a theory that says there are necessary physical laws does not predict that *these* physical laws are necessary; again, far greater complexity is required for that, and adopting such complexity doesn't come free, but drastically lowers the internal likelihood of such a theory being true.

In other words, for naturalism to beef up its explanatory power in one area, it complicates itself and loses explanatory comprehensiveness overall. In this sense, it becomes almost worse than many grand-scale conspiracy theories.

That is the primary claim of this section, anyway, and it is best substantiated through a series of illustrations. That is, by looking at the relevant features of the world requiring explanation and then seeing what naturalism leads us to expect concerning this feature, and how, in the face of poor expectations, naturalism must complicate itself to keep up.

There are, as always, complications in this debate that must be noted. One complication concerns which data requires explanation. Before continuing in our analysis, several points must be made on this score.

For example, part of the problem of engaging worldview comparison is agreement upon data and how much a prior commitment to a worldview can influence what the features of the world actually are (in other words, the theory winds up determining the data, rather than the data determining the theory). Some data — for instance, that something exists — is undeniable. But other data may be more contentious.

This complication is well illustrated through moral features. We'll be discussing morality at length later, but for now, let's just ask: are there moral facts? Certainly, most people seem to act and believe as if there are. Indeed, many naturalists are themselves moral realists, not moral anti-realists. If the atheist and theist agree upon the data of moral facts, they can then see which metaphysical theory makes better sense of this data, is more explanatorily comprehensive and hopefully just as simple if not simpler, and so on.

Moral realism is the position that most people (at least implicitly) affirm: namely, that moral facts exist, which are represented by true moral claims such as, "It is wrong to kill everybody in the world even if you wanted to."[134] Moral realists are committed to moral *objectivity* — that is to say, the idea that moral truths exist independently of our attitudes toward them. In everyday language, some things are truly good (or bad) regardless of whether we desire them, and moreover, we ought to desire what is truly good.

Moral anti-realism is the position that there are no moral facts. Some anti-realists are called noncognitivists, claiming that moral statements (like those that assert an *ought* or an *ought not*) cannot be either true of false; hence they do not belong in the sphere of knowledge at all. Other anti-realists are error theorists, who accept that moral judgments are cognitive (that is, capable of being true or false) but hold that they are never actually true.

Here, I want to grant that naturalistic evolutionary theory provides something of a decent account of this, where evolutionary pressures put beliefs into us that, while not corresponding to anything objective concerning human nature or God's commands or some Platonic realm or what have you, nevertheless help us to "avoid bears and have sex." False, but useful.

---

[134] Lieuwe Zijlstra, "Are People Implicitly Moral Objectivists?" *Review of Philosophy and Psychology* 14, no. 1 (2023), 229–47.

That account flows nicely from a naturalistic paradigm (which is why so many naturalists, old and new, maintain it); but it also shows how much a theory affects one's accounting of the data. For it seems strange that anybody would deny moral facts unless some prior theory that appeared inconsistent with moral facts is compelling them to do so, especially since the moral realm is intuitively obvious. Personally, I believe this is clearly an instance of the theory determining the data, rather than the data determining the theory. Of course, I am not saying this is irrational, as one might have other good reasons, including other data, for thinking that a theory must be true.

If that is where the conversation is, then worldview comparison becomes more difficult, because the disagreement is not about what best explains some feature of the world but what the features of the world are. If the theist says moral facts are better explained by theism but the atheist doesn't think there are any moral facts to explain — well, you can see the problem. This means that one of two things must happen. Either the dispute must be settled concerning the status of moral facts, which shifts the debate toward issues concerning moral realism or moral anti-realism, or the respective worldview competitors must agree to set that issue aside and list the features of the world that they do agree on, and then see which worldview provides a better explanation of those.

For obvious reasons, I cannot settle this rather large dispute here. In just a moment, I will list what I believe are basic features of reality that any worldview contenders should be able to make adequate sense of. To the extent that the reader agrees that the list includes real features of the world, they will find the following arguments of greater interest and, I think, persuasive force. If they deny such features are real, there is little I can do at that point to convince them otherwise, except to insist that denying such features of the world is probably some indication that prior worldview commitments are allowing one to determine the data, rather than one allowing the data to determine their worldview commitments.

Anyway, we've covered a lot of territory so far. Let's briefly zoom back out, recap a few basic concepts, and then transition into a different phase of our overall argument for the existence of God.

Recall that one way of thinking about God is to start with the world in front of us and ask what its necessary condition is for its very existence. Reason might reveal something special if this approach is taken. In fact, that is just what has been argued above in Part One.

But there is another approach, and that is one of treating God as a sort of Big Picture hypothesis and then inquiring as to whether certain aspects or experiences of our world are better predicted, expected, and made sense of according to the God Hypothesis than any rival hypotheses. The major rival hypothesis to classical theism, at least concerning Big Pictures of reality or worldviews, is naturalism, which, as you'll recall, tells us that fundamental reality is run by a principle of indifference — that there is no agency at bottom, no personal force either benevolent or malevolent. Naturalism essentially maintains that we should not go beyond the science; whatever we know, at least with any real confidence, is what comes from science, and whatever exists is the sort of stuff that science talks about (stuff like what physics and chemistry describe). Nothing else we affirm, like human consciousness or ethical values, should be in any sense repugnant (nonreducible) to this physical base. If so, we have an explanatory problem, an instance of what might appear like something coming from nothing.

In the broadest sense, we might think that classical theism posits a principle of perfection (pure actuality) at the bottom of reality, whereas naturalism posits a principle of indifference (and obviously imperfection) at the bottom of reality.

From there, we can generate broad degrees of expectation with respect to what each principle might lead to: that is, we can begin to ask whether certain features of our world are better anticipated if fundamental reality is a principle of perfection or indifference. For our purposes, we might think of these considerations as additional confirmation of what we have already been arguing for — that is, by seeing how the God Hypothesis shaped by the investigation above leads us to expect many if not most of the features of the world that we in fact do encounter. This should strengthen our confidence that we have the correct worldview theory in hand, at least insofar as naturalism does not lead us to expect as many of the features of the world that we in fact encounter.

So, that is where we are heading. We are going to look at some of the very broad features of reality that we believe any worldview should be able to explain and then make the case that these features are better expected in (predicted by/explained by) the classical theistic worldview than the naturalistic worldview.

The question, ultimately, is which worldview makes better sense of the phenomena or features of this world. What are these phenomena or features? For all the relevant phenomena, it can be argued with reasonable assurance that each is better expected to occur if God exists than if God does not exist. If this can be established, then each of the phenomena counts as evidential weight in favor of a theistic worldview, or from our perspective, additional confirmation of the theory already determined by the cosmological argument.

Of course, I cannot be too extensive in this section, and so what follows is a nonexhaustive (but hopefully sufficiently impressive) list of broad features of the world that are either undeniably true or extremely well evidenced. If any worldview cannot account for these facts, that is a major problem.

- That there is something existing that is causally capable.
- That there is something contingent (something not required to exist).
- That there is continued existence among things not required to exist.
- That there is order and organization among existing things.
- That there is consciousness.
- That there is reason.
- That there is knowledge.
- That there is morality (moral facts and knowledge).
- That there is suffering and evil.

The existence of contingent things we have already considered. Shortly, I will defend four of the features listed above as additional confirmatory evidence for the existence of God: order, consciousness, morality, and suffering/evil. The others I leave to the reader's own investigation.

However, as a quick note: all or most of these features are logically independent, at least in certain directions. That there is some concrete entity does not *entail* that anything exists contingently or continues existing if contingent, *nor* that there are beings which are conscious, *nor* that the universe is physically fine-tuned for the emergence of interactive intelligent biological life, and so on. In other words, you could have one of these things (say, some concrete existent) without the other (a finely tuned universe). Moreover, physical fine-tuning, to the best of my knowledge, does not entail complexly structured biological life. Fine-tuning strikes me as water to fish: a necessary but not sufficient condition.[135] No fish without water, of course, but water can come without fish. Moreover, there could be — however strangely it seems to us — moral facts without anybody coming into reliable cognitive contact with (that is, knowing) those facts, so moral knowledge must be accounted for as well, which I think we obviously have. But so must knowledge in general, especially since there could be instances of knowledge of things other than moral facts. Likewise, there could be consciousness without rationality, as is presumably the case with brute animals. (It might turn out that I'm wrong concerning the independence of some of these facts — say, the relation between fine-tuning and biological complexity — but surely not all of them. Thus, I believe my general point is secure.)

Nevertheless, some of these features could not occur without prior features, such as complexly structured biological life apart from physical fine-tuning or suffering and evil without causally capable entities. This is an important consideration, for if some worldview cannot possibly account for some necessary prior feature, then that worldview is dropped to probability zero, which is sticky, even if it might seem to better explain latter features. For example, if it were shown that naturalism cannot possibly account for why there are any concrete causally capable entities, then naturalism is "stuck" there. Further evidential considerations, including those concerning suffering and evil, which are logically posterior, are irrelevant unless and until a naturalistic theory can be made unstuck. Here, obviously, I am hinting at the force of cosmological reasoning, which, as we have seen, maintains that nothing apart from the existence and activity of a transcendent first cause (immaterial, simple, eternal, etc.) can possibly explain the existence of things.

The point for now is just this. It strikes me that the features above are non-negotiable, so obviously true or so well evidenced that if there is a true theory of everything, it must be able to account, and account well, for each of these features, and not be forced or inclined to eliminate any of them.

---

[135] Even if the fine-tuning of our universe makes life like ours arising at least somewhere probable.

Overall, theism explains these features with elegance and ease; it does so extremely simply. (The only initially problematic feature for the theistic hypothesis is suffering and evil, which will be treated last and at length.) After all, our conceptual understanding of God leads us to a not insignificant anticipation of these features. God, as a being of pure perfection, would have reason to create beings like us (in fact, an entire hierarchy of being, as the philosophical tradition has it) and ensure we have appropriate moral knowledge; moral facts are grounded in the natures of things, natures that are explained as finite (limited) participations of being brought into existence by God.[136] God would be capable of doing this, obviously, given His omnipotence. Along for the ride is physical fine-tuning, biological complexity, and more generally, a world of order, stability, and harmony, a world that isn't utterly chaotic or doesn't just randomly blip out of existence. God makes good sense of all this, and only one basic entity is needed. Thus, God is not only a powerful explanatory theory, but a remarkably simple and unifying explanatory theory.

On the other hand, naturalism struggles seriously with most of these features, must frequently adopt auxiliary hypotheses to maintain that struggle, and cannot in principle explain several of them, such as contingent being. I will do my best to illustrate this criticism through several examples. The difficulty, of course, is that many of these complications are obscure unless somebody delves into the tall grass of naturalistic theories. We must remember that what might appear just as simple or even simpler superficially may be far more complicated beneath.

Since we spent so much time previously with cosmological reasoning, let us briefly return to that, just to concretize some of these otherwise abstract points. There, it was argued that naturalism has no available adequate explanation concerning the data of contingency. But let us set that conclusion aside momentarily to explore the issue we are now interested in — namely, even if naturalism *could* provide an alternative explanation, is it really an explanation

---

[136] For a popular level introduction to the traditional idea of God creating a "Great Chain of Being" see David Oderberg, "Recovering the Hierarchy of Being," YouTube video, from Ian Ramsey Centre, on May 12, 2020, at www.youtube.com/watch?v=AUV9dfmIr8I. For a written summary, see Pat Flynn, "Are You More Advanced than a Crab?," Catholic Answers, May 20, 2021, at www.catholic.com/magazine/online-edition/are-you-more-advanced-than-a-crab.

that is just as simple or even simpler, *and* that itself could just as well account for everything else requiring explanation *without* positing further complexity? As we'll see, I believe the answer is no: I insist that once the details of such proposed alternative explanations are unpacked, we see the naturalistic account is decidedly *not* simpler.

To draw this point out, we must entertain different ways this debate could go. Concerning simplicity, suppose the naturalist wants to charge the theist with having a more complicated theory because the theist maintains not just that there are contingent concrete entities but necessary concrete entities, whereas the naturalist has only the former. Here the theist can say several things in response, returning to territory covered in the previous section. First, without that necessary concrete entity, no contingent concrete entity can be, in principle, explained, so what the naturalistic view gains concerning simplicity in that respect is entirely negated by what it loses concerning explanatory power. Someone might just as well say their theory that "nothing exists" is simpler, but who cares? It's clearly explanatorily inadequate.

Even setting that aside, the matter is not so simple. Again, recall a point made in the previous section: the theist, in having a necessary concrete entity, can explain all contingent concrete entities through a broadly casual connection. The naturalist, in rejecting a necessary reality, cannot do so, and must ultimately rest — in this instance, anyway — upon having *both* caused contingent concrete entities and uncaused or brute contingent concrete entities, which are presumably different kinds of things. In this sense, the naturalist is committed to something the theist is not, and that something should presumably have a deeper explanation but cannot, given the approach the naturalist is here adopting.

Or suppose the naturalist does admit to some necessary reality — some necessary initial physical state of the universe, say. Here, we encounter other problems. For one, something being necessary (if it is necessary, as in it had to exist or occur no matter what) does not automatically mean that something is not caused or does not have a deeper explanation. If we supposed it were necessary (say, because of His nature) that God *had* to create certain things, those certain things would be necessary by an extension of God's activity, though their necessity would still be caused, derivative, and explained more deeply by God.

THE BEST ARGUMENT FOR GOD

Obviously, I do not think that picture is the correct one. As I maintained before, God did not *have* to create, even if God was strongly inclined to. Nevertheless, it seems a coherent enough supposition and is one that various theistic thinkers have held. It shows that things can be necessary and still have some deeper explanation. The same is true of other necessary realities, or truths — for example, certain moral and mathematical truths. Philosophers often explain more specific moral principles (which are often thought to be necessary) by way of more general moral principles (also thought to be necessary). Also, there are many necessary mathematical truths that not only *can* have a deeper explanation but of which we *have* figured out their deeper explanation.[137]

The point is this: Something being necessary does not automatically exempt it from having any further explanation, so it is not altogether useful just to deem something necessary and think that this reconciles the explanatory conundrum. What is wanted concerning ultimate explanation is something only theism provides — namely, something that is both necessary *and* can provide a principled explanation of its necessity in virtue of its nature. As we saw through cosmological reasoning, no naturalistic reality can do this.

To reiterate, the cosmological argument claims no physical reality can be the ultimate explanation for why any concrete contingent thing exists, but for now we are setting that conclusion aside for the sake of entertaining another argument, the one concerning simplicity, because we can still ask, even if the naturalistic theory is explanatorily inadequate, whether positing some necessary physical reality is simpler than God in the relevant respects.

The answer is no, for reasons given in the previous section.

Even if the naturalist posits a necessary reality to explain subsequent contingent realities, it will be a necessary reality that itself crucially calls out for a deeper explanation and is itself more complicated than the theistic necessary reality. The naturalistic, for example, would have both explained necessities and unexplained necessities — or maybe just unexplained necessities — whereas the theist has only explained necessities. One need only think back to how the argument from the Principle of Sufficient Reason

---

[137] Pearce offers a fun example of mathematical explanation in Oppy and Pearce, *Is There a God*, 185–86.

could be tied into the ontological argument to get a deeper explanation of God's necessity. That is a path unavailable to the naturalist.

It seems that naturalism doubly strikes out concerning the feature of contingent concrete entities. Even when strapped with greater complexity, naturalism still cannot adequately account for the phenomenon under consideration.

Apart from the cosmological argument, the problem for the naturalist concerning the data of contingency is that they either must assume contingency as something fundamental (in which case they cannot explain contingency and are stuck with however many and however complicated brute facts), or they must posit something necessary, but then lack the resources to both explain how that something could be necessary *and* how that necessary something could give rise to anything contingent. If they assume contingency, they have not explained contingency (and whatever their fundamental contingent thing, or things, is/are, much complication follows). If, on the other hand, they posit something necessary, they cannot give an adequate explanation for how their naturalistic entity can be necessary — as we've argued, only something with a very special nature could fit the bill.

Worse, the naturalist positing something necessary, so far as the physical world is concerned, seems to be going against their own rules, since the best of contemporary science tells us that the physical world could have been otherwise.

As Pearce points out:

> One of the fundamental theories in current physics is general relativity. This theory describes the nature and behavior of spacetime. Spacetime, according to this theory, is not an inert container for matter: Spacetime is itself an entity that interacts with material objects. In particular, spacetime bends in the presence of mass. This bending affects the motion of objects within spacetime, which is the origin of what we call 'gravity.'
>
> The equations that describe the bending of spacetime are called Einstein's Field Equations. A solution to these equations describes a possible way spacetime and mass could be in some region. A global solution describes a possible shape for the totality of spacetime.... A background assumption ... is that most solutions to Einstein's Field Equations — the non-bizarre solutions — do

describe physical possibilities. If, then, we're taking our cures from current, well-established science, we should endorse the following principle: any solution to Einstein's Field Equations should be assumed to describe a physical possibility unless there are compelling reasons to the contrary.[138]

In other words, if naturalists are supposed to take their cues from science — if they are not to go *beyond* science, which is pretty much just a statement of what it means to be a naturalist — then they should *not* be positing any necessary physical structure or state, initial or otherwise. So not only can the naturalist not explain how something could be necessary if naturalism is true, but their own naturalistic criteria should deter them from doing so, given that most scientists believe there are multiple possible solutions to Einstein's field equations, which describe ways that physical reality could have been (implying ours is not necessary). Their move of positing a necessary physical reality is, by all appearances, contrived, adds considerable complication, and *still* fails to provide an adequate explanation in this particular context.

God fares *far* better in all respects, because through God we can explain contingency by the free action of a necessary being, which is relevantly different than all contingent beings such that its own necessity can be explained. We have seen reasons for thinking that contingency demands necessity, but then we must also ask how necessity can give rise to contingency. The answer is this: the necessary being is a free and personal agent, if analogously.

God is the best and simplest explanation of contingency. But we already knew that, as we discovered in Part Two.

Let us now move on to other considerations.

---

[138] Ibid, 61–62.

CHAPTER EIGHT

Stability and Order

NOT ONLY DOES GOD offer a nice explanation for how anything contingent exists at all, but He also serves to explain how anything contingent continues to exist and doesn't just blip out of existence randomly. God acts for reasons, and God being perfectly good and rational would not create a nonsensical world. If God creates a world and orders it toward an end, God is not going to blip it out of existence randomly. Such an irrational act would contradict God's nature and even God acts according to His nature. Thus, if theism is true, we should expect creation to continue. And creation does continue — at least it has continued so far. Another accurate prediction. If God exists, we can rest easy at night concerning whether we are going to spontaneously snap out of existence.

There is nothing about naturalism, run by a principle of indifference, that predicts anything will endure in existence, even if something is brought into existence somehow. Indifference doesn't care if things keep existing or not. Thus, further complication, like some thesis of "existential inertia," would have to be added to the base theory of naturalism to make sense of continued existence.[139] For these reasons, that anything continues to exist is considerable confirmatory support of classical theism. A simple point, but a powerful one.

---

[139] Though as we'll see later, we have strong reason to think a thesis of existential inertia is impossible.

Order

Why does the world consist of just the natures (specific types of things) it does? Why do they seem to interact so well? Even if one accepts an *essentialist* paradigm, where things have stable and abiding centers of activity — "organizing principles" or more simply "forms," as Aristotle called them — there should be some further explanation of why the world consists of just the natures it does and why they seem to interact so well. God offers a nice explanation for this. God knows what created things would play well together and how to organize them just so for a nonchaotic world. This makes sense because God, as an ontologically simple and supreme intellect (unrestricted idea), can order things without having any parts of His own that require ordering. He can serve as an "undirected director," which is a principled explanatory stopping point for how a complex story requiring much direction should ever have taken hold. That we live in an ordered world of various natures is great confirmatory evidence of God's existence, because such order is expected if God exists but not expected if God does not exist.

Moreover, we can get a nice, relatively slim explanation of the forms themselves, as ultimately contained in the mind of God, who is the Form of Being, the infinite plentitude of existence as such. If a naturalist accepts that there even are such forms to begin with (many naturalists do not, though I will argue later that denying this is absurd), they will lack some ultimate grounding for them — they will have to be brute attaining: just there and that's all.

Naturalism makes no similar predictions, offering nowhere near as adequate an explanation. It is not only quite inexplicable how any forms or natures exist at all if naturalism is true; it is also unclear why the world includes just the forms or natures it does, and in the particular arrangement it does — an arrangement that seems remarkably (dare we say?) providential. Nothing about mindless naturalism, run by a principle of indifference, leads us to expect a world that is quite so well behaved as ours, insofar as regular order and interactions go among existing things.

Theism predicts order (and natural regularity) because these are necessary conditions for human beings to get around, for discovery and for learning and for science, for sharing and for adventure. These are all good things, whereas complete chaos would not be. God predicts the better outcome and we experience the better outcome — our world is orderly and not chaotic. It has regularity.

This is a general point, observable and confirmable by all. However, for those who might be familiar, the consideration above is not quite the argument from physical fine-tuning, but nevertheless one might think that our universe exhibiting an unfathomably precise physical order that seems necessary for the emergence of intelligent biological life to emerge is also much more expected if God exists than not, because we might think that God would want beings like us to emerge for the simple reason that we are good.

For those unfamiliar, an understanding of fine-tuning is best accomplished through expert testimony. Fine-tuning, of course, is not something observable by all, but is overwhelmingly agreed upon by the relevant experts.[140] And since I am not myself one of these experts, I must ask the reader to entertain several quotations from those who are to impress the point about fine-tuning.

Consider the following from physicist John Polkinghorne:

> Four fundamental forces of nature operate in our universe. Their intrinsic strengths are determined by the values of four corresponding constants of nature…. The magnitudes of all these constants are tightly constrained if the universe is to be capable of producing life. If [one of these] were a little smaller, the early universe would have converted all its hydrogen into helium before it had cooled below the temperature at which cosmic nuclear processes ceased. Not only would this have meant no water, so essential to life, but there would also only have been helium-burning stars, which would not have lived long enough to support the development of life on one of their planets. If [it] had been somewhat bigger, supernova explosions would have been inhibited.

And the following from physicist Luke Barnes:

> A universe that has just small tweaks in the fundamental constants might not have any of the chemical bonds that give us molecules, so say farewell to DNA, and also to rocks, water, and planets. Other

---

[140] To list just a few of the eminent scholars who accept that our universe is fine-tuned for life (even if they do not accept any wider philosophical or theological implications): Stephen Hawking, Roger Penrose, Max Tegmark, Frank Tipler, Alexander Vilenkin, Paul Davies, George Ellise, Brian Green. For more and for references see Luke Barnes, "Fine-Tuning of the Universe for Intelligent Life," in *A Fortunate Universe*, ed. Geraint Lewis and Luke Barnes (Cambridge: Cambridge University Press, 2020), 531.

tweaks could make the formation of stars or even atoms impossible. And with some values for the physical constants, the universe would have flickered out of existence in a fraction of a second. That the constants are all arranged in what is, mathematically speaking, the very improbable combination that makes our grand, complex, life-bearing universe possible is what physicists mean when they talk about the 'fine-tuning' of the universe for life.

Moving to a more precise definition, physicist James Sinclaire offers the following:

> We are now in a position to define fine-tuning. This expression refers specifically to fine-tuning for the emergence of life within our universe — or within any universe with physical laws similar to those of our universe. An instance of fine-tuning for life occurs if a free parameter has a value needed for the emergence of life-forms, and if such a value is exceedingly improbable within the total available parameter space of our universe. So, for example, if the total free parameter space for the values of a given free parameter (say, the electromagnetic charge or the Q nonuniformity of mass-energy density) could be mapped on a grid that is three miles by three miles, but the parameter space permitting life is only one millimeter by one millimeter on that grid (exceedingly improbable), and the value of the free parameter in our universe just happens to fall within that relatively small area, it appears to be an instance of fine-tuning for life.

He concludes:

> There is a multiplicity of these exceedingly improbable coincidences, all of which are necessary for life to emerge.... The deeper we go in the probing of the laws of nature to explain the higher levels of fine-tuning, the more we find additional instances of fine-tuning. This is what has led many physicists and philosophers to appeal to the above natural and transcendent causal options.[141]

Finally, as astronomer Fred Hoyle (a former atheist) once remarked:

---

[141] Graham Oppy and Joseph Koterski (eds), *Our Universe: Theism in Theism and Atheism* (New York: MacMillan Reference, 2019).

> If this were a purely scientific question and not one that touched on
> the religious problem, I do not believe that any scientist who exam-
> ined the evidence would fail to draw the inference that the laws of
> nuclear physics have been deliberately designed.... A common-
> sense interpretation of the facts suggests that a superintellect has
> monkeyed with physics, as well as with chemistry and biology.[142]

Hoyle's language is telling, especially when he speaks of a commonsense in-
terpretation. What he is saying is "this is just the sort of thing I would expect
to find in physics if there is some transcendent, super-intellective force behind
it." Alternatively stated, "this is not at all what we would expect if naturalism
were true."

The point? Our universe appears "set up" for the emergence of interactive, intelligent biological life, and it seems these conditions are dialed in to an
extent that defies comprehension. We are in something of a Goldilocks situation, it looks like. *And for all we know*, things could have been different, with
the overwhelming odds being against a universe finely tuned for the existence
of interactive, intelligent life. At the level of common sense, one would think
it is far more likely that there would be a life-permitting universe given a supreme intellect at the foundation, especially if that supreme intellect has motivation to bring about creatures like us (which God does). The motive is
there, and the capability is there; thus, a universe finely tuned for life like us is
not surprising if God exists. It is, however, extremely surprising, given all the
ways things could have been otherwise, if reality were indifferent at the fundamental level, not aiming toward any particular outcome.

In fact, philosopher Michael Rota has issued a powerful demonstration,
using the standard Bayesian formula, focusing on just one aspect of physical
fine-tuning — namely that the effective cosmological constant falls within the
life-permitting range — to show one would have to have lower prior expectations of God down at over 1 over 10^{32} (meaning they would have to think the
existence of God is *that* unlikely before considering the evidence of fine-tuning) to neutralize the force of the fine-tuning evidence in favor of theism.[143]

---

[142] Fred Hoyle, "The Universe: Past and Present Reflections," Annual Review of As-
tronomy and Astrophysics 20 (1982), 1–36.

[143] See Michael Rota, *Taking Pascal's Wager* (Westmont, IL: InterVarsity Press, 2016).

What this means, for all intents and purposes, is that from physical fine-tuning one should be virtually certain that God exists.[144] So, we might find the discovery of physical fine-tuning to be additional confirmatory evidence of God's existence.

That said, naturalists don't just take such arguments lying down — they have rejoinders, of course.

The most prominent naturalistic attempt to explain fine-tuning is the multiverse theory, which posits an enormously, perhaps infinitely, large number of universes, with the notion being that probably, if not inevitably, you wind up with a universe like ours. From there, we happen to be the lucky ones.

Skeptical philosopher Michael Ruse puts it like this:

> The fact that it is our universe or part of the universe in which there is life is no more improbable than that someone holds a winning lottery ticket. Given enough rolls of the dice or the drum, there was bound to be a winner eventually. The same with livable universes. Obviously, if we didn't have the winning ticket, we wouldn't be around to tell everyone about it. That's no miracle, any more than that the person who won the lottery is the person who quits work and goes to live in the south of France.[145]

Here, a few remarks should suffice to show why the naturalist is unable to provide a plausible alternative explanation by appealing to the multiverse.

First, positing an infinite number of universes, without qualification, fails to solve the larger issue, for that could mean an infinite number of non–finely tuned universes — that is, non–finely tuned for life like us. An infinite number

---

[144] Importantly, Rota's calculation even considers the suggestion — often made as a counter by atheists — that physical fine-tuning was necessary rather than contingent. Rota shows the necessity objection does virtually nothing to block the enormous evidential weight fine-tuning provides for the existence of God. Another basic problem with the necessity proposal is this: just positing that whatever the initial physical set up is as being necessary does not itself predict that it will have *the precise set up that it does*; it only predicts that whatever the initial set up is, it is necessary that it is that way. Unless a naturalist greatly complicates his theory to specify the initial conditions as necessary (in which case, such inherent complication renders the theory entirely untenable) the necessity proposal does not help against fine-tuning.

[145] Brian Davies and Michael Ruse, *Taking God Seriously: Two Different Voices* (Cambridge: Cambridge University Press, 2021), 72.

of something is no guarantee you'll get what you want — you could just as well have an infinite number of universes with just one atom, and nothing more. Nor will it do to posit a multiverse theory that includes all possibilities, since some possibilities preclude other possibilities — for example, the possibility that nothing exists precludes the possibility that something exists. So, just positing all possibilities is contradictory.[146]

Another fundamental issue is that — so far as we can tell — any theoretically workable multiverse proposal itself requires specification and fine-tuning, which only relocates the problem, rather than solving it.

As physicist Robin Collins summarizes the point:

> In all current worked-out proposals for what this 'universe generator' could be — such as the oscillating big bang and the vacuum fluctuation models explained above — the 'generator' itself is governed by a complex set of physical laws that allow it to produce the universes. It stands to reason, therefore, that if these laws were slightly different the generator probably would not be able to produce any universes that could sustain life. After all, even my bread machine has to be made just right in order to work properly, and it only produces loaves of bread, not 12 universes! Or consider a device as simple as a mouse trap: it requires that all the parts, such as the spring and hammer, be arranged just right in order to function. It is doubtful, therefore, whether the atheistic many-universe theory can entirely eliminate the problem of design the atheist faces; rather, at least to some extent, it seems simply to move the problem of design up one level.[147]

As Collins affirms elsewhere:

> Even if an inflationary/superstring many-universe generator exists, it must have just the right combination of laws and fields for the production of life-permitting universes: if one of the components were missing or different, such as Einstein's equation or the Pauli-exclusion principle, it is unlikely that any life-permitting universes could be produced. In the absence of alternative explanations, the

[146] Rasmussen, *Best Explanation*, 145.
[147] See Robin Collins, "The Fine-Tuning Design Argument" at rintintin.colorado. edu/~vancecd/phil201/Collins.pdf.

existence of such a system counts as evidence for design since it seems very surprising that such a system would exist with just the right components under the hypothesis that the universe exists as a brute fact without any explanation, but not surprising under the theistic hypothesis. Thus, it does not seem that one can completely escape the evidence of design merely by hypothesizing some sort of many-universe generator.[148]

Second, it goes without saying that the multiverse comes with an impressive increase of ontological commitments (this concerns quantitative simplicity). Perhaps this is not terrible however, if the ballooning number of entities are not basic or fundamental. Still, for the multiverse theory to generate such a range of universes to eventually wind up with one like ours, as a theory it must be very complicated in ways that significantly decrease its believability.

Here is another issue. Those who think fine-tuning is explained by the multiverse appear to commit a probabilistic fallacy. This fallacy is related to the well-known gambler's fallacy: i.e., where after throwing a pair of dice repeatedly without getting a double six, the gambler concludes he has a better chance of getting double sixes on the next roll. The reason this is fallacious is because the outcome of getting double sixes is probabilistically independent of the outcomes of previous rolls.

As it happens, the fallacy related to fine-tuning is something of an inverse gambler's fallacy. For example, imagine the gambler is asked if some pair of dice has been rolled before and he asks to see the dice rolled before he makes a judgement and that they land double six. From that observation the gambler concludes that they must have been rolled many times before, since it is so unlikely that they land double six in a single roll. Again, this is clearly a fallacy, since the outcome in this instance is probabilistically independent of previous rolls.

Notice the similarity to those positing a multiverse regarding fine-tuning: they think that because it is so unlikely that our universe is fine-tuned, there must have been many (perhaps infinitely many) "rolls," as it were; that our universe is just one universe in a rather extended sequence of universes. The

<hr/>

[148] Robin Collins, "The Many-Worlds Hypothesis as an Explanation of Cosmic Fine-Tuning: An Alternative to Design?" *Faith and Philosophy* 22, no. 5 (2005), 654–66, esp. 659.

basic point is this: the fact that something improbable happened is not evidence for there being multiple independent rolls. Philosophers have argued from considerations like these that fine-tuning not only counts against the naturalistic multiverse proposal but counts against the theistic multiverse proposal as well — that is, fine-tuning is evidence for the theistic single universe hypothesis.[149] In short, the discovery of fine-tuning should cause us to think probably there is *just one* God-produced universe.

The final point I want to make about the multiverse is this. Even if fine-tuning could equally be seen as evidence for the multiverse as for the existence of God, there are, as this book has already contended and will continue to contend, strong independent reasons to believe in God (for example, the cosmological argument). There is not, however, independent reason to accept a multiverse.

For all these reasons, the multiverse is not as good an explanation of fine-tuning as classical theism.

For the sake of completeness, let us consider a few additional objections. After all, skeptical philosophers, like Ruse, are ready with another retort. Like this one: "Are we convinced that the only kind of life-form we know — carbon-based and so forth — is the only viable life-form? What about the Horta in *Star Trek*?"[150]

But as Collins said about this objection years before Ruse raised it:

> Another objection people commonly raise to the fine-tuning argument is that as far as we know, other forms of life could exist even if the parameters of physics were different. So, it is claimed, the fine-tuning argument ends up presupposing that all forms of intelligent life must be like us. The answer to this objection is that most cases of fine-tuning do not make this presupposition. Consider, for instance, the case of the fine-tuning of the strong nuclear force. If it were slightly larger or smaller, no atoms could exist other than hydrogen. Contrary to what one might see on *Star Trek*, an intelligent life form cannot be composed merely of hydrogen gas: there is

[149] Kenny Boyce, "The Fine-Tuning Argument Against the Multiverse," The Blog of the American Philosophical Association, March 28, 2023, at blog.apaonline.org/2023/03/28/the-fine-tuning-argument-against-the-multiverse/.
[150] Davis and Rouse, *Taking God*, 73.

simply not enough stable complexity. So, in general the fine-tuning argument merely presupposes that intelligent life requires some degree of stable, reproducible organized complexity. This is certainly a very reasonable assumption.[151]

Okay, but what about *this* objection? Fine-tuning doesn't require an explanation, because if the universe wasn't fine-tuned, we wouldn't be here to ask about it. In other words, the universe must be fine-tuned since that is the only universe where we could discover fine-tuning (after all, you couldn't exist in a universe not fine-tuned for your existence).

This objection — flat out — is not a good one. Obviously, we could not be aware of fine-tuning if the universe were not fine-tuned; nobody denies that. So, fine-tuning must occur for us to raise questions about it. That, however, does not itself explain the occurrence of fine-tuning, even if it explains how we came to discover fine-tuning. Consider: you're set to be executed by a firing squad of a hundred sharpshooters. Somehow, after all the shots are fired, you survive. Against all odds, not a single bullet hit you. Obviously, if you didn't survive, you wouldn't be able to ask the question — *however did I survive the execution attempt?* That said, your being alive does not explain why you survived the execution attempt. Surely, it is reasonable to demand an explanation of this, and likely that explanation has to do with the execution attempt being something of a ruse (someone giving the command for all the shooters to miss, say).

Perhaps the skeptic could accept the probabilistic force of fine-tuning in favor of theism at this point, but respond, as some naturalists have, that quantum cosmology gives counterevidence for atheism, since it implies only the probability of a life-permitting universe and not the certainty thereof, alongside the claim that this would be an irrational way for God to create. Unfortunately for the skeptic, this objection assumes too much, including that God doesn't have control over outcomes based in natural propensities. Of course, God, given that He creates and sustains all nature(s) in existence, can hit whatever outcome He wants with certainty. As Rob Koons explains, "What exactly is irrational about God's creating a condition C with the natural propensity of producing E with probability p (<1), and then actualizing E with probability 1? I suppose God does that sort of thing all the time. Presumably there was some small, finite probability that the water of Lake Galilee would support Jesus's weight in an upright position, but God intervened so as to bring about this result with probability 1."[152]

Next objection: Perhaps the dials of fine-tuning can be explained by deeper physical laws, more basic physical features? Perhaps, but this objection is one that falls prey to the relocation problem as well. Why does this deeper physics happen to give rise to just the fine-tuning necessary for the emergence of interactive intelligent life?

Rasmussen gives a nice illustration:

> Calling features basic only relabels the mystery. Suppose astronomers discover a star constellation that forms the following words: 'the foundation of the universe caused these starts to exist.' We might wonder why or how those starts managed to be arranged like that.... Now suppose someone gives the following hypothesis: the star arrangement is an inevitable consequence of the most basic features of reality. This hypothesis doesn't remove the mystery. It only relabels it. Why would reality have features that happen to give rise to a message in the stars. Calling them 'basic' does nothing to answer this deeper question.[153]

Collins summarizes the point more technically:

> Although many physicists had hoped that superstring theory would entail all the current laws and constants of physics, that hope has almost completely faded as string theorists have come to recognize that superstring theory (and its proposed successor, M-Theory) has many, many solutions, estimated at 10^{500} or more. Consequently, the prospects of discovering such a fundamental law are much dimmer than they once were. Second, such a fundamental law would not explain the fine tuning of the initial conditions of the universe. Finally,

---

[152] Robert Koons, Review of *Logic and Theism: Arguments For and Against Beliefs in God*, by John Howard Sobel (Cambridge: Cambridge University Press, 2003), at robkoons. net/uploads/1/3/5/2/135276253/sobel_review_logic_and_theism.pdf.

[153] Rasmussen, *How Reason*. 98.

hypothesizing such a law merely moves the epistemic improbability of the fine-tuning to the laws and constants up one level, to that of the postulated fundamental law itself. Even if such a law existed, it would still be a huge coincidence that the fundamental law implied just those lower-level laws and values of the constants of physics that are life-permitting, instead of some other laws or values.[154]

Finally, one might ask if positing God just relocates the issue as well, for wouldn't God be something quite complex and requiring a designer, as well? But for those who attended carefully to the cosmological argument the answer to this query is obviously no. God is in no way complex, either physically or metaphysically. Given divine simplicity, God's act and object of understanding are identical — God has no parts that require coordinating, nor is God directed toward some end other than Himself by anything beyond Himself. This shows the theoretical superiority of classical theism, as it escapes the concern of positing something more complex, in the sense requiring extrinsic explanation, than the phenomena before us, yet is still something with infinite, intellectual capability, which is the best if not only possible explanation of physical fine-tuning. Classical theism offers the best of all worlds — or the best of all multiverses, if one prefers.

In summary: even when strapped with greater complexity, naturalism fails to provide as good an explanation of physical fine-tuning as theism does, since theism is more predictive of fine-tuning than any plausible naturalistic variant, including multiverse scenarios. While much more can be said about the fine-tuning debate, my evaluation is that physical fine-tuning is far better explained by theism than naturalism and provides overpowering confirmatory weight in favor of a theistic worldview.[155]

[154] Robin Collins, "The Teleological Argument," in *The Blackwell Companion to Natural Theology*, ed. William Lane Craig and J.P. Moreland (Hoboken: Wiley-Blackwell, 2012).
[155] Another issue worth mentioning concerns what is sometimes known as the normalization problem. For those familiar with this objection, the normalization problem is cogently addressed by John Hawthorne and Yoaav Isaacs, "Misapprehensions about the Fine-Tuning Argument," *Religious Epistemology* 81 (2017), 133–55. Collins has an insightful response as well (Collins, "Teleological Argument," in *The Blackwell Companion to Natural Theology*, ed. William Lane Craig and J.P. Moreland [Hoboken: Wiley-Blackwell, 2012]), *as* does Plantinga (Alvin Plantiga, *Where the Conflict Really Lies* [Oxford: Oxford University Press, 2011] 204–211). For ease, McIntosh canvasses replies: Chad McIntosh, "The Normalization Objection to Fine-Tuning

Whether we look broadly at the fact that our world exhibits wonderful order and arrangement concerning the natures it includes, or more specifically at the findings of physics, we can argue that God is by far the better explanation of such phenomena. The order of our world is much better expected if the foundation is perfect than if it is indifferent. For this reason, theism gains significant evidential confirmation.

Arguments," *Appeared to Blogly* (blog), at appearedtoblogly.files.wordpress.com. For another response and a rather comprehensive book on fine-tuning as evidence for theism in general, see Lewis and Barnes, *A Fortunate Universe.*

CHAPTER NINE

Morality

WE NOW MOVE ON to consider our human moral experiences, and whether classical theism or metaphysical naturalism is the better explanation of such experiences. The explanatory targets are *objective* moral goodness or value, obligation, and knowledge thereof.

Objective in this context means mind-independent and hence not contingent upon our thinking about it. For example, the squirrel Robert outside my window is an objective reality (though his name is my invention): He would exist, even if I thought about or looked at something else. Further, Robert is the original cause of my thinking about him, not the other way around.

Conversely, if we say something is *subjective*, we mean it is rooted in the person (subject) alone, like a personal preference. For example, I, Pat Flynn, prefer unsweetened iced tea on hot summer days to Diet Tang, though I would not say anybody who does not share this preference is wrong in the sense that somebody who denies the squirrel outside my window is wrong.

Finally, *moral value* refers to something's goodness (like when we say it is better, in some very real sense, to be a human than a pig or a pebble, or that every human life is infinitely valuable), whereas *moral obligation* relates to prohibitions or prescriptions regarding behaviors pertaining to rational agents that can set themselves on courses of action that promote, or frustrate, their attainment of the objectively good life.[156]

With all this in mind, when we say there are objective moral facts, we mean there are moral statements (concerning goodness or obligation) that are made true entirely apart from our personal stance, preference, or attitude. For example, we take as an objective moral fact that rape is inherently evil and that we should not commit such an act, since rape does not and could not become a good act or morally permissible just because somebody desired it — in fact, no matter how many people desired it. Nor do certain other actions, such as genocide, become good acts or morally permissible just because a certain number of people, perhaps even the majority of a given population, desire it or consent to it or advocate for it. Some things are inherently bad or prohibited wholly independently of personal or collective attitudes. This position is known as *moral realism*, which holds that there are moral facts or moral elements of reality represented by true moral claims such as, "it is wrong to kill everybody in the world even if you are having a really bad day."

Moral anti-realists deny there are any objective moral facts or moral elements of reality represented by true moral claims. Many moral anti-realists are error theorists, who accept that moral judgments are capable of being true or false but are just never actually true.[157] Error theorists essentially think people making moral claims are like people talking about unicorns, with the difference being that while most people realize statements about unicorns are not grounded in anything beyond their imagination, most people do not realize their moral claims are not grounded in anything beyond their imagination. Ultimately, for moral anti-realists, moral claims are no more binding or objective than people's statements of preferences, like those who claim vanilla yogurt is better than blueberry. If such a statement is true, it is true only insofar as *that*

---

[156] The term *value* is something of a modern moral notion. Traditional philosophers tended to think and talk simply about the good. The problem for some is that value may seem to imply a certain subjectivity, of the goodness of something depending upon the valuer, rather than being inherent in the thing itself. While I don't think this has to be the case, I would not insist upon the use of value if push came to shove and one simply wanted to eschew the term altogether and stick just with goodness or the good.

[157] Other moral anti-realists are non-cognitivists claiming that moral statements cannot be either true nor false and don't belong in the sphere of knowledge.

person prefers vanilla yogurt, but not true for everyone and definitely not something that reflects anything beyond what's going on in that person's head.

I take it that most people think moral realism is correct. Certainly, this is how most people act and speak. (Moreover, moral realism has expert consensus on its side since most philosophers in this debate accept moral realism and reject moral anti-realism.)[158] People do not act and speak as if certain beliefs or actions are totally on par with preferences, like how people feel about flavors of yogurt. People do not think that rapists and genocidaires just have different tastes and, like, that's all good. No. They think they are doing something objectively wrong and ought to refrain from doing such things, no matter how much they desire to perform actions of that sort and no matter if they believe they can get away with them. Even people who otherwise pronounce that morality is relative or just a social construct are often rather quick to condemn certain actions as morally impermissible, such that people who commit such acts are evil or atrocious or repugnant or deplorable and should be punished and condemned. Such language, of course, reflects a commitment to moral realism. Really, all one needs to confirm this claim is to take the sophomore out of their Intro to Ethics class and begin to ask their opinion of certain politicians. Within seconds you will hear a slew of moral commendations more obviously committed to morality being an objective enterprise than you would hear from a Baptist preacher outside Planned Parenthood. And behavior like this — that is, living or acting inconsistently with what one professes to be the case — is what we call a performative contradiction.

---

[158] 62 percent of philosophers either accept or lean toward moral realism according to the latest survey I've seen. While appeals to authority may be, in the grand scheme, not completely decisive, and in certain contexts even fallacious, most think that expert testimony does count for something. But aren't most philosophers also atheists, and so wouldn't this point come back to bite the theist? That may be true, among all philosophers. But once we look at the most relevant experts, that is among philosophers of religion, who specialize in looking at the question of God's existence, a different picture emerges, where most are theists — 73 percent. So, I think appeal to relevant experts in both cases supports the positions I myself endorse. Of course, the skeptic may claim selection bias in both cases, but I'm more inclined to think it's a matter of studying these matters more carefully. Unfortunately, space does not permit us to settle this dispute here, so I simply note the survey results and pass on. D. Bourget and D. J. Chalmers (forthcoming) Philosophers on Philosophy: The PhilPapers2020 Survey. *Philosophers' Imprint.*

But maybe such people just cannot help themselves. Perhaps these false but useful beliefs are so deeply ingrained by evolutionary forces that they are all too easy to slide back into. And just because a person cannot live consistently as a nihilist, is this enough to say that nihilism isn't true?

Fortunately, there are many good arguments against nihilism and for moral realism.[159] I will rehearse a few (though not all) of these arguments in just a moment. For the most part, however, I will take it that the genuinely sincere reader will agree that morality does certainly *seem* like a real feature of the world, that it is not entirely determined by individual preferences or cultural attitudes, that some things really are inherently valuable (i.e., they are good and so we ought to desire them, not only good because we do desire them), some actions really right and others wrong, and that if some theory could make good sense of all this, we should prefer that theory to some other theory which cannot, other things equal.

Nevertheless, let me at least address what many consider to be the strongest reason for denying objective morality, and then tease some of the costs that come along with doing so.

That reason has to do with morality being something that evolved and helped us to survive. There is, however, an immediate problem with thinking that just because our moral beliefs have (at least partial) evolutionary history, they are not reliable windows into the world. It begs the question, even if unintentionally, against certain positions, including the theistic one. For why couldn't God guide the evolutionary process such that moral beliefs are not only conducive for survival (at least generally) but really are windows into moral features of reality? The only reason to deny the latter, so far as I can tell, is because one is assuming (beyond what science tells us) that everything is ultimately blind behind the scenes.

In other words, just as our sense of vision evolved and is generally reliable in telling us about something beyond our head, so we can say our moral sense

---

[159] I've written a popular level summary of arguments for moral realism, including how rational argumentation itself seems inexplicably bound up with moral objectivity. Pat Flynn, "Morality Has to Be Objective" at Catholic Answers (July 27, 2021), www.catholic.com/magazine/online-edition/morality-has-to-be-objective. For a more robust defense, see Terence Cunneo, *The Normative Web* (Oxford: Oxford University Press, 2010).

evolved and is generally reliable in telling us about something beyond our head. Moreover, there is no reason to think our moral sense is not picking out things (even if not infallibly) that really are good, bad, permissible, prohibited, and so on, *and* that such beliefs tend to be useful for survival.

Here's the point: just because something helps us to survive does not preclude that same something telling us about reality as it is. Our sense of sight helps us to survive, and it also tells us about something objectively real: that there is a squirrel in the front yard. It is frequently useful *and* true. Why assume that our moral sense is not similarly evolved, that it comes with a host of survival and reproductive benefits, but also helps us to discern what the good life truly is, given the sorts of creatures we are? Things can have an evolutionary history and still be windows into the world, and it is not enough to tell any just-so evolutionary origin story of something (senses of sight, reason, morality, etc.) to bear doubt upon the reliability of it. We would need further considerations to justify the latter inference, and apart from assuming (rather than proving) naturalism in addition to evolutionary theory, the evolutionary account is, for the most part, irrelevant and cannot decide the issue either way.

On the theistic worldview, there is no conflict between these commitments — the scientific, on one hand, and what we might call the metaethical on the other. The theist can fully maintain all evolutionary and social theory, if they feel these theories are well evidenced, alongside a robust moral realism. They are not required to eliminate any of the data; the theist can explain it all.

What is more, as soon as someone starts claiming that evolutionary forces could have given us unreliable but useful sensory powers or cognitive states, he is going to have a difficult time preventing that line of argument from dealing skeptical destruction to all human powers of sense and probably reason itself.

Few arguments could be given from an evolutionary origins standpoint that cast doubt on the reliability of our moral power without also casting doubt on the reliability of everything else — that is, all of our belief-forming mechanics. And if our belief-forming mechanisms are generally unreliable (or if we are otherwise quite unsure of them), and especially if false beliefs can just as well help a person survive as true beliefs, then we should be doubtful of the truth of any of our beliefs, including *that* belief. Self-defeat is knocking at the skeptic's door.

What's more, notice this: it won't do for the skeptic to say we can at least test our other senses or powers, say, by touching and feeling things, because all such tests already assume the reliability of the senses in question, in which case the skeptic will be arguing in a circle. In fact, our sense powers *must* be generally reliable to make a case for evolutionary theory in the first place.

Our powers of sense appear to be something of a package deal. In other words, if we begin to cast doubt on the general reliability of any of the senses, we ruin most, if not all, of them. In such a case, say goodbye to any legitimate basis for science, empirical reasoning, truth, and so on. Ironically or tragically, many naturalists not only see this implication but embrace it, accepting nihilism not just with respect to morality but everything else, including meaning and truth.[160]

To put it another way, to say *nothing* has any objective value would apply, quite obviously, to statements and opinions. But if no statement nor opinion has any value, why adopt it? Also obviously, the reason we *do* adopt statements or opinions is because we believe them to be true or at least probably true *and* that we believe it is objectively better and more valuable (for whatever reason) to believe true and not false things. Moreover, if there are no moral obligations either, then why should anybody accept any statement (even if it is true), especially if they prefer otherwise? What response could one give except that we ought to believe true and not false things no matter how we feel about them? This, I confidently profess, is just the response I think every one of us would give.

However, there is no way to sustain such an assertion unless the moral skeptic retracts his claim of there being no objective moral values or obligations to begin with. One way or another, the skeptic throws himself into a series of intellectual knots that cannot be undone from within his skeptical position. Ultimately, one must forsake skepticism to escape the mess. And that, I suggest, is precisely what one *should* (there's that moral language!) do.

[160] For example, Alex Rosenberg, *The Atheist's Guide to Reality* (New York: W. W. Norton & Company, 2012). And for a critique, see Edward Feser, "Rosenberg Roundup" at *Edward Feser* (blog), 2 May 2012, at edwardfeser.blogspot.com.

THE FINER POINTS

Consider, as well, the case philosopher Terrence Cuneo makes concerning the "package deal" of moral and epistemic facts—namely, that moral and epistemic facts appear to be "companions in guilt," where if you reject one, you must reject the other.[161] For those unfamiliar with this line of argument, let me briefly explain. Moral facts are what we've been talking about—that is, moral facts represented by true moral claims, such as, "It is wrong to kill everybody on earth even if you wanted to." Epistemic facts are represented by true epistemic claims, such as, "Sam's belief in UFOs is irrational." As Cuneo points out, if facts of either of these sorts exist, they provide categorical reason (independent of an agent's desires or attitudes) to act a certain way: that is, to not kill everybody on earth (even if you wanted to) and that Sam ought not to believe in UFOs. While I cannot fully defend the case Cuneo makes, the simple summary point is this. The moral and epistemic (rational) domains are tightly interwoven and deeply interpenetrating, and, in some cases, norms are even hybrid in nature (such as intellectual honesty, intellectual humility, fairness in evaluating another person's views, etc.), such that there is not enough conceptual space to divide them. If one goes down, then so does the other. However, we cannot possibly relinquish epistemic or rational norms to nihilism, for then we lose all ability to evaluate arguments and rational discourse. The anti-realist position concerning epistemic facts is self-defeating and absurd. But if that is the ultimate consequence of being a moral anti-realist, as Cuneo (I think convincingly) argues, then being a moral anti-realist is ultimately self-defeating and absurd.

Here's a question. Once we see that these evolutionary debunking arguments, as they are often called, fail, what other reason do we have for denying that morality is objective apart from assuming a worldview that either strictly precludes it or makes it improbable? The answer is hard to find. Arguments from moral disagreement are weak: we disagree about many things we believe can be adjudicated by some objective standard, even if those adjudications are difficult. Plus, one does not need to have perfect sight of everything (whether every situation is right or wrong) to have clear sight of some things (that at

---

[161] Again, see Cunneo, *The Normative Web* (Oxford: Oxford University Press, 2010).

least *some* situations are wrong). Combine that with our obvious, everyday grasp that at least some things *are* wrong (say, torture and the murder of innocents) or even good (say, acts of self-sacrificing love), and we have almost no other reason, aside from a prior commitment to naturalism, to abandon moral realism.

No surprise then that many naturalists find the nihilistic result unsatisfactory. In fact, naturalists are often boldly willing to go against the "inner logic" of naturalism, if only because they consider the obviousness of moral facts to be, well, *more obvious* than the truth of any premise in any argument that could lead one to deny moral realism. They cannot, even with all the pressure from their worldview urging them to do so, let go of the idea that there is something really and truly wrong with rape, bigotry, genocide, intellectual dishonesty, and so forth.

Thus, if we can find a story that gives a nice account of morality as we commonly think of it, then we should, other things being equal, prefer *that* story to the one that tries to resign morality to the realm of useful delusion. I claim that theism can provide such a story and naturalism (without enormous ad hoc complication) cannot.

With all that in mind, I will now tell a story about morality that I believe makes good sense of our experience, jibes with common sense, is not in conflict with science, and has strong support among some of the greatest philosophers in history. My aim is not to argue that, for the theist, no other moral theory is available, only that this moral theory seems highly plausible, is just what is to be expected if God exists and naturalism does not predict anything remotely similar concerning moral experience. If this theory is correct, then we can say that our moral experience is confirmatory evidence for the existence of God.

Let us suppose, then, that God exists, as classical theists understand God. Let us further suppose that God desires to create as we have argued He would. God then creates *things;* that is, natures with determinate ends, beings that operate in some regular fashion and strive toward their fulfillment through a range of activities. Trees sink roots to suck nutrients from the ground, lions eat meat, and humans read books and love each other. We suppose, generally speaking, that these activities are good for each of these beings, because they work toward perfecting those beings as the kinds of things they are. Humans *need* knowledge and love, and lions and trees *need* nutrition.

Things like the above (trees, lions, humans) are perfected insofar as they acquire being or actuality, particularly along the lines of their most relevant features (or specifying potency, to use the technical term), that is, along the lines of what most makes such things to be what they are. Now, since ethics is thought of as a rational enterprise, we should focus our attention on the most common rational beings of our acquaintance: human beings. If anybody is in more regular acquaintance with angels, I leave it to them to tell us about that experience.

From Aristotle onward, human beings have traditionally been classified as rational animals. We are animals, yes, falling under that wider category (or genus, to use the traditional term). But our specific difference (species) — what makes us *specifically different* from other animals — is our rationality. So, while there are many things that animals need in order to flourish that we as humans also need (food, water, shelter, etc.), we tend to think that what matters most to our ultimate perfection, as humans, has something to do with our rationality. Being well fed but lacking in knowledge, we feel, is a failure to fully flourish as humans. Meeting just the animal requirements is not enough for the truly good life. Rather we feel we are ultimately perfected to the extent that we exercise our rationality well, that we come to know the truth about things (including our human nature) and what is really (as opposed to just apparently) good for us, and that we choose to act accordingly. By *really good* for us, I mean our needs or inherent desires, things that, given human nature, are necessary for our flourishing, excellence, and happiness. Contrast needs with wants, which are *acquired* rather than *natural* desires, like preferences in yogurt. Many wants are innocuous and do not interfere with needs; we believe these wants can be pursued without any moral infraction. But not all wants are innocuous, some do interfere with our needs, and these are the sorts of acquired desires we should resist pursuing.

To differentiate, needs are things we ought to desire, whether we desire them or not; wants are things we simply do desire, whether we ought to desire them or not. We ought to desire everything we need, and we ought not to desire anything that interferes with the satisfaction of our needs; however, we may pursue wants when they are otherwise innocuous. That is really the entire crux of the traditional ethical position, where needs are something spelled out by human nature, the fulfillment of which is essential for our flourishing as the kinds of beings we are.

This account assumes what philosophers call teleology (or natural directedness), the ways in which things inherently "aim" toward certain ends, effects, or ranges of effects, given their nature or form. In virtue of what they are, trees aim at sinking roots, hearts aim at pumping blood, reason aims at truth, and so forth.

We may wonder if it is coherent to deny teleology altogether, as many naturalists do, if only because they find no basis for it in their reductive scientistic perspective. My answer is that it almost certainly is not, or at least it is not coherent to deny it all the way through — for even intellect or reason itself seems to have an undeniable *natural* aim, which we take to be *toward* the truth of things. If we say truth is not, in fact, the natural aim of the human intellect, then we immediately lose any basis for saying somebody's reasoning is better or worse. We would no longer have any objective standard by which to say any act of reason is better than any other. At this point, we must bid farewell to all rational argumentation of any kind, including any argumentation against teleology. The attempt at banishing teleology completely is absurd and self-defeating; nevertheless, I will not pursue the argument further here, since it is clear that theism can make sense of teleology (God creating natures with inherent ends and putting them into operation) and that teleology seems impeccably obvious.[162]

The relation of all this to morality is as follows: by understanding our rational nature, particularly its most relevant feature of rationality, we find that our intellects have the knowledge of the truth of things as their inherent end, whereas the will has the pursuit of what the intellect perceives to be good as its inherent end. Thus, a person acting rationally is someone who will grasp what is really (not just apparently) good for them and pursue it. And so, a well-functioning rational agent apprised of the relevant facts will naturally see that certain things, like gluttony or dishonesty, are really *not* good and seek to

---

[162] Here one could, I think, run another argument through in confirmation of God's existence just from teleology, one that is quite independent of the moral considerations which are the primary focus of our chapter. But let's not get greedy.

avoid them, pursuing instead virtues like temperance and other good states.[163] To the extent these operations are performed, this person sees a real increase of actuality with respect to rationality, and thus is objectively better (objectively "more good") because of it. Conversely, to the extent that a person engages in gluttony and becomes increasingly obese, they are failing to actualize their rational capacity and, to that extent, are becoming worse off. We are better to the extent that we perfect our rational capacity and, by extension, the human virtues. We are worse to the extent that we fail to perfect our rational capacities, act irrationally, and acquire vice.

Eleonore Stump summarizes this traditional ethical position as follows:

> By converting the specific potentiality of a human being into actuality, an agent's actions in accordance with reason increase the extent to which the agent has being *as a human being*; and so, given the connection between being and goodness, such actions increase the extent to which the agent has goodness as a human being. And this is moral goodness. Human or moral goodness, then, like any other goodness appropriate to one species, is acquired in performing instances of the operation specific to that species; in the case of humanity, this is the rational employment of the rational powers, intellect and will.[164]

Recall that for the classical theist, being and goodness are convertible: identical in reference but differing only in sense. Goodness, for the classical theist,

---

[163] I chose to focus on obesity because, while Aquinas and others want to say being and goodness are convertible, which is true, that doesn't mean our acquiring more being full stop amounts to our perfection — which would seem to have the odd implication of encouraging people to become as fat as possible (more being, right?). Rather, it is being along the lines of our specifying potency that matters most — being, we might say, along the most relevant features. Thus, to the extent that being gluttonous and becoming obese is an irrational act (which it is, given the negative health effects), we are failing to become as good as we could be along the most relevant features. Aquinas spells this matter out by drawing a distinction between first and second actuality. Under the aspect of first actuality, a human being is good just insofar as they exist — no doubt there. Under the aspect of second actuality, however, a human being is good to the extent they actualize their rational capacity, since rationality is their species-specifying potentiality or property. For a further defense of this theory, see Eleonore Stump, "Aquinas's Theory of Goodness," *The Monist* 105, no. 3 (2022).

[164] Ibid.

not only runs all the way down to the very root of reality, but finds its extreme manifestation there, where God stands as the very paradigm of goodness, just as God stands as the very paradigm of existence. For the classical theist, goodness never has to suddenly emerge from prior things lacking goodness. Goodness already, always, and automatically exists in perfect actuality at the foundation of reality, and is subsequently doled out, or shared, with everything else brought into existence.

Where does moral obligation or duty come into play? For humans, it emerges from our innate desire to be happy, the inevitable drive to pursue our own fulfilment.[165] For if we want to be happy — if we truly want to flourish — then we should follow the dictates of the laws of human nature, since that spells out what must happen for us to be happy, to flourish. However, all of us, unexceptionally, by nature, *do* want to be happy; we all *do*, inescapably, want to flourish. And so, what started as a conditional ("*if* we want to flourish...") is now categorical ("we *do* want to flourish"). Thus, we ought to follow the dictates of the laws of human nature.

For what it's worth, the above account allows someone to coherently traverse what is known as the *is–ought gap*, an objection often brought against ethical theory. The objection, stemming from David Hume, claims that from matters of fact alone, matters of merely what *is*, we cannot validly reason to any true prescriptive conclusion or matters about what one *ought* or *ought not* to do.

In other words, even if it is a matter of fact that human beings universally desire knowledge, how are we to infer that we really ought to desire or really ought to pursue knowledge? The answer? The inference comes from the observation that we ought to seek what is really good for us given human nature *together* with the fact that we inevitably want to flourish.

In other words, *if* we want to be happy, *then* we should follow the dictates of natural law — particularly human nature. By nature, we all *do* want to be happy. Therefore, we should follow the dictates of human nature. That is, we

---

[165] As many have pointed out, this truth is quite undeniable; even among those who (tragically, and I believe, mistakenly) consider or even commit suicide, they consider suicide because they believe they would be better off not living anymore. It is that inevitable drive to be better off that I am here highlighting.

should pursue what we need (what is *really* good for us) given the sort of creatures that we are.[166]

Given that it is a self-evident truth that we ought to desire what is really good for us, the remaining question is simply this: What, given human nature, is really good for us? And while we may not have certainty just through philosophical or scientific reflection on the complete range of real goods for human beings (maybe revelation is required?), surely we have reasonably high assurance of many of them: physical health, knowledge, loving and trusting relationships, a stable and just society, and such like. Some goods, as you might have noticed, are possessions (external goods, like wealth, societal institutions, etc.), whereas other goods are perfections (personal goods, like virtue).

Personal goods concern the good we desire to *be* rather than goods we desire to *have*, and chiefly the habit of desiring what one really ought to desire and not desiring anything that interferes with obtaining the goods one needs. As Mortimer Adler tells us, personal goods "amplify our very being through actualizing our potentialities. The man or woman who has become a good human being through acquiring the personal perfections that everyone should desire to have is also the good man or woman that everyone should desire to be."[167]

Once we have reasonable assurance that something is really good for us, we have an obligation to pursue it, given the facts about human nature, including our innate drive to fulfillment. For those familiar with ethical theories, they will undoubtedly see a certain virtue ethics picture in this account. Virtues are stable dispositions ("good habits") related to the perfection of our

---

[166] To hedge against a common but silly objection, when we speak of following the natural law, we do not mean that humans should take their moral cues from just anything that goes on in nature at large — like from sharks that forcibly copulate with other sharks. No, what we mean is that human needs are determined by human nature (not shark nature, not monkey nature, etc.), and so our flourishing is set by the ends toward which our nature or form is inherently directed. What sharks or other animals do is quite irrelevant, because we are not sharks or any other animal. Nor is it any objection against this view that we should not use anything that isn't "natural," like eyeglasses. This too is just an equivocation on what we mean by natural in this sense. Eyeglasses help to restore proper function, or sight, to the eyes. Eyes are aimed at vision, thus eyeglasses are a good thing, since they help to facilitate the good of eyesight, though they are something we construct.

[167] Mortimer Adler, *Six Great Ideas* (New York: Touchstone, 1997), 91.

powers, with some of the traditional cardinal virtues being prudence, justice, temperance, and fortitude.

Our purpose is not to spell out an entire ethical theory here, only to present a story—a story of how objective morality flows quite naturally from a classical theistic perspective, a world populated with natures, developing through time and space, moving toward their fulfillment by having their being amplified along the relevant features. Classical theism predicts (makes sense of) a world where our common moral experiences are not illusory but rather track something vitally important, namely, some general understanding of how to lead an objectively good human life. That, after all, is what ethics amounts to: the study of the good life.

Notice, as well, that none of the above requires any immediate appeal to God such that if we don't *believe* in God, we are helpless concerning ethical action or ethical knowledge. The question we are considering is not whether we need to believe in God to know certain moral facts, but whether we can make sense of morality as objective if God does not exist. These are different questions. God may exist and may have caused the world to be structured in such a way that much of our moral knowledge can be gained apart from immediate belief in God or divine revelation—in fact, I believe that this describes just the world that God created. Nevertheless, I believe the conditions for morality to be objective are only possible if God exists, or at least they are far more probable if God exists.

This follows largely from what was considered in the cosmological argument, including the fact that no finite nature guarantees its existence. Moreover, because finite natures, including human nature, are oriented toward some end that they at present do not yet possess, this means they are oriented toward some *being* or *actuality* they currently do not have. So, anything that is directed toward some further state of actuality is not everything that it can be: it is not purely actual, as God is, but is a composite of act and potency, if we're putting the matter in metaphysical terms (which we should).[168] We have already

---

[168] God, after all, is supposed to be the ultimate explanation of being, or why anything exists at all. Thus, I don't think it should be surprising if various considerations, including moral considerations, often just bleed into the cosmological argument; that is, just offer another way of considering the being of things and what ultimately explains that. In this case, the being which things do not yet possess but are naturally oriented toward. This discloses, once again, a sort of metaphysical composition that points back toward God as the metaphysically simple being that brings these act–potency composites about.

argued that beings of this sort point ineluctably back to God as the ultimate source of their existence, and so it turns out that God, who undergirds this entire system of natures, is responsible not just for the current existence of any such being but their being directed toward some further being (perfection) as well.[169] And that, I suggest, is the more sophisticated way of seeing the necessary link between morality and God. It is not that if we do not believe in God, then we would be hopelessly ignorant of how to behave; it is rather that if God did not exist, then there would be no ultimate adequate way to explain the metaphysical system that is itself necessary to undergird objective morality (of natures and ends) however we come to learn of the moral rules which provide the blueprint for our flourishing as humans.

I should, however, make the brief remark that none of the above means that revelation is not important. For it might be the case — in fact, I believe it is the case — that we have an obligation, for our own good, to worship and obey God, not only as a matter of justice, but to attain our highest supernatural end of union with the divine. Thus, it may be necessary for God to reveal certain things to us, including specifically how God wants us to relate to Him, and therein lies the possibility, not just of divine revelation, but also "organized religion," assuming any religious tradition can argue for itself being the intended expression of how God wants us to relate to Him. But we'll have to save all that for another time.

In short, then: from the traditional classical theistic perspective, we expect a world where our moral experiences generally align with how things in fact really are. Our moral judgments about things (humans included) being good or bad, better or worse, are not just statements of preferences, even if they are not always correct judgments for various reasons. Of course, there is room for statements of preferences, since we have room for acquired and not just natural desires. But the theory above also helps to make sense of why we do not think of certain horrible actions, like murder or molestation, to be merely a matter of

---

[169] What's more, given that God is pure actuality, whose essence just is His existence, there would be no end God Himself is naturally directed toward. God, then, is the undirected director; that which orients all other natural things toward their fulfillment without Himself requiring orientation from anything else, being already completely actual and perfectly realized.

taste: we believe they are objectively evil because they are objectively irrational and contrary to the needs of the human person. And we have the grounds by which to say they are prohibited, as explained above.[170]

Further, nothing of the above account conflicts in any way with the sciences. If anything, one might think science itself requires many of the metaphysical starting points of the moral theory just briefly explained, including, most particularly, that things really have natures or stable, abiding centers of activity. And if theism best predicts or explains these metaphysical starting points, then the success of science and the genuine knowledge it offers us of the world is another point of confirmation for classical theism, assuming naturalism does not make equally good predictions on this score (which it does not).

Naturalism does not make a similar prediction concerning objective morality; in fact, many naturalists, new and old, are moral nihilists.

As naturalist Alex Rosenberg explains:

> Nihilism consists in the following claims: a) normative terms — good, bad, right, duty, etc. — do not name real properties of events or things, either natural nor non-natural ones; b) all claims about what is good in itself, or about categorical moral rights or duties, are either false or meaningless; c) the almost universal beliefs that there are such properties and that such claims are true can be 'explained away' by appropriate scientific theory.[171]

Rosenberg continues:

> Nihilism takes the form of what Mackie (1977) calls an 'error theory.' It does not deny that beliefs about norms and values can motivate people's actions. It does not deny the felt 'internalism' of moral claims, nor does it deny that normative beliefs confer benefits on the people who hold them. Indeed nihilism is consistent with the claim that such beliefs are necessary for human survival, welfare and flourishing. Nihilism only claims that these beliefs, where they exist,

---

[170] Though further grounds may be provided as well if, in fact, we believe God acts as something of an additional enforcer of the natural moral law — if, as it happens, things are not appropriately settled or squared away.

[171] Alex Rosenberg and Tamler Sommers, "Darwin's nihilistic idea: evolution and the meaninglessness of life," *Biology and Philosophy* 18 (2003), 653–68.

are false. It treats morality as instrumentally useful — instrumentally useful for our nonmoral ends or perhaps the nonmoral ends of some other biological systems, such as our genes for example.[172]

Why think, as Rosenberg does, that nihilism is the right result if naturalism is true? Because it flows naturally (if not inevitably) from the grand story of naturalism: that our universe began with the Big Bang, from which various bodies formed according to physical laws. Life itself began in a primitive soup of chemicals, and evolution caused the emergence of the incredible lifeforms we see today. There was no design nor intention behind any of this — everything is governed by indifference. Thus, any appearance of design is explained by selection pressures working upon random genetic variation — that is, whatever traits an organism might have, from its claws to its feathers to its brain, it has them because it contributed to reproductive fitness ("have sex, avoid bears"), in some way or another.

"Considered as a rationally justifiable set of claims about an objective something," says naturalist Michael Ruse, "ethics is illusory. Morality is just an aid to survival and reproduction … and any deeper meaning is illusory."[173]

The point is that if naturalists are not supposed to go beyond science, their grand narrative pushes in an obvious direction concerning morality, and that is in the direction of its denial or negation. Hence why many atheists are willing to eliminate the data of moral experience, seeing (clearly, I think) that it isn't something that can be reasonably located in the naturalistic worldview, but rather is something the naturalistic worldview causes us to think is a programmed false belief, one that is useful to survival but not true in any way apart from describing our attitudes about things. Naturalists typically do not accept essences or natures or forms, at least not on the level we need them in order to make sense of objective moral experience for human beings; naturalists think that everything is effectively reducible to what the hard sciences give us, and the hard sciences do not give us human nature. They give us atoms. And there is no getting any robust system of ethics from mere recombinations

---

[172] Ibid.

[173] Michael Ruse, "Evolutionary Theory and Christian Ethics," in *The Darwinian Paradigm* (London: Routlege, 1989), 268–69.

of atoms. If that is *all* there is to the story — atoms and the laws we use to combine them — then morality is surely illusory, just as many a naturalist claim. (Should I also emphasize the theoretical problem of the brute stopping point and inherent complication of having *just* the atoms and the laws we do?)

THE FINER POINTS

Philosopher Sharon Street, for example, argues that the naturalistic grand narrative should cause naturalists to prefer what is called an "adaptive link account" between fitness and moral beliefs, which means embracing some variety of moral anti-realism (like constructivism).[174] She disregards a "tracking account" where fitness somehow follows mind-independent moral truths as scientifically implausible. It is far more consistent with evolutionary theory and naturalism to go the route of moral anti-realism. (My only qualification on Street's remark is that it is not *scientifically* implausible to adopt a tracking account, rather it is just naturalistically implausible, where we assume behind everything is a principle of indifference alongside an otherwise reductive, mechanistic view of the world.)

Mark Linville reinforces Street's proposal in arguing against moral supervenience theories among naturalists, where, somehow, moral facts supervene upon natural facts, since what Darwin's theory conjoined to naturalism should cause us to do is "glance back over our shoulder" to see if our widely held judgments might be unreliable, *including* supervenience of moral facts upon natural facts.[175] In other words, if the naturalist is assuming some sort of dependence thesis between moral and natural facts to undergird a system of moral objectivity, then what thinkers like Street and Linville are proposing is a strong reason, from the inner logic of naturalism, for doubting that any judgments about the dependence thesis itself are true.

Things only become more difficult for the naturalist, assuming that they aren't eager to embrace moral anti-realism, when a story must be told of how *unguided*

[174] Sharon Street, "A Darwinian dilemma for realist theories of value," *Philosophical Studies* 127, no. 1 (2006), 109–166.
[175] Mark Linville, "The Moral Argument," in *The Blackwell Companion to Natural Theology*, ed. William Lane Craig and J.P. Moreland (Hoboken: Wiley-Blackwell, 2012), 407.

evolutionary forces somehow bring us into reliable cognitive contact with moral facts about the world. After all, moral facts and moral knowledge are not the same, and one does not entail the other. Even if we granted a naturalistic account, whereby we could affirm a slew of objective moral facts, that does nothing to entail our ever coming to *know* such facts. Thus, what we want is a theory which makes sense — hopefully, in a relatively simple way — of both. Theism does this; naturalism cannot.

This is a subtle but important point, so let me illustrate through analogy. Suppose I form the belief that it is 3:15 based upon looking at a broken clock. Does that belief count as knowledge? Most philosophers would say it does not, because the process by which that belief was formed was too unreliable. Even if by some happy accident it really *were* 3:15 when I look at the broken clock, the truth of my belief is not enough for me to say that I *know* it is 3:15, given the inherent unreliability of how that belief was formed — and how much more likely it is that my belief would be false.

What's required for knowledge is not just true belief but a generally reliable (even if not infallible) process for arriving at that true belief. Naturalistic evolution does not care about connecting human beings with objective moral truths, even if there are objective moral truths, because it is run by a principle of indifference, ultimately *aiming* at nothing. It therefore clearly cannot be taken as a reliable process for arriving at moral truths.

Going further, the notion of "Darwinian counterfactuals" provides further reason to see naturalistic evolution as unreliable in respects relevant for securing moral knowledge, since, if evolutionary circumstances were different and we were raised (as Darwin himself suggested) under the conditions of hive bees, we might have very different moral beliefs, including beliefs that, say, patricide is moral (or infanticide or inequity, if we look toward other species).

As people like to quote Darwin himself on this score, so do I: "If men were reared under precisely the same conditions as hive-bees ... our unmarried females would, like the worker-bees, think it a sacred duty to kill their brothers, and mothers would strive to kill their fertile daughters, and no one would think of interfering."[176]

---

[176] Charles Darwin, *The Descent of Man*.

The point? For naturalistic evolution, what matters is not necessarily the truth of the matter but what conduces for survival, and there is no reason, especially concerning the formation of moral beliefs, that these two need not coincidence, either for most of the time or ever. For naturalism, moral truth (if there is any) doesn't seem to be connected in the right way to reproductive fitness for such a process to produce knowledge. This means naturalism fails to explain moral knowledge, which is something we all think we have at least some of. We think we know, for example, that molestation of children is wrong.

The most promising — but still hopelessly contrived, I think — attempt naturalists have made to avoid this difficulty is to postulate that natural processes, while not aimed at moral accuracy, are nevertheless pointed at some "third thing" that itself is roughly correlated with moral accuracy. For example, evolutionary forces surely aim (unintentionally, of course, and so only metaphorically speaking) at survival, but things which promote survival, the naturalist will say, are generally good. Thus, if we wind up believing things that promote survival and those things are generally good, then there is the connection we need to secure moral knowledge.

The problem with this proposal should be obvious: it seems not just wrong, according to what Darwin himself suggested considering Darwinian counterfactuals and behaviors observed throughout the wider animal kingdom (behaviors which have been conducive to fitness but that we would consider morally repugnant), but it also begs the question. We assume *certain* behaviors that promote survival are good based on our moral intuitions that they are good; however, the argument at hand has just called those intuitions into question. Yet the naturalist is here just relying upon those intuitions to reassert their theory, thus stepping into a circle of notably small diameter.

While we may be justified in generally trusting our faculties without first proving that they are reliable — and this includes moral intuitions — we cannot just reassert that general trust if there is some independent reason calling into question the reliability of that intuition, which is the case here concerning naturalism, evolutionary forces, and moral belief.

Nevertheless, we again see complications beginning to arise for the naturalistic hypothesis, where many things must coordinate in what appears to be a rather improbable fashion.

Comparing naturalism with conspiracy theories is becoming increasingly sensical, as I hope you can see. Let's push that illustration a little further. Coming back to moral knowledge, our grasping abstract moral properties within the inner logic of a naturalistic framework would undoubtedly require something — as atheist philosopher J. L. Mackie called it — "queer." By that Mackie means "some special faculty of moral perception or intuition, utterly different from our ordinary ways of knowing everything else."[177]

Of course, this rational intuition is not queer according to the inner logic of classical theism, but as philosopher J. P. Moreland says about naturalists adopting this strategy, "It would be a case of helping himself to an entity that just can't be located in the most reasonable naturalist epistemology, Grand Story, and result ontology, bereft of queer brute entities."[178] Moreland then references atheist philosopher Thomas Nagel on how adopting the ability of any such rational intuition is one that is "secularly uncomfortable, should make naturalists nervous, and is suspiciously religious or quasi-religious."[179]

All this links back to the remarks from Street and Linville, where the inner logic of naturalism should push one away from moral realism. Thus, it is not surprising that for naturalism to secure moral facts and moral knowledge, things have to become complicated. Where so many auxiliary components are introduced and subsequently wired together, resulting in so many apparent ways for things to go wrong, it just no longer seems like a credible story. It is too improbable.

Worse, these naturalistic accounts for making sense of the moral features of our world introduce other aspects into the naturalist world picture which not only are *not* a natural fit within naturalism but can no longer find an adequate explanation *according to* naturalism (for example, strong emergence), appearing instead like magic, ultimately replacing one explanatory difficulty with another.

What we are left with, at least for the naturalist trying not to abandon objective morality, is an impressive metaphysical mess, with components

---

[177] J. L. Mackie, *Inventing Ethics* (New York: Penguin Books, 1977), 38.
[178] William Lane Craig and Eric Weilenberg, *A Debate on God and Morality* (London: Routledge, 2020), 101.
[179] Ibid.

scattered all over the place, themselves brutely obtaining or brutely connected or both, and — worse still — ultimately failing to make sense of the very datum they were brought in to explain. In this sense, naturalism is worse than a grand-scale conspiracy theory, since most conspiracy theories do have the requisite explanatory power, even if their complications make them ultimately unbelievable.

Theism is the better explanation of moral facts and knowledge. Our moral experience is thus considerable evidence for the existence of God.

CHAPTER TEN

Beings Like Us

Is it surprising that beings like us exist? I think not, so long as God exists. God would have reason to create us, the good and infinitely precious things that we are, because God is perfectly good and inclined to share His goodness. By God's very existence, good and omnipotent as He is, beings like us are made highly probable.

It would, however, be extraordinarily surprising that beings like us exist if naturalism were true and God did not exist. There is no inherent drive within naturalism — that is, within mindless mass and force — to produce beings like us; no reason, even if we thought naturalism had the resources to make sense of the emergence of minded entities, that such an emergence should ever occur. Further, naturalism does not have the resources to make sense of the emergence of beings like us. It fails to get even the idea of us off the ground.

"What even are we?" one might ask.

Minimally, we are beings that can sense (feel), think, know, reason, choose, communicate, love, and be consciously aware of ourselves doing these things. If God — and by extension, mind — is fundamental to reality, it is far more likely that other minded beings would crop up, at least at some point, especially since an omnipotent mind would have all the resources and motivations to bring forth other minded entities. If, however, mind (in some sense) is not fundamental to reality, it becomes seriously unlikely that other minded beings would emerge anywhere ever.

That is the *prima facie* case, admitted by almost everyone. But I should like to strengthen the case by focusing on two aspects of the human person that naturalism struggles seriously to explain — qualitative experience (*qualia*) and thought (mental content) — and highlight how the proposed naturalistic explanations of these phenomena are riddled with what appear to be insuperable difficulties and do nothing to increase the probability that beings like us would emerge. For this reason, conscious beings like us count as strong confirmatory evidence for the existence of God.

At the outset, I must admit that the issue of explaining aspects of human consciousness from a naturalistic perspective has spawned an enormous literature, probably because it has proven to be something of an intractable project. That being so, I must content myself with offering just the highlights of arguments (and objections against them) that I find to be quite persuasive against the possibility of a naturalistic explanation of consciousness. We'll work through qualitative experience first.

Qualitative Experience

We feel things. We are aware of sensations, and moreover, we are aware of our awareness. We have a private inner mental life that nobody else can access directly. When you pinch me, you may be able to correlate my pain with activity in my brain, but the feeling aspect of pain — of *my* pain — is mine alone. Only I *feel* the pain of the pinch you gave me.

Philosophers use the term qualia (plural for the Latin *quale*, as in "quality") as a label for our subjective private impressions of things — in other words, the "what's it like" to experience something, whether a pinch, a fragrance, a color, a logical argument, a personal mood, or what have you. Qualia *define* and *differentiate* our experiences, apart from which we could not distinguish between colors or sounds or sights or arguments. That we have this qualitative dimension of experiences is undeniable and absolute bedrock. Everything comes to us through this experiential dimension, everything is ultimately made sense of within it.

Physical bits of matter have no qualitative experiences, let alone experiences of experiencing; they have no "quale." Dust is in motion when it swirls, yet one would search in vain for *emotion* in that motion. There is no "what's it like" for dust to swirl — for the dust, I mean. Humans can experience dust swirling; dust itself cannot.

The problem for the naturalist is how to take stuff that is just like dust — which is to say, mindless mass and force — and get it to produce that which is virtually its qualitative opposite: a unified center of conscious activity, capable of feeling and thinking.

Actually, there are two problems for the naturalist in this regard. The first is one of an in-principle construction constraint, which is often called the "hard problem of consciousness": how can subjective first-person sensations be generated from material that entirely lacks senses? The second is one of explanatory irrelevance or redundancy. Let's start with the second consideration.

For the naturalist, the qualitative dimension of experience would not seem to add anything causally relevant to their picture of the human person or history of the world. In turn, this makes it difficult to explain why the qualitive dimension would emerge, even *if* it could emerge.

As Hart points out:

> Could not a very sophisticated automaton or even some kind of 'soulless' human replicant have all the same functional relations without possessing subjective awareness as well? Could not either be programmed to withdraw its titanium pincers or biotechnical digits from the flame or to flee wildly before the teeth of the bear, in either case uttering the appropriate howls of pain or terror, even though within each of them there existed only an absolute affective void? And, then again, are there not also innumerable qualia that seem clearly to have no functional purpose at all, but simply are — such as that odd and poignantly buoyant melancholy that I derive from a great deal of music written in the key of D-minor?[180]

In fact, many naturalists are *epiphenomenalists* about the experiential dimension, which means they believe that our mental life simply "floats atop" the underlying physical base, ultimately playing no causal role in the history of the world. An

---

[180] David Bentley Hart, *The Experience of God: Being, Consciousness, Bliss* (New Haven: Yale University Press, 2013).

epiphenomenon is something caused by something else but itself unable to cause anything. Thus, for the epiphenomenalist, all conscious experience is something of an affective "residue" fortuitously thrown off by unconscious physical events that it cannot causally influence. The experiential dimension is, in other words, a byproduct of brain activity, causally dissociated in the downward direction. According to such naturalists, our experiences — including our apparent experiences of choosing — make no actual difference to the world.

Naturalists often hold this epiphenomenalist perspective because that is just what is to be expected if naturalism is true. Assuming our mental life is something to be explained, it must (to be consistent with the inner logic of naturalism) be explained by the underlying physical states, which means the physical states must somehow precede and determine it, and not the other way around. Mind, for the naturalist, is something "late and local"; physical reality comes first. Epiphenomenalists take seriously (perhaps too seriously, though what other choice do they have?) the naturalistic commitment that mindless blocks of reality (atoms) are the real actors.

The problem with epiphenomenalism is just that it is as obviously false as anything can be. Think about it: according to the epiphenomenalist, while I may think my experience of desiring to drink coffee is what makes the difference in my walking over to pour myself a cup, that really has nothing to do with it. Rather all such action is the result of unthinking physical processes, which somehow seem to be the result of, and coincidentally line up with, conscious desires or choice or what have you.

In case you need something to refute this (I think self-evidently false) position, try this: picture in your mind a blue square. Now, begin to rotate that blue square. Isn't that something? You can, by a basic intentional action, generate a blue square before your mind. You can then rotate the blue square. Yet according to so many naturalist philosophers of mind, we are supposed to believe this is all coincidence, not the result of your mental intention but rather mindless forces that just so happened to cause you to visualize the blue square the moment you decided to (and mindless forces caused this desire as well) but also aligned perfectly to produce a rotating blue square the moment you intended to rotate it. There is no need to be coy here: does anybody find that story even remotely plausible? I don't. Clearly, your intentions make a difference to the world, and are both basic and immediate. There is no imaginable story (let alone any actual established science) of how physics or chemistry can make sense of even the simplest intentional acts like the one above without appealing to an unfathomable array of inexplicable coincidences.

Not only is epiphenomenalism false — even if it were true, we would have no good explanation (from a naturalistic perspective) for the emergence of our mental life, since our mental life plays no indispensable causal role. Such experiences would be functionally unnecessary in the naturalistic grand narrative. After all, following Hart's example, the functional relations needed for survival and procreation could occur with no problem entirely apart from an entity having any actual experience of those relations.

In other words, even if conscious experience could be constructed from a purely physical base, there is no good evolutionary explanation for why any conscious experience *would* be constructed — if anything, the experiential dimension seems entirely wasteful. So, in other words, even if naturalism had the resources to make sense of how mind could emerge from matter, we have no reason for thinking mind actually *would* emerge from matter, given the grand narrative of naturalism.

But I said naturalism doesn't have the resources to make sense of mind, which brings us to considering the construction problem. This I take to be the more fundamental issue concerning consciousness and naturalistic explanation.

Let us begin by noting that some constructions are not just improbable but impossible. You cannot, for example, construct a purple tower from white blocks alone, and it doesn't matter how many blocks you have, nor does it matter how much time you have to rearrange them. If all you have are white blocks, a purple tower is never going to emerge.

We can say the same concerning naturalism and consciousness: if all you have is mindless mass and force, you are never going to be able to construct — no matter the amount of mindless material and no matter the time available — minded entities like us. There is too profound of a categorical difference between the stuff naturalists suppose reality is ultimately composed of and beings like us to suddenly leap from one to the other through mere recombination — shifting blocks, as it were. For the naturalist, whatever is bottommost is nothing like us: it does not feel or sense, it is not aware, it does not think, it does not aim, it is not unified, and so on, yet we are told that, if given enough time and chances at recombination, eventually beings like us will emerge. This error is clearly no different — if anything, it is worse — than thinking that, with enough chances at recombination, eventually a purple tower will emerge from white blocks.

To draw out the profundity of this categorical difference between the mental and the physical, consider the following:

✣ There is a raw qualitative feel — a "what it is like" — to having mental states or conscious experiences (pain, joy, familiarity, etc.). No physical state exhibits this feature. There is no "what it is like" to exist as an atom.

✣ Mental states exhibit intentionality or directedness toward an object (when we think, we think *about* things, like cats or dogs or liberty or justice). No physical state exhibits this feature, either. Fire isn't "about" anything.

✣ Mental states are private, accessible only to the subject having them. No physical state is private; all physical states are public, accessible in principle to all. While everyone can look at a CT scan of my brain, nobody except me can know what I'm thinking (unless I tell you and we map correlations).

✣ Mental states also clearly lack features physical states have — for example, spatial extension, location, and being composed of parts. My thought of justice has no physical dimension, location, and isn't made of simpler parts.

Mental states or the experiential qualitative dimension are clearly not *identical* to physical states, for what is true of one is not true of the other. While I am directly aware of my thoughts, I am not directly aware of any associated physical brain activity. But if mental states were identical to physical states, then I should be directly aware of the former when I am directly aware of the latter — but I am not.

This is *not* to say the mental and physical might not be really distinct aspects of the same underlying reality, like two sides of the same coin. It is simply to point out that one is not (identically) the other, just as the heads of the coin is really different from the tails of the coin.

Someone might object to the above point by bringing in the example of Superman and Clark Kent. In some cases, the objection holds; one thing may in fact be identical to another, but we somehow fail to notice it, as apparently is the

case with Lois Lane not being able to identify the superl
she works with. But there *are* differences between Supei
even if only a pair of glasses and tights. These are really d
aspects. Wearing glasses is really not the same as not we
being appeared to by someone with glasses on is really dif   ..... being appeared to by someone without glasses on) even if the underlying reality these
properties attach to is one and the same individual. So, the proposed counterexample fails.[181] Mental states really are not physical states, even if they are really
distinct aspects of the same underlying reality, as I maintain they are — the reality which is you. The considerations so far are not claiming there is no single
underlying reality, only that one aspect of us (the mental or experiential) is not
identical to, or even generable from, another aspect of us (the physical).

Again, reason reveals that some constructions are impossible, and we can
see this apart from having to run experiments. We know prime numbers cannot
add up into a prime minister, to use a classic example. That is not something we
need to test. Same with mindless mass rearranging into first-person experience,
of the physical generating the mental. We can see that just as prime numbers
cannot add up into a prime minister, purely third-person aspects — masses, mo-
tions, and so on — cannot construct first-person subjective experiences. (Or
minimally we can see that if a conscious being resulted from the rearrangement
of mindless mass, we would be confident that there was more to the story than
just those molecules, molecules being themselves insufficient.)

We have used the terms "emerge" and "emergent" quite a bit. So, let me
pause a moment to insist that the naturalist claiming consciousness is

[181] Joshua Rasmussen also points out the relevant difference between direct and indirect awareness, and how indirect awareness is less reliable. When Lois Lane sees
Superman, she is not directly aware of Superman. "She experiences an image of his
face, his cape, and the way he talks. This experience is inside her, and she is aware
of it directly. Superman, by contrast, is not wholly inside her mind. For this reason,
while her awareness of Superman's appearance is direct, her awareness of Superman
is indirect. Her lack of direct awareness of Superman explains why she fails to realize
that Superman is the same as Clark Kent. She is not directly aware of Superman.
She is only directly aware of her experience of his attributes. By contrast, you have
direct awareness of some aspects of your own thoughts and feelings." And yet we
have no direct awareness of any associated physical event which we would if these
aspects were identical. Rasmussen, *How Reason*, 86–87.

mergent" is not an adequate *explanation*, for two reasons. First, when it comes to examples of emergence that we know of — for example, water emerging from a certain arrangement of molecules — either a fully reductive account is available in which an adequate functional analysis can be given (for example, the property of liquidity can be analyzed entirely in terms of the water's molecular structure and more basic laws) *or* the problem of qualitative experience — the felt aspect, as it were — is smuggled into the causes. Wetness, as the *felt* phenomena associated with water, is clearly not explicable, reducible, or analyzable via entirely non-wet qualities. And so, the qualia problem is either ignored or pushed around by emergentist proposals rather than being explained.[182]

To summarize the issues so far: naturalism has no good account for why beings with conscious experiences would emerge even if it were possible for them to from a naturalistic framework. More fundamentally, it does not actually seem possible for conscious beings to emerge if the only materials available are mindless mass and force. The construction is impossible. How does one convert material that is unconscious and unaware and disparate (not unified) into a unified center of conscious awareness? How does one take stuff that is fundamentally unlike us in virtually every respect and invert it, qualitatively speaking, through a series of entirely quantitative steps, into... *us*? Invoking terms like emergence, as has been pointed out, is not an explanation of *how* such an emergence, if it occurs, is possible. What we are looking for are the necessary conditions for the possibility of the emergence of beings

---

[182] One might wonder if there can be *sui generis* emergence of mind from a mindless base. The problem isn't that emergence of mind isn't or can't be possible, the problem is that calling something emergent ignores the question of how such emergence is possible. In our case, emergence of mind just labels (or relabels) the mystery insofar as what emerges is quite repugnant (not reducible) to its physical, non-sensing base. If, for example, we saw fire shooting from somebody's hand, calling it emergent doesn't really tell us anything. In fact, we know enough about the nature of people to say they can't shoot fire from their hands, so even if the fire emerged, we know there is more to the story than just the person's hand. The same, of course, can be said with respect to the emergence of minds; even if emergence is possible, then we can say there must be more to the story than mindless mass. Alternatively, if the naturalist just wants to insist upon brute strong emergence of minds, so be it: but at that point they have really given up offering an actual explanation and lost whatever epistemological advantage they think is afforded to naturalism concerning the power of scientific explanation.

like us, and thus far naturalism does not seem to have them. Nothing about naturalism leads us expect the emergence of beings like us, and everything about naturalism, including its commitment to source physicalism, tells against this happening. If fundamental reality is unconscious matter, there is no reason at all to expect the sort of things that we are — conscious entities.

Let us turn now to another aspect of conscious experience that naturalism fails to explain: mental content or concept possession.

Mental Content (Concept Possession)

By mental content I mean the *meaning* of thought. When we say we have mental content, we are saying that our thoughts have meaning for us, which is obvious. When I think, for example, of my being a father, I have a clear understanding of what I am thinking about — namely, my being a father. When I think of *modus ponens*, again, I have an unambiguous grasp of the object of my thought — in this case, a logical rule. When I think of triangularity, my thought again has determinate meaning: there is some specific concept that I currently possess.

When I say a person possesses a concept I mean, to paraphrase Mortimer J. Adler, that they have acquired a *disposition* to pick out perceived objects as being *this kind or that kind* and to *understand* what this kind or that kind of object *is like*, and to perceive a number of particulars as being the same in kind, and *discriminate* between them and other sensible particulars that are different in kind. Moreover, as Adler points out, "concepts are acquired dispositions to understand what certain kinds of objects are like both (a) when the objects, though perceptible, are not actually perceived, and (b) when they are not perceptible at all, as is the case with all the conceptual constructs we employ in physics, mathematics, and metaphysics."[183]

Our thoughts are about things (they exhibit intentionality, to use common philosophical parlance), and what they are about — cats, dogs, liberty, justice, addition, multiplication, and so forth — is often clear and exact. We know just what we are thinking about when we are thinking about it.

The intuitive problem that determinate meaning of thought (call it concept possession) poses for naturalism is this: everything physical is inherently

---

[183] Mortimer Adler, *Ten Philosophical Mistakes*, (Touchstone Reprint, 1997), 51.

particular, imprecise, ambiguous, or inexact. But concepts are not. Concepts are universal and determinate (or exact) in their meaning. There is no perfect physical instance of triangularity as such, only particular *triangles* that more or less approximate triangularity depending on how well they are drawn.

Universals are general ideas or abstract patterns or common natures, shared among various kinds of things. For example, *redness* is shared by stop signs, fire hydrants, and Irish foreheads, and triangularity is shared in common with particular triangles drawn in various places (books, chalkboards, scrap paper) using differing material (ink, chalk, graphite). Universals are *abstract* insofar as when we consider them, we ignore the particularizing features that the concrete objects exhibiting the pattern may have — for instance, a particular point in spacetime, or the matter something is made of (ink or chalk). In Aristotelian speak, we pull form from matter when abstracting a universal concept.

Of course, there have been objections posed to the idea that there really are universals (general ideas, common natures, etc.), famously from David Hume, who writes, "Let any man try to conceive a triangle in general, which is neither isosceles nor scalene, nor has any particular length or proportion of sides; and he will soon perceive the absurdity of all the scholastic notions with regard to abstraction and general ideas."

Hume's mistake is fairly basic, really; he is failing to differentiate between understanding (or conceiving) and perceiving (or imagining). Granted, one cannot picture or imagine ("image") a triangle without engaging the sense power and thus having the picture become bound as either isosceles or scalene, but that is not what understanding is about; Hume is overlooking the difference between intellect and sense. We obviously can and do conceive of triangularity by understanding (not picturing) what is common to all particular triangles, be they isosceles or scalene, red or white, drawn in chalk or ink, and so forth. What's more, there are many things we can conceive of, yet can definitely form no mental image of — for example, a chiliagon (a thousand-sided polygon).

To deny the existence of general ideas, abstract patterns, or common nature is just to endorse a position called nominalism (essentially the claim that there is no sameness that is not identity; everything is individual, nothing has a shared or common nature), which itself is deeply tied to naturalism. And the recurring issue with nominalism is that it inevitably seems to lead either to self-defeat or self-refutation. For we have every right to ask why we call such particulars (this triangle, that triangle) by a common name (triangle), and what other reason could a person provide aside from the fact they share certain characteristics in common (triangularity, trilaterality, etc.)?

If we admit to understanding such characteristics, then nominalism is refuted because we have conceded to having a universal and determinate understanding of something, such as our triangularity example, apart from particulars (being isosceles or scalene, drawn in chalk or ink), which is what Hume denies. If we do not admit to understanding such characteristics, then there is no basis for calling various particular things *triangles* in the first place — which is required for Hume to get his objection started. Ironically, Hume demonstrates both the reality of and his understanding of universals (triangularity) in his very attempt to refute them; otherwise his assertion would be meaningless. Hume is simply confusing picture thinking (sense power) with conception (intellectual power).[184]

Returning to the original point, we possess concepts, and in possessing concepts, we are able to entertain clear, unambiguous thoughts of general ideas. A powerful shot against materialism — and by extension, naturalism, since the most promising naturalistic account of mind is the materialist one — is that if everything material is concrete and particular, then thought

---

[184] Ed Feser summarizes the self-defeat issue for nominalism, a position which denies the reality of universals, as follows:

Where we think there are universals, the nominalist says, there are really only general names, words we apply to many things. Hence, there is, for instance, the general term 'red,' which we apply to various objects but no such thing as redness. Of course, this raises the question why we apply the term 'red' to just the things we do, and it is hard to see how there could be any plausible answer other than 'because they all have redness in common,' which just brings us back to affirming the existence of universals after all. The nominalist might seek to avoid this by saying that the reason we label different things 'red' is that they resemble each other, without specifying the respect in which they resemble each other. This is implausible on its face — isn't it obvious that they resemble each other with respect to their redness?

Feser, *Five Proofs*, 92. Notice that *resemblance* is itself a universal. Nominalism again reverses itself.

itself cannot be material, since thought is abstract and universal. This would disqualify thought from being identical with any particular brain state.

In simple language: everything material is particular. But some thoughts are universal. Ergo some thoughts are not material.[185]

The first premise is uncontentious because every material thing is obviously restricted to this or that particular instantiation. There is, for example, *this* triangle drawn on this chalk board and there is *that* triangle drawn on that chalkboard, but never do we encounter in the material world *triangularity as such*. Further, every material thing in relation to its universal characteristic — that is, for example, every particular triangle in relation to triangularity as such — is always to some inevitable degree imperfect (having less than perfectly straight sides, for example), however precise the tools are that we use to draw it.

But we can know and entertain the concept of triangularity and do not rely on any restricted mental image or representation to do so, because such images or representations (as we argued alongside Hume) will always be particular and therefore not universal (and to some degree imperfect). We grasp what triangularity is, and this grasping transcends the material because everything material — including brain states — is particular. One is not reducible to the other. Hence at least some of our thinking cannot be entirely material. Because our thoughts are something no material thing can be (universal and, as we'll soon see, determinate or exact in conceptual content), our thoughts cannot themselves be material.[186]

For the naturalist, this is a serious problem, because our universal thought content must *for the naturalist* ultimately be accounted for by some physical representation in the brain (certain patterns of neural firing or what have you), but as Feser explains, "no physical representation could possibly count as the universal *triangularity*, because like any other physical representation of a triangle, this one too would be just one particular material

---

[185] For a more detailed development of this argument see Edward Feser, *Aquinas: A Beginner's Guide*, (London: OneWorld Publishing, 2009), chapter 4.

[186] The argument is that if thought has property X, and property X cannot be material, then thought cannot be material.

thing among others, and not universal at all. Thus the operations of the intellect cannot consist of purely material processes."[187]

This point is reinforced not just by focusing on the particularity of material things but the inherent ambiguity of material things. Just as all material things are particular rather than universal, so all material things are ambiguous as to what they could "stand for" or represent. Again, this is a problem for the naturalist, since thought — probably all thought, but certainly all formal thought — is not ambiguous but determinate or exact concerning conceptual content. This is a subtle point and somewhat easy to miss, so let me draw it out carefully.

Consider again some particular triangle drawn on a chalkboard. Now ask, what does it represent? Does it represent triangularity, or trilaterality, or three straight sides, or small triangle (because it is relatively small), or red triangle (because it is drawn in red, say), or does it represent (more obscurely, as Feser suggests) the forgotten pop band Triangle? The point is that anything material, in and of itself, is always indeterminate and ambiguous as to what it does (or could) conceptually represent. This is not only true for mental images, but anything we want to claim is purely material, including logical and mathematical examples, as well.

By contrast, when we are thinking of triangularity or addition or modus ponens or what have you, there is nothing inexact or approximate about it. Our grasp of triangularity is a grasp of perfect triangularity, with clear meaning. But no material thing, as should now be obvious — no material picture, symbol, or representation in the brain — is ever determinate or exact; all material things are always, to some extent, imperfect, fuzzy, ambiguous, and could stand to represent many different things. It follows from this that no thought, at least concerning our conceptual understanding of things, is material. There is, at least concerning our power of concept possession and formal thinking, an undeniably immaterial aspect about us, an aspect fundamentally irreducible to physics and that could not itself have evolved.

Of course, naturalists don't just let the problem of mental content sit there; they have their proposals. And probably the most promising way naturalists have thought to secure determinate meaning of thought (concept

[187] Feser, *Aquinas*, 182.

possession) is by appealing to causal relations. That is to say, the reason I possess the concept that there is coffee in a cup before me is because that belief is caused by the presence of coffee in a cup before me.

While this may seem initially plausible, there are *many* problems with causal theories of meaning, as many philosophers (including naturalists) have pointed out. For one, I can entertain a clear concept of something — for example, Pegasus — that could not have been caused by that something, because that something, being fictional, does not exist anywhere. Or I might hold a concept of something that does exist somewhere in reality, like a cup of coffee, but instead my entertaining that concept is caused, not by a cup of coffee before me, but by some hallucinogenic or a mad scientist stimulating my brain or what have you. And if our thoughts can be about coffee regardless of what is causing those thoughts, it then becomes entirely unclear how such causal roles are supposed to generate any determinate meaning at all.

Secondly, and independent of the previous point, causal relations are clearly insufficient to account for the determinacy of meaning, because at the very least, causal relations cannot account for conceptual differences among properties that have the same logical extension. For example, whatever the thing or circumstance is that instantiates triangularity (as we know through geometrical reasoning) always instantiates triangularity — that is, we know that these concepts are truly distinct but not separable (wherever one is, the other is also). And as John Haldane explains, "to the extent that he can even concede that there are distinct properties the naturalist will want to insist that the causal powers ... of trilaterals and triangulars are identical. Thus, he cannot explain the difference between the concepts by invoking causal differences between the members of their extensions."[188]

Haldane's point is that there are clear instances of conceptual differences that could not possibly be explained by invoking causal differences, hence the latter is insufficient to account for the former.[189]

---

[188] Smart and Haldane, *Atheism and Theism*, 107.
[189] Could *evolution* fix determinacy of meaning? Not hardly, and a deeper consideration of this should tell against any purely naturalistic account of evolution, as well, since evolution would just be an efficient causal story and (as we've already argued) no efficient causal story can solve the issue of determinate meaning for the physicalist. Are frogs selected for catching bugs or small flying things? Naturalistic evolution — that

Finally, causal relations themselves seem to require a prior conceptual understanding of things, in which case the former could not possibly explain the latter. After all, the impression of a coffee cup before me is itself quite ambiguous from a purely physical description, particularly as to just where that causal event begins and where it ends.

Here an extended quote from Feser will serve our purposes well:

> The problem is this: in the external physical world as it is in itself, apart from human purposes and interests, there seems to be nothing more than an ongoing causal flux, comprising an unimaginably complex sequence of events. Nothing in this flux is objectively either the determinate starting point of a particular sequence of events or the determinate ending point. It is we who pick out certain events and count them as beginnings and endings; their status as beginnings and endings is relative to certain purposes and interests of ours. This is as true of A and B as of anything else: there is no objective reason why A should be the cat rather than the cat's fur or a particular photon in the stream leading from the cat to our retinas, and no objective reason why B should be this particular brain state rather than the one immediately before or after it in the causal sequence of brain processes. So the 'fact' that the causal chain purportedly explaining your perceptual experience of the cat begins with A and ends with B would appear to be mind-dependent fact, determined by human purposes and interests — that is to say, it appears to presuppose intentionality (concept possession). But then, the characterization of all such causal chains would presuppose intentionality — in which case, no appeal to such causal chains could truly explain it after all.[190]

---

is, blind selection working on mutation — has no way *in principle* of knowing or telling us, which indicates, given that here is some determinate fact of the matter of just what selection pressures have selected for, that evolution itself must be determinate, which tells against it being a purely physicalist phenomenon. Again, I leave the completion of this argument to others. What has just been said should be enough for our purposes.

[190] Edward Feser, *Philosophy of Mind: A Beginner's Guide* (Berkeley: University of California Press, 2006), 183.

In summary, because physical causes cannot fix mental content, the naturalist cannot make sense of the determinacy of meaning or concept possession. In fact, the issue surrounding the determinacy of meaning has led several naturalistic thinkers (famously, Quine) to say there really are no "facts of the matter" when it comes to what it is that we mean by various statements and thought processes.[191] But this is untenable. For one thing, denying that our thoughts have real determinate meaning would make reasoning impossible, since arguments are only valid if they follow the formal rules of logic, not mere approximations. For another, to say we do not really have a grasp of, say, triangularity appears to implicitly suppose that we *do* have a grasp of triangularity. How could we say we don't grasp triangularity unless we already knew what triangularity really (determinately) is? The whole idea of saying we only have an approximation of something in thought seems to demand that we don't just have an approximation of something in thought, for the whole idea of an approximation requires knowing what that something is an approximate *of*.

The point, simply put, is that if naturalism does not have the resources to make sense of meaning or mental content, then one should abandon naturalism before abandoning the obvious truth that our thoughts have clear meaning for us.

At this point, we have discovered something quite significant. There is an aspect about us, related primarily to intellectual activity, that is not reducible to physics or chemistry but appears to be an immaterial operation, whatever else that may entail (in other words, whether we have an immortal soul or survive bodily death is not something we shall attempt to resolve here).

For now, we can say this: the above considerations suggest that even if we cannot think without our brains, we do not think (understand) with our brains. Our brains, while perhaps a necessary condition, are not themselves a sufficient condition for the functioning of the human mind, at least in relation to formal thought and conceptual content. This gives good reason to believe that naturalism cannot adequately explain conscious, thinking beings like us, neither how we are possible nor how we are likely to have emerged. In turn, the existence of beings like us provides considerable confirmatory evidence

---

[191] Edward Feser, "Kripke, Ross, and the Immaterial Aspects of Thought" *American Catholic Philosophical Quarterly* 87, no. 1 (2013), 1–32.

for the existence of God, since a classical theistic perspective, not restricted to purely material causes, can make sense of beings like us, and makes it probable that other conscious thinking entities would emerge.

Let us take one final look at the difficulties mental content poses for naturalism, using philosopher Richard Taylor's illustration concerning mind, meaning, and origin stories.

Taylor asks us to imagine we encounter, during a train ride into Wales, a particular arrangement of stones on a hillside that reads, "THE BRITISH RAILWAY WELCOMES YOU TO WALES."[192] Upon seeing this, we naturally form the belief that the arrangement of stones is telling us something — namely, that we are entering Wales and are welcome there. There is meaning to the formation, or so it seems.

Could this arrangement of stones, which we assume was the result of intentional agency, come about through accidental processes? Taylor admits that it could — greatly improbably, sure, but nevertheless it seems logically possible. Maybe (again, however unlikely) the message formed just by rocks randomly tumbling down the hill and becoming lodged just so.

Here's the problem, however. As Taylor points out, the moment we assume the arrangement of stones came about through unintentional accidental processes is the moment it no longer becomes rational to believe the stones *are really telling us something,* let alone something accurate about the world. Obviously, to believe we are really being welcomed to Wales, we must believe there was purposeful agency or intention behind the arrangement of the stones.

As Taylor writes, "It would be irrational for you to regard the arrangement of the stones as evidence that you were entering Wales, and at the same time to suppose that they might have come to have that arrangement accidentally, that is, as the result of the ordinary interactions of natural or physical forces."[193]

We take it for granted that our cognitive powers "tell us" things, and generally what they tell us is accurate. There is real and determinate meaning in all this — or at least that is how we operate. This is true for perception, memory, and, I would add, logical and moral intuition. We see something and we form the belief that that thing exists. We hear things, we infer things, and so on. We

---

[192] Richard Taylor, *Metaphysics* (Hoboken, NJ: Prentice Hall, 1991), 114.
[193] Ibid, 115.

rely on our cognitive powers to discover the world, including what we suppose exists independently of those cognitive powers. Again, for the most part, we take it that what our cognitive powers "tell us" — that is, the mental content they deliver to us — is true (and of course we still rely on those same cognitive powers to correct instances where we believe we've erred).

However, the naturalist is committed to these senses and cognitive powers coming about through unintentional, accidental processes. This puts the naturalist into the same awkward situation as believing that the stones along the hillside at the Welsh border were accidentally arranged. That is, it puts them into the situation of making it irrational to believe *both* that our cognitive powers are telling us something (let alone something generally reliable) *and* that they were brought about through purposeless forces.

Equally problematic is the fact that any possible evidence that could be gathered in favor of naturalism is gathered through cognitive powers that the naturalist must take to be generally reliable (which they cannot rationally do if Taylor's point is correct) in conjunction with the naturalistic thesis of the origins of those cognitive powers. The entirely naturalistic position smacks of being self-undermining, such that even if naturalism were true, it would ruin the conditions for our being able to say we knew it to be true. (This, by the way, is also the conclusion of Alvin Plantinga's famous evolutionary argument against naturalism, though I take Taylor's argumentative approach to be more clear-cut.)

As Edward Feser emphasizes in developing Taylor's argument:

> This is not a point about probabilities, but rather a conceptual and metaphysical truth. Neither stones nor marks on a rock have any inherent connection with any semantic content we might decide to convey through them. The content they might have *must derive from a mind* which uses them for the purpose of conveying such content. Delete such a mind from an explanation of the arrangements of stones or marks, and you delete the semantic content along with it.[194]

---

[194] Edward Feser, "Taylor on cognition, teleology, and God," *Edward Feser* (blog), February 25, 2022, at edwardfeser.blogspot.com/2022/02/taylor-on-cognition-teleology-and-god.html.

Moreover, as Mortimer Adler stresses concerning the connection between meaning and ideas, "our ideas do not *have* meaning, they do not *acquire* meaning, they do not *change, gain,* or *lose* meaning. Each of our ideas *is* a meaning and that is all it is. Mind is the realm in which meanings exist and through which everything else that has meaning acquires meaning."[195] In other words: no mind, no meaning. Therefore, if the foundation of reality is fundamentally mindless, we can reasonably infer that everything above it would be fundamentally meaningless, yet this is not the case.[196]

Here it seems we have encountered another limitation in principle for naturalism, but for the sake of modesty, we could simply say that theism much better anticipates a world of meaning, since mind (and subsequently meaning, given that God is an unrestricted idea) is fundamentally bedrock for the classical theist. For that reason, our experiencing such things is considerable confirmatory evidence for the existence of God.

---

[195] Adler, *Philosophical Mistakes*, 66.
[196] How, ultimately, should we understand meaning? This, as expected, is a huge area of philosophical debate, but I believe the traditional Thomistic-Aristotelian answer is the correct one: we acknowledge the existence of intentional entities (namely concepts and senses) that organize thought and meaning in a way similar to how natural forms organize the material world. For example, the concept "dog" stands to the thought of a dog just as the form dog stands to a dog. Each is a structuring principle, making something to be of a certain sort. For Thomists, concepts and forms are ultimately two ways of being the same nature.

CHAPTER ELEVEN

Suffering and Evil

THE PROBLEM OF EVIL, an argument against theism because bad stuff happens, should be called the *problems* of evil, because there is more than one. I use the term "bad stuff," not to be coy, but to impress the broad scope of what is meant by "evil." Traditionally, evil meant any negative state of affairs, including natural destruction and decay, rather than merely the evil that people do.

There is, for example, the *logical* problem of evil, which asserts the strongest incompatibility between God and evil: that evil and God cannot possibly exist together. This argument can be traced back at least to the ancient Greek philosopher Epicurus, as quoted by David Hume in the *Dialogues Concerning Natural Religion*: "Is [God] willing to prevent evil, but not able? Then he is impotent. Is he able, but not willing? Then he is malevolent. Is he both able and willing? Whence then is evil?"[197]

Philosophers have increasingly abandoned the logical problem of evil, however, because no one has been able to show that God could not possibly have a morally justifying reason for allowing suffering and evil to occur.[198] More on that soon.

---

[197] David Hume, *Dialogues Concerning Natural Religion* (New York: Penguin Classics, 1990), 186. See also J. L. Mackie, "Evil and Omnipotence," *Mind*, New Series, 64, No. 254. (April 1955), 200–212.

[198] Largely, but not entirely. For a recent discussion on the logical problem of evil, see James Sterba (ed), *Is the God of Traditional Theism Logically Compatible with All the*

More modest is the *evidential* problem of evil, which suggests that the suffering and evil of our experience is evidence against the existence of God. Philosopher William Rowe, for example, proposes the evidential argument from evil in his article "The Problem of Evil and Some Varieties of Atheism," contending there are some evils that God could have prevented (famously, a fawn burned to death by a tree fire caused by a lightning strike) without any loss of some greater good, and, because of this, the nature of these presumably gratuitous (some may call them mysterious) evils cannot be made sense of if God exists.[199] The idea is that the evil and suffering we experience — even if not strictly incompatible with God — should be considered evidence against God to some extent, and perhaps, as many skeptics maintain, a very strong extent.

THE FINER POINTS

As an immediate response the evidential problem of evil, it should be insisted that just because we may not see the reason for God permitting this or that instance of suffering, this does not justify us in inferring that there is, or probably is, no reason. Just as a neophyte might not see the reason for any particular move a chess master makes, this does not permit the neophyte to infer that there is *no* reason. In fact, the neophyte should expect not to see the reason, because he is not skilled at chess. Rather, he should expect that the master's chess moves will not be wholly predictable or analyzable to him, since the master's ability to envision reasons for the moves he makes far exceeds the grasp of the beginning player. All this should cause the novice to realize that he is not in any position to make a sound judgment about whether the chess master is making a reasonable move or not. This is not a position of extreme skepticism, mind you, for knowing someone is a master chess player, we expect the moves he makes to be very good and reasonable; yet we would not always expect to see how they were very good and reasonable in the moment, assuming we are not ourselves master chess players. If the analogy isn't obvious, how much more would this be true of God, who is omnipotent, omniscient, and in charge of the whole of creation?

Evil in the World? Special issue of *Religions*, no. 12 (2021).

[199] William Rowe, "The Problem of Evil and Some Varieties of Atheism," *American Philosophical Quarterly*, at https://www.kul.pl/.

Whatever the distance between a chess master and a neophyte, this chasm is ridiculously miniscule compared to the difference between God and man in the relevant domain (divine reasons for permitting suffering and evil). We know enough about God to expect that whatever He permits is for some very good reason; we also know enough about the differences between our cognitive powers and God's to expect that we should not always be able to see how any particular move God makes is a very good one. But our not seeing that reason is not good grounds for concluding that there is no reason.

There is a third problem of evil, one which occupied the mind of many earlier thinkers but has also fallen somewhat out of fashion lately. That's the *metaphysical* problem of evil, which is concerned with how, ontologically speaking, God, who is all good, creates any actual *thing* that is evil.

The following discussion will deal with all three problems of evil. My responses to the evidential and metaphysical problems of evil will also address the logical problem of evil. This will be accomplished by showing that the suffering and evil of our experience is not only *not* incompatible with God, but is better expected if God exists than if mindless naturalism is true. This is, no doubt, a bold claim, as it amounts to the position that the suffering and evil of our experience is evidence *for* the existence of God and against naturalism, contra the skeptics.

Let's get right to it.

God, Christianity, and the Expectation of Evil

To begin to address the problems of evil, I should like to consider them from a specifically Christian perspective, because I am of the mind that a fully robust response to these problems can and probably *must* make use of religious teaching. Moreover, to determine whether certain events or actions are justified requires a clear value system, a certain ordering of what the highest goods (including the highest good) are. Simply put, we cannot answer what is a morally sufficient reason for allowing evil without first committing ourselves to a moral system. Christianity provides just this.

After all, for Christians, the ultimate purpose for God allowing suffering, including natural evils like skin rashes or cancer, is not just to build virtue (such as courage or fortitude) but more fundamentally to save us from a sort of spiritual cancer, an inherent or at least inherited disorder of the will, and thus make possible the necessary conditions for union with God. For Christians, the ultimate *revealed* purpose of life, that is the highest good, is to attain union with God, and whether somebody has an actually good life, on the whole, depends entirely on whether he attains that end or not in the afterlife (which, of course, is largely dependent upon what occurs in this life).

In other words, if the ultimate lower bound any human being can hit is to fail to attain union with God, then it might well be the case that other evils, including very appalling evil, may be permissible insofar as those evils are the best or only available means to prevent some human person from failing to attain relationship with God.[200] Some of these evils, such as moral evil (evils people do), may be inevitable or highly probable consequences of creating other free beings in the first place, and some of these evils, such as natural evils (evils people suffer), may be the best or only available means for getting these creatures to freely relinquish an evil orientation of the will and to ultimately love God. Either way, Christianity has an objective value scale, a clear upper and lower bound for human goodness or flourishing. The upper bound is freely willed union with God; the lower bound is freely willed separation from God.[201] According to Christianity, every human

---

[200] Importantly, the best or only available means does not guarantee 100 percent effectiveness. Sometimes the best or only available means may produce no effect toward the desired outcome or sometimes the opposite effect, as we see in cases where people, instead of coming to seek God through suffering, come to detest God. This unfortunate outcome, however, does not prove suffering was still not the best or only available means to get man to become dissatisfied with his current condition, recognize his own evil, and begin to allow God's grace into his life. It may well still be the best means yet because of human free will not being effective in certain or even many instances.

[201] Obviously, the former is Heaven, and the latter is Hell. Heaven is an essential part of this response to the problem of evil; Hell, however, may not be. Although I think a coherent defense of Hell as compatible with an all-loving God can be given (see Eleonore Stump, "The God Of Love," at Church Life Journal [April 13, 2023], at churchlifejournal.nd.edu/articles/can-hell-and-the-god-of-love-coexist/), I believe one could swap in other conceivable lower-bounds that would not affect this defense much or at all — annihilationism, for example, where God just releases from existence anybody who fails to attain union with Him.

person will wind up either in union with God or separation from God; there is no in between.[202]

Naturally, one might wonder if appealing to Christianity at this point is contrived or complicates the hypothesis. I would say neither, for there is a strong case to be made that what Christianity teaches (some forms of Christianity, anyway) is rather a probable consequence of classical theism, even if we don't immediately see it — except for after the fact by way of revelation — and consequences of theories are not complications of theories.[203] This follows from the fact that God, as supremely generous, would not just want to bring other beings into creation but ultimately to share the greatest good of all, which is Himself. This means that God would aim at uniting creation with Himself (recall, if you will, that God brings beings like us into union with Himself as a means for bringing all creation into union with Him). Christianity teaches this.

The further philosophical link to Christianity is this: God pulling humanity into union with Himself might well involve God assuming a human nature — that is, God incarnating. In God becoming man, man might become, or rather share in the life of, God.

Why so?

If only because, as Norris Clarke explains, "to share our journey with us, to show us the best and surest way to walk it, and to ensure its final transcendent success beyond this present world. This God-with-us-now becomes the great, perfected Mediator and High Priest (The Pontifex Maximus = supreme Bridge-Builder) between the entire created world and its Ultimate Source and Goal."[204]

---

[202] Though I should note theologians have maintained there are degrees of each of these two end-states. People in Heaven can love God more than other people in Heaven, and people in Hell can be further from God than other people in Hell. Dante is the go-to for an exposition of this.

[203] Plausible consequences of a theory do not reduce the prior probability of that theory, because consequences of a theory are not the same as the internal complexity of the theory. Alternatively, if these Christian commitments do complicate the hypothesis, they do not complicate theism nearly to the extent which naturalism must be complicated to make sense of worldly phenomena, including, as we'll see, the data of suffering.

[204] Clarke, The One, 307.

From a consideration of God's nature, particularly God's goodness, something like the Incarnation begins to make a lot of philosophical sense as the best or most befitting means for God to bring creation to its ultimate perfection and into union with the divine. We can see it as being a probable consequence of our root classical theistic theory, because this is clearly a good act, if not the very best kind of act, and those are just the sorts of acts we can expect God to do.

THE FINER POINTS

We might not be able to predict the Incarnation *just* from thinking about classical theism in the abstract, insofar as the Incarnation (God assuming a human nature) might not be something we ever thought would even be possible. However, if there is evidence that the Incarnation has occurred (historical claims), and we thereafter think of the Incarnation as possible, it is by no means illegitimate to then see this as being a supremely good act that does, in fact, flow from the classical theistic hypothesis. All this is to say, we might not be able to immediately see something being a consequence of a particular theory, but after that something has occurred (or seems to have), we can then look back and see how befitting it was, how it makes perfect sense.

Recall the chess analogy. We might not be able to predict *ahead of time* any particular move a master chess player will make; however, after certain moves are made, after the game has played out a bit, we might then be able to look back and see that the moves the chess player made were, in fact, extremely good moves, just what was expected from a person of that skillset.

Moreover, given that humanity is presumably fallen — or, if one does not buy into the account of the Fall, one can swap in whatever account one likes for our undeniable inclination to pursue power and immediate pleasure over self-sacrificial love, our propensity to evil — the Incarnation serves the further role of having God enter our dejected situation, show solidarity with us, and provide the means for redemption. In fact, many Christians have argued that, given God's aim of uniting creation with Himself, the Incarnation would have happened even if the Fall had not occurred. But given that the Fall *did* happen and we now have an inherent tendency toward evil, the Incarnation becomes all the more fitting as a means of God expressing His radical love for us.

In other words, the Incarnation and subsequent Crucifixion become extremely fitting when we consider that the primary barrier to salvation is on the side of humanity, not the side of God. We have an inherent proneness to evil, not created by God but generated by us, and since evil is incompatible with God, we are thus resistant to God, even if unknowingly so.[205] Given the difficulties of this world, we are prone to want to shake our fist at God, even if we believe in Him. But it is difficult to shake our fist at the God who allowed Himself to be hung from the Cross for us, the God who was not indifferent to creation but entered into it, bore the worst of it alongside us, who went "all the way down" in order to pull us up.

What we are detailing so far is a story that is minimally true *for all we know* and has been told by many religious people over the course of time. This story does not conflict with anything we know about the world via scientific knowledge, is reasonable and consistent with the classical theism paradigm, and begins to show us why the suffering and evil of this world is not that surprising, given the existence of an all-good God.[206]

---

[205] The metaphysical root of sin begins in our not considering a particular moral rule that we really could have considered when deliberating courses of action. This non-consideration, being an absence, is not something that requires being caused by God, but neither is it a sin (privation), since we are not required, nor even capable of, always considering all things. However, we are required to consider the appropriate moral when we make a particular judgment where that moral rule applies, and our failure to not consider and apply that moral rule in a judgment where it is due, is when the mere negation becomes a privation, when actual sin occurs. But again, all this involves an absence, or a hole in being, where it otherwise should be, and it was within our power to consider the rule, and so we alone, not God, are the first cause of sin, and (in most instances) culpable for it. For a detailed defense of this view, see Michael Torre, "The Grace of God and the Sin of Man," in *Aquinas and Maritain on Evil*, ed. James Hanink (Washington, D.C.: American Maritain Association/Catholic University of America Press, 2013).

[206] Some might think the idea of the doctrine of the Fall is at odds with modern evolutionary theory. This is false. Nothing in evolutionary theory is incompatible with the claim that "at some time in the past as a result of their own choices human beings altered their nature for the worse" or even an historical Adam and Eve. For a recent study on the matter, see William Lane Craig, *In Quest of the Historical Adam* (Grand Rapids, MI: Eerdmans Publishing, 2021).

What's more, the suffering of our experience is of the sort that should actually cause us to think the story we are detailing, at least broadly, *is* true, not just "true for all we know," because it is expected should God exist. And if the story we are telling is only told by Christianity, this gives us reason not just to think that God exists, but that Christianity is true as well. (For the sake of modesty, however, I should say "for all we know" is enough to defeat the problem of evil, so one need not follow me in the stronger claim, though I hope the reader will consider it.)

Our (Proper) Ultimate End and the Possibility of Sin

Now, suppose that God is motivated to share His goodness by bringing other beings about, and especially other rational beings that can share in His divine life, enter into communion with Him, and love Him for eternity. That is the classical theistic story told by many, including Aquinas, and it is certainly the theism of Catholicism, though other religions share a similar story. It is motivated again by metaphysical principles like the principle of diffusiveness (namely, that the good naturally seeks to communicate itself) and the principle of convertibility between being and goodness (that goodness is being under the aspect of desirability), which we considered earlier.[207]

Recall that if God is going to create, we should expect a wide range of beings to result; the existence of God anticipates the Great Chain of Being. This relates to natural evil since — as we'll discuss shortly — we can expect God to bring about beings that are not just incorruptible (as angels or other immaterial realities are taken to be) but material and inherently corruptible entities, for it is better to have these than not.

As Aquinas tells us:

> Now, one grade of goodness is that of the good which cannot fail. Another grade of goodness is that of the good which can fail in goodness, and this grade is to be found in existence itself; for some things are which cannot lose their existence as incorruptible things, while some there are which can lose it, as things corruptible. As,

---

[207] It should be noted that other philosophers think you can get the same or similar expectations from God from theism in conjunction with other principles, like moral motivation internalism.

therefore, the perfection of the universe requires that there should
be not only beings incorruptible, but also corruptible beings; so the
perfection of the universe requires that here should be some which
can fail in goodness, and thence it follows that sometimes they do
fail. Now it is in this that evil consists, namely, in the fact that a thing
fails in goodness.[208]

That material beings are naturally corruptible is no reason for God not to bring
them about, insofar as they are still good to have — which they definitely are,
as everyone can plainly see. But that story by itself is incomplete. While it is
good to bring many and various things into existence, the very best thing God
could share is Himself, with the aim of bringing a creature's existence into an
intimate relationship with Him. And so, God's purpose is not just to bring
things into existence, but to bring things into union with Himself, and for that,
God must make other conscious agents — beings, that is, like us.

However, there are constraints to even what an omnipotent God can
achieve, constraints that may make negative states of affairs (i.e., evil) inevitable, or at least highly probable. Recall that arguments for classical theism tell us
there is just one being that is purely actual and is the subsistent good itself.
That being is God. Everything else is a metaphysical composite of potency and
act, and essence and existence, and so is finite in being, existentially fallible, a
being whose existence is derivative, who merely participates in existence — unlike God, who just *is* His existence. Since God is absolutely simple, God's will
is identical to God's nature, *is identical* to God's goodness, and so on.[209] Thus,
only God's will is perfect, impeccable, and infallible.

Every other free-willing created entity, in virtue of being a fallible composite entity that cannot know or consider everything at once, must always
"look beyond itself" for the source of all goodness and for the moral rule. It
can only choose to consider some things at certain times and other things at

---

[208] *ST,* I, q. 48, a. 2.
[209] That God is identical to goodness also supplies a response to another theistic objection, coming from Plato's *Euthyphro*: is something good because the gods (God)
will it, or do the gods (God) will something because it is good? The answer, for the
classical theist, is neither. God wills what He wills because God just is the Good
itself. God neither wills arbitrarily nor must He look beyond Himself for the moral
rule; God *is* the moral rule.

other times. Moreover, it can also choose not to take some knowledge into consideration when making a moral judgment. This being may know it's wrong to drink and drive, yet it does so anyway. In other words, it can engage in voluntary ignorance and make a moral miscalculation. It can sin.

As Aquinas teaches:

> The agent whose will has its own nature as its ultimate end is pre-serve from any possibility of defect in its voluntary activity but that is the property of God alone. For the divine goodness, the ultimate end of all things, is the very nature of God. As regards all other agents endowed with will, on the contrary, their nature is not their last end; and consequently it is possible for them to commit faults in their voluntary actions. This takes place if their will remains fixed in their own good without tending on beyond it towards the Sover-eign Good who is the ultimate end. All created intellectual sub-stances have in themselves, therefore, the possibility of failing in their voluntary activity.[210]

THE FINER POINTS

Importantly, the creature's will is not just free to choose means to an end, but may choose the ultimate end itself. And there are two choices for our ultimate end: self or God.[211] God is our proper ulti-mate end, as only He can truly fulfill and perfect us. Conversely, the creature only has the power to pursue something as its ultimate end—that is, to choose the means to attaining their end, proper or not. And so, we can make ourselves the ultimate end, by which we mean pursuing any good less than God that we (falsely) take as ulti-mately fulfilling. This decision is an error, following a false rule—but nevertheless, it is in our power to pursue self over God. God is not free *in this sense*, because of the great metaphysical difference be-tween God and everything else—that is, as something that is the end of everything (God) against something that is directed toward that end (creature). For God just is His own end, as the fullness of

---

[210] Thomas Aquinas, *Compendium Theologiae*, I, c. 113. Quoted by Jacques Maritain in *The Sin of the Angel* (Providence, RI: Cluny, 2023), 39.

[211] For a further account of this form of voluntarism, see Thomas Ward, *Ordered by Love* (Brooklyn, NY: Angelico Press, 2022).

being and goodness and truth. For this reason, only God's will is *naturally* infallible, for everything, including God, acts according to its nature, but only God's nature (which is God) is the ultimate proper end of everything, the Supreme Good. Everything else is directed toward the end, which is God, and free creatures can either employ reason well to act in accord with nature and align their will with God's, or not.

"Sin" happens when a rational agent does something other than it should, when it moves away from its perfection or proper end. The proper end at which every rational agent aims is the Good itself — God. God cannot move from His proper end because God is identical to it; thus the only free being *internally incapable* of sinning is God. Moreover, sin entails having a privation of a due perfection of the rational will (failure to consider the moral rule or proper end when making a moral choice), but God, insofar as He is purely actual, cannot have any privations. Creatures, on the other hand, in virtue of being act–potency composites, absolutely can and do suffer such privations, since a privation is just an unactualized potency (a potency that *should* be actualized). The metaphysical picture that Aquinas paints reveals that the possibility of sin is just a necessary consequence of creating free rational agents, itself a necessary condition for love between persons and God. It's a bundle deal.

And so, this possibility of sin is an inevitable consequence of God pursuing love with creatures, for He "cannot make any creature who is naturally impeccable, any more than He can create a squared circle."[212] God's will alone is naturally impeccable. Creatures? Not so much.

THE FINER POINTS

Aquinas gives the analogy of a carpenter to illustrate this critical point. To cut a piece of wood straight, the carpenter must hold the ruler in his hand. Of course, it is not a sin that the carpenter is not always holding the ruler in hand; that is an absence, but not a privation (a due good gone missing = evil). The carpenter is not expected to always be holding the ruler, like when he's going to the bathroom.

[212] Jacques Maritain, *St. Thomas and the Problem of Evil* (Milwaukee, WI: Marquette University Press, 1942), 16.

However, the absence of the ruler will nevertheless become the cause in virtue of which the craftsman will saw a piece of wood poorly, if the ruler is not picked up and applied when it should be.[213] The privation or evil occurs in the application or operation it-self—that is, the act of cutting wood, when the ruler is not picked up and applied.

God can never fail to consider the measure of things, since God just is the measure of things, the Supreme Good itself. Human be-ings, on the other hand, are more like the carpenter in being finite participants in existence: they must pick up and apply the moral rule when making a moral choice, a rule supplied through the use of right reason, of acting in accord with our nature. Of course, it is not evil to not have this or that rule (for instance, don't drive after drinking) always under consideration, because not everything can be consid-ered at once when it comes to finite beings like us. That is a mere negation, not a privation. However, if one makes a moral choice (say, to drive after many drinks, which is to act unreasonably, out of line with the ultimate proper end of charity or divine nature) without taking up and applying the appropriate rule that they habitually knew and really could have considered (don't drink and drive!), the nega-tion then becomes a privation, because something is missing in the act of judgement that ought to have been there. Then, and only then, has sin occurred.

Does It Have to Be This Way?

Couldn't God help creatures make the right moral choice always, even if by a miracle? Some think so, others not. However, even if God could do this, should we expect that God *would* do this? Almost certainly not.[214] For God

---

[213] Jacques Maritain, *God and the Permission of Evil* (Milwaukee, WI: The Bruce Publish-ing Company, 1966), 35.

[214] An additional question for Catholics: But what of Our Lady and the saints in Heaven, where we think sin could not occur? The answer may be that Our Lady could have said no to forming a higher-order desire to will what God wills, and, if that were the case, we would have had a different Blessed Mother, someone who did say yes. (This account is not just offered to be consistent with the philosophy of freedom but theologically, as well, since we are supposed to see Mary as reversing Eve. But if Mary was not free to say no just as Eve was, then how was Mary a genuine reversal?) Saints in Heaven, too, have freely formed the higher-order desire to will what God wills, so God securing them in that (particularly after the process of sanctification where the human cooperates

orders creatures toward their end in accordance with what they are. God works with natures; He "plays fair" with what He creates by governing things according to their mode of being. If we are beings of a naturally fallible liberty, in general, God will govern us accordingly, allowing us to be what we are as He guides us providentially toward our final end. So, even if God *could* cause us to choose rightly all the time, God *would not*, since that is not in accord with God's providential wisdom.[215] Even if a talking donkey once served some important providential purpose (Numbers 22:22–40), God is not going to make all donkeys talk all the time. Rather, God is going to let them operate according to their nonrational donkey nature. Aquinas writes:

> God moves everything in accordance with its own manner ... and so he also moves human beings to justice in accordance with the condition of human nature. But in accordance with his own nature a human being has free choice. And so in a human being who has the use of free choice, there is no motion from God to justice without a motion of free choice.[216]

Our nature is one of *fallible* liberty, one where moral miscalculation is inherently possible. God permits our transition into a sinful state if we initiate it by

---

with God's grace) is not a destruction of their freedom but a terminal perfection of it, since God is helping them to will what they want to will. Indeed, a free will is one free from restraint: to will freely is to be able to will what one wants. If one forms the desire to will in alignment with God, there is no violation of one's freedom if God provides special help and grace in securing that higher order desire; it is, in fact, a perfection of one's freedom. And it is still ultimately free because whether such help is provided is within the control of any person the help is provided to, either by resisting or not resisting God's grace. Another perhaps more basic answer for how someone can be free in Heaven but unable to sin is this: Someone can attain a morally perfect character that makes sin impossible, and that character was the result of prior libertarian free choices — thus even in their perfected state where sin is impossible, they are free in choosing right over wrong in a derivative sense. For a development of this account, see Kevin Timpe and Timothy Pawl, "Incompatibilism, Sin, and Free Will in Heaven," *Faith and Philosophy* 26, no. 4 (2009), 396–417.

[215] Is it wise for God to allow something of such significance to fall upon finite, fallible creatures? Yes, because for love there is no other possibility than the uniting of two free independent wills, and because God supplies us with everything we need to attain union with Him, without coercing us.

[216] As quoted by Stump, *Aquinas*, 390.

failing to consider *what we really could have done*. Sin is ignorance; true enough, but it is *voluntary* ignorance, it is our *ignoring* something we really could have paid attention to, something we habitually knew. The ignorance involved in sin — what makes sin culpable — is not the ignorance of not knowing something, but ignoring what one already knew.

Perhaps, however, we have conceded too much, since many philosophers have argued that there is no such help that God could give, however occasionally. Their argument is that it is logically impossible to force a free creature to choose such a certain way.[217] It is, after all, one thing for God to add something to a thing's nature, like having a donkey talk; it is quite another to contradict something's nature, like *determining* a *free* choice. (Determining in the sense of introducing some factor that is both explanatorily prior and logically sufficient for some act.)[218] If God does that, if God introduces some factor, grace or otherwise, that is both explanatorily prior and logically sufficient for some act, then we are not free in such an act.[219]

THE FINER THINGS

At this point, for those wondering how human freedom is compatible with the universal causality of God, consider the following from philosopher James Ross: "God produces, for each individual being, the one that does such and such (whatever it does) through its whole time in being.... God does not make the person act; he makes the so acting person be. Still, to say that freedom or human

---

[217] Eleonore Stump, for example, maintains, "But it is logically impossible for anyone to make a person freely will something, and therefore even God in his omnipotence cannot directly and miraculously remove the defect in free will, without destroying the very freedom of the will he wants to fix." Eleonore Stump, "The Problem of Evil," *Faith and Philosophy* 2, no. 4 (1985), 392–423. John Haldane claims something similar, remarking that God "empowers beings freely to direct their lives toward moral perfection, but it is logically impossible that he should compel such a movement toward the good." Smart and Haldane, *Theism and Atheism*, 141.

[218] Explanatorily prior in the sense that some factor is either temporally or logical prior to some act, and logically sufficient in the sense that if that factor attains, then the act attains inevitably as well.

[219] For a defense of how God can be the universal cause of everything apart from Himself and there still be room for genuine libertarian freedom, see Matthews Grant, *Free Will and God's Universal Causality* (London: Bloomsbury Academic, 2020).

agency is thereby impeded is absurd. Nothing can be or come about unless caused to be by the Creator. So the fact that God's causing is necessary for whatever happens cannot impede liberty; it is a condition for it. Similarly, in no way is our liberty impeded by its necessary conditions.... God did not make Adam to be the first man to defy God; God made Adam, who was the first man to defy God, to be. God made Adam, who undertook to sin.... God makes all the free things that do as they do, instead of doing otherwise as in their power, by their own undertaking. So God does not make Adam sin. But God makes the sinning Adam, the person who, able not to sin, does sin. It follows logically that if Adam had not sinned, God would have made a person who, though able to sin, did not. And, surely, God might have made a person who, though able to sin, did not.... It is the whole being, doing as it does, whether a free being or not, that is entirely produced and sustained for its time by God."[220]

We will have more to say about the relevance of human freedom in relation to suffering in just a moment. For now, let's address another objection: even if one concedes free will, they might still wonder why God doesn't just cancel out the negative consequences of free choices without impeding the free choice itself. For example, God could turn a knife to jelly immediately before some killer decides to use it. Wouldn't that be a solution to the conundrum? Could we not retain free will but avoid the harmful consequences of people choosing evil?

In response, consider the following from C. S. Lewis:

> We can, perhaps, conceive of a world in which God corrected the results of this abuse of free will by His creatures at every moment: so that a wooden beam became soft as grass when it was used as a weapon, and the air refused to obey me if I attempted to set up in it the sound-waves that carried lies or insults. But such a world would be one in which wrong actions were impossible, and which, therefore, freedom of the will would be void.... That God can and does, on occasions, modify the behavior of matter and produce what we call miracles, is part and parcel of the Christian faith; but the very conception of a common, and therefore stable, world,

[220] As quoted by Davies, *Introduction to Philosophy of Religion*, 266.

demands that these occasionally should be extremely rare.... Try to exclude the possibility of suffering ... and you will find that you have excluded life itself.[221]

Likewise, God generally permits our acting out on sin, not only to avoid creating a massively chaotic world if He constantly intervened (itself a necessary condition for meaningful moral community and relationship formation), but because God knows that He can bring greater goods from even the evil that we introduce into the world, goods such as compassion, empathy, and perhaps even, in Christian belief, the Incarnation and atonement. Notice that many of these goods are *logically dependent* goods, which is to say goods that are only possible with a backdrop of negative states (no courage without danger, no compassion without hurt, no forgiveness without trespass, and, most obviously, no overcoming adversity without adversity).

Importantly, God does not cause bad things *so that* people can be courageous or overcome adversity. Rather, God runs the risk of love, which entails the possibility that beings like us could morally fail. Once such failure has occurred, *then* God works with it, bringing other goods — such as courage, compassion, mercy, and so on — from it. But the fundamental thing that God takes the proverbial chance on is love. And surely that is worth it. If anything is worth a chance, it is love.

God supplies each of us with genuine free will, which is a necessary condition for love between persons, including love between humans and God. He respects the natures of things, and since our freedom is fallible, God permits

[221] C. S. Lewis, "The Problem of Pain," in *C. S. Lewis Signature Classics* (New York: HarperOne, 2017), 565. Lewis's point relates to a response provided by Peter van Inwagen concerning the defect of creating a *massively irregular world* (one with constant supernatural intervention/miracles) and what things of intrinsic value might be impossible and why God would be justified in creating a generally stable world over a massively irregular world, even if that meant all the evils and suffering we see. "For all we know, either the disutility, intrinsic or extrinsic, of massive irregularity in the world is greater than the intrinsic disutility that is a consequence of containing vast amounts of animal suffering, or else the disutility of massive irregularity and the disutility of containing vast amounts of animal suffering are incomparable." Peter van Inwagen, *The Problem of Evil* (Oxford: Oxford University Press, 2008), 113–23.

our moral miscalculations. (This is the traditional Dionysian principle, that God's Providence works to save natures, not destroy them.)

Earlier I entertained the possibility that God might directly move our will from rejecting Him to loving Him. But now we should ask: is this *really* possible? Here's one important reason many philosophers think not: if God unilaterally overrode our otherwise resistant will in order to make us forsake evil and love Him, then there would just be one will there — namely, God's — instead of two. But two wills are required for love, and so if genuine love is to be had, this unilateral move is not possible on God's part. In such a case, the best that God might be able to do is create a natural arena that is maximally conducive for the treatment of our inherent propensity to evil, offering the best possible shot at treating a disordered will or getting us to freely omit our evil acts and abandon resistance to God. Not implausibly — highly probably, in fact — the allowance of suffering may be the best available means for facilitating greater spiritual goods, culminating in opening the human psyche to the love of God.

Let us pause here to emphasize a point: we often think it is acceptable to permit bad things, including very bad things, if permitting those bad things is the best or only available means to prevent something worse. However, we often do not think it is acceptable to permit bad things just to get some good things. It is not okay to shove my child across the street and risk his getting hit by a bus just so he can get first in line at some job interview, a job which might be good for him to have. But it *is* okay to shove my child off the street and risk him breaking his arm if he might otherwise get hit by a bus and die. Some people have suggested that God allows suffering and evil *just* so that we can acquire virtue — build courage and empathy and all that. These are good things, no doubt, and perhaps a case *could* be made that it would be acceptable for *God* to permit an arena of challenge, evil, and suffering, so long as said arena helped us move along in attaining some otherwise unattainable (extremely valuable) good, assuming this arena is the best or only available means to help us move along in attaining some genuinely *good* goods.

But that is not the story Christianity gives us, so it is not the case that *must* be made for the Christian response to the problem of evil. The story Christianity gives us is in a certain sense bleaker, but simultaneously more beautiful. Instead, God permits suffering and evil, if not as a necessary concomitant of something created (like free beings), then primarily to save us from something truly terrible. We have a sort of cancer of the soul, something we are incapable of fixing on our own — namely, a disorder of the will. Should this spiritual cancer be left untreated, it will result in our eternal alienation of ourselves from God, leading us to Hell. And according to Christianity, Hell is the absolute lower bound so far as the human condition goes. Nothing is objectively worse than freely willing against God eternally, but for Christianity that is a real human possibility.

Three Ways the Will Can Go

The story, however, is a little more complicated than that. Because isn't it always? After all, Christians have long maintained two positions concerning salvation that initially seem at odds. Namely:

1. Salvation depends significantly upon what we (freely) do.

2. Apart from God's grace, human beings can do nothing good, including merit salvation.

We should work through this apparent paradox, because in doing so, more will be revealed as to why God permits the suffering of this world.

So, how are these commitments harmonized? The answer is found within Aquinas's subtle understanding of the human will. Here, the story is that the human will effectively has three "gears": we can either will for something, will against something, or omit an act of will entirely. In this sense, the will is like bodily motion. Just as we can walk east or west, we can cease walking altogether. Notice that our ceasing to walk is not itself a form of walking; rather it is just an inactivity of the relevant body parts. The same goes for omitting an act of will, such as an inactivity or acquiescence of the power, not an actual use of the power.

The immediate upshot of this understanding of the will is that omitting resistance to God (that is, broadly speaking, giving up an evil orientation of will, or refusing grace) *is* within our control but it does not itself amount to doing something *good* apart from God; it is not by itself enough to attain salvation. Again, omitting an evil orientation of will is not itself an act but the absence of an act, and absences have no being (and thus no goodness, given the convertibility between the two). It is like ceasing to walk: a mere inactivity. What would be good is willing to turn from evil *and toward God*, and this, so Christians have long claimed, human beings cannot do on our own but only once we omit resistance and God supplies the necessary help, with which we can then cooperate.

This account provides the philosopher with "metaphysical space" to harmonize two commitments that seem initially at odds. Because we can either freely resist or not resist God's help, salvation does significantly depend upon what we freely do. Nevertheless, salvation is not something we can attain without God.

If one accepts this perspective on the human will *and* that suffering can be humbling, spiritually medicinal, and perhaps the best or only available means to facilitate acquiescence of our will in relation to the continual grace that God offers every existing person, then the suffering in the world begins to appear far less surprising. Once we stop actively resisting God, God can infuse grace into the human will without coercion, supplying the means by which the human person can accept and further cooperate with God's grace, thus beginning the process of sanctification, of getting to Heaven.[222] On this account, the process of becoming holy cannot begin without God's initiative, thus preserving that fundamental Christian commitment that we really cannot do anything good without God, since a merely inactive will is not yet a good will; nevertheless, because omitting resistance to God is within our

---

[222] Is this grace of justification consistent with libertarian freedom? Yes, and here's how to see this. God first provides antecedent grace — help that is explanatorily prior to some human action — that itself inclines us toward some good act (say the act of detesting sin and loving God). However, that grace can be freely resisted and is not itself sufficient for the good act. Nevertheless, if we do not resist but reach a point of relevant acquiescence, God then gives concurrent grace (help that is simultaneous with some human action), which is God just directly bringing about the good act in us. The latter is logically sufficient for the act, since it simply consists in God bringing about the act directly (God is the universal cause of everything with positive being, remember); nevertheless, this concurrent act is still free in the libertarian sense since no factor was introduced that was *both* explanatorily prior and logically sufficient for the act, both of which are required to say some act was determined. Concurrent grace is sufficient but not prior. Antecedent grace is prior but not sufficient, and whether we received concurrent grace depends upon whether we resist God's help or not. For a defense, see Grant, *Free Will*, 158–66.

control, the attainment of our ultimate happiness (that is, union with God) *does* significantly depend upon us in some sense.[223]

So, we can will for something, will against something, or simply omit an act of will altogether. God cannot directly cause us — as in unilaterally override our will — to go from willing against God (refusing grace) to willing for God (accepting grace). That would be coercive, which is incompatible with free choice. Instead, what God must do is providentially guide us to a point of acquiescence, where we freely abandon our resistance to God, but a point where we are not yet willing what God wills and actively detesting sin. Once that resistance is dropped, God can then put operative grace in us and cause us to detest sin and love Him. That God inserts a form or configuration into the will that wasn't there previously is not a violation of our freedom so long as that form has not shoved out another form but simply filled a void. An acquiescent will presents such a void. Suffering can lead us to a relevant acquiescence — that is one important reason God permits it: so that He can begin to draw us freely to Himself and keep us from Hell.

Granted, this has all been presented in a rather abstract manner. Nevertheless, there are everyday examples showing how someone can work with an acquiescent will to the benefit of someone else in a noncoercive manner. To borrow one such example from Eleonore Stump, imagine someone who is extremely fearful of needles being in urgent need of an inoculation. Given their intense fear of needles, this person may not be able to actively will that the doctor gives them the inoculation. Nevertheless, they may, through sufficient prodding, reach a point where they acquiesce, where they are no longer shouting, "No, no, no!" The doctor then provides the injection upon the recognition that their resistance has been quelled. If someone asked the doctor if that person

---

[223] True, a will not willing evil is better than a will willing evil, but one thing (or state) can be better than another without yet being good. Comparatives don't demand a positive: For example, someone can be taller than someone else without himself being tall. Nor is acquiescence of will itself a good, since lapsing into inactivity, like ceasing to speak, is not itself an act but just the absence thereof. Such considerations should be enough for Christians to avoid the worry of Pelagianism or semi-Pelagianism. For humans, what is in our control is either to reject grace or to accept it. But this is enough to make sense of the fact that we really have a significant say in our salvation, and yet it is still true that we can do nothing good apart from God (and, of course, this is true in a deep metaphysical sense, insofar as all positive being is the result of God's causality).

asked for the shot, the doctor would probably laugh and say, "Yeah, right!" On the other hand, if someone asked the doctor if they *forced* the shot upon the person, the doctor would definitely, and rightly, deny that charge as well.[224]

To reiterate, the Christian claim is that God allows suffering, including natural suffering, not foremost that we acquire virtues like courage but that we predominantly omit resistance to God and subsequently allow God to fix our disordered will *without breaking or coercing our will*, which is necessary for avoiding eternal separation (Hell) and achieving union with the divine (Heaven).[225]

And What about Natural Evil?

It has been widely acknowledged that free will can make sense of moral evil — that is, the evil that *people* do — for the obvious reason that we can judge falsely about the proper ultimate good, pursue power over the love of other persons, and introduce a horrendous amount of violence and abuse into creation. It is no surprise that many of the worst evils people suffer are because of the sinful choices of others — murder, rape, torture, genocide, and so on. And given that God has reason to allow the significant exercise of free will, we should expect that, generally, God is not going to thwart our acting upon sinful judgments.

---

[224] Stump, *Aquinas*, 395.

[225] What's more, allowing God to fix our will to the point of us willing and loving as God wills and loves helps make sense of how we attain eternal security in Heaven — this, of course, is by God's special help (grace), but this special help is not incompatible with our free will, because it is through our free will that we receive it. If we resist it, such help is not provided. The other point often made for the permanence of one being in Heaven or Hell has to do with the postmortem fixity of the will. In simple terms, the account of postmortem fixity is this: to change our minds, we must either come across new information or consider the information we have from a new perspective. But a traditional understanding of the human person maintains that neither of these conditions attains upon death, when the intellect is separated from the body. In effect, we "angelize" upon death, and the orientation of our will at that point remains thereafter. Nothing "new" or "different" is going to come along to get us to consider things afresh. Although God could perform a "spiritual lobotomy" on everybody who makes the faulty judgment of willing against Him, God — in His perfectly wise governance — orders things toward their end *in accord with their nature*. And our nature is one of a *fallible liberty* — we are free, and we are free to make mistakes, which we do. For a popular level overview, see Pat Flynn, "You Can't Have an All Good God without Hell," at Catholic Answers (December 6, 2022), at www.catholic.com/magazine/online-edition/you-cant-have-an-all-good-god-without-hell.

However, it has also been widely acknowledged that not all evils are the result of free moral failing, at least not at first blush.[226] Natural evils — hurricanes, famine, and so on — must also be accounted for. But again, the Christian claim is that suffering of all kinds can help us recognize that we are in an objectively evil state and so lead us to desire a better one. In order to accept God and allow Him to fix our disordered will, suffering is the means through which we become sufficiently humbled, a necessary prerequisite for eternal union with the divine.

And so, if it's true that suffering may be spiritually beneficial for us, then the allowance of natural evil may also be the best or only available means for facilitating greater spiritual goods, including our highest good (union with God), the only means of bringing us to the requisite point of free acquiescence.

As Stump explains:

> Natural evil — the pain of disease, the intermittent and unpredictable destruction of natural disasters, the decay of old age, the imminence of death — takes away a person's satisfaction with himself. It tends to humble him, show him his frailty, make him reflect on the transience of temporal goods, and turn his affections towards other-worldly things, away from the things of this world. No amount of moral or natural evil, of course, can guarantee that a man will seek God's help. If it could, the willing it produced would not be free. But evil of this sort is the best hope, I think, and maybe the only effective means, for bringing men to such a state.[227]

God would know just the right conditions to put us in — concerning the general distribution of suffering required to best facilitate the treatment of whatever

---

[226] "At first blush" because one should one dismiss the possibility, as has been traditionally held by classical theists, that many if not all natural evils are themselves the result of other prior failed willing entities that are spiritual but play a nevertheless critical role in the unfurling and governing of the cosmos — namely, angels and demons. While I do not believe this account is necessary for the success of the story we are developing here, it does seem plausible given a classical theistic paradigm, along with the assumption that in creating, God might delegate important roles to intellectual agents, which he seems to do with us, so why not with higher spiritual entities?

[227] Stump, "Problem."

spiritual disease we acquire from faulty moral decision making — in order to best get us to freely realize our ultimate end of union with Him.

We know suffering *can* produce heroes and saints *because it has*. Suffering has cracked open hardened hearts, brought people to repentance, including surrender to God, reduced self-centeredness and narcissism, turned otherwise callous people empathetic, and so forth. We have seen this on the grand scale and in our own lives many times over. Personal experience confirms the sanctifying effects of suffering. We can all think of times when suffering seemed pointless, but looking back, we are surprisingly grateful for it. We can see that suffering caused us to relinquish false notions of independence, understand our inherent fragility, release narcissism and egoistical tendencies, seek out community, forgo merely apparent goods for real goods, and often return to God or at least become open (nonresistant) to God's help.

Unfortunately, we also know not everyone who suffers becomes a hero or a saint, at least not in this life. But maybe not even God can control this outcome. If we are genuinely free, perhaps God can visit suffering upon us as the best available means for attaining salvation (the right sort of loving, virtuous character needed to enter into union with God as our ultimate beatitude), but which may ultimately be ineffective, due to our failure to respond in the right way. In such cases, no greater good was actually had, which means that God could have prevented the suffering without the loss of a greater good or permitting some evil equally bad or worse. Nevertheless, we still take God to be justified in His allowing the suffering to occur, assuming it was the best or only means available.

Ultimately, evil is permitted for *multiple* reasons in the Christian story. Some of it is an unavoidable risk of creating fallibly free creatures, which is itself a necessary condition for friendships, love, and communion with God.[228] That risk is moral evil, the evil that people do. The rest of it — natural evil, the evil that people suffer — is because, among other things, it is the best or only available means to save us from spiritual cancer, which, if left unchecked, can cause us to fail to achieve our proper ultimate end.

---

[228] That Hell is a real possibility does not mean anybody actually winds up there. So far, this story is consistent with the idea that God's providential ordering is so magnificent and wise that it actually succeeds in getting every human being freely to Heaven.

Is Some Suffering Arbitrary?

I said "among other things" because there is one final complication that we must consider. Once this complication is considered, a particular light will shine upon the more difficult and mysterious instances of suffering, cases where some justifying reason is not immediately obvious.

To create an orderly world where moral development and meaningful interaction between beings is possible, God has good reason for letting natures take their course of action in the general run, without divine intervention or frequent interference in the significant exercise of free will, even knowing much suffering may result. Such a "general policy" is justified by the overall good it generates or sets the conditions for, especially if that condition is (1) the only one available to avoid a massively chaotic world and (2) the best available rescue plan from spiritual cancer and our self-alienation from God. God could almost certainly intervene in any instance of suffering without subverting the general policy. But even more certainly, God could not intervene in all instances of suffering without subverting the general policy, leading to a totally incoherent creation. Ultimately, God will have to draw the line somewhere concerning suffering and natural interaction, and that line is arbitrary but not unreasonable.[229] This means some instances of suffering will occur that *could* have been prevented without the general policy being subverted; nevertheless, we should take God to be justified in permitting them because some line must be drawn and because the general policy justifies God's refraining. This means we have some general reason to think — in some cases, though certainly not all — that there may be no specific reason for why some instance of suffering occurred to some particular being, even if God exists.

Allow me to explain: some suffering *in particular* might be arbitrary, even if it is not arbitrary that there be suffering *in general*. Said differently, there may be a *general reason* for why there is not a *specific reason* for this or that *particular* person or being's suffering; rather, the reason may be that some suffering

---

[229] By natural interaction I simply mean the interaction between co-existing things as they express their powers and liabilities — lions and gazelles, plate tectonics. Really, just the general goings on of a universe.

must occur even if that reason does not specify who bears it. This point is best illustrated through familiar examples, like the economy.

John Haldane puts it this way:

> Suppose it is logically the case that certain ranges of high benefit economies require patterns of innovation that mean that at any given time a certain percentage of the population is unemployed or otherwise suffering. It will then be true that very good economies involve temporary suffering. Together with certain empirical facts, this will be a sufficient explanation of why some particular individuals suffer as and when they do. Even so, the structural feature does not necessitate that it be THESE individuals who suffer.

As Haldane explains, any victim may rightly point out that the overall good did not demand that he or she *in particular* must suffer; nevertheless, it remains the case that someone needed to suffer to facilitate the overall good. While arrangements might have been such that other people were the ones who suffered, it might be the case that things could *not* have been arranged such that nobody suffered. Said differently, while the specific assignment of suffering might have no particular reason in *some instances*, there may be a *general reason* for the lack of *specific reason*, which is that suffering on the larger scale was logically unavoidable to facilitate the overall good.[230]

[230] Related to Haldane's point, and in response to God avoiding a totally chaotic world and why God would allow the suffering of what seem to be innocents (children, animals, etc.), Van Inwagen offers the following analogy:

Atlantis is sinking. Russel is in charge of the last refugee ship. There are one thousand people left in Atlantis (all men, let us say). They are standing in a queue — position in the queue was determined by a fair lottery and is now unalterable — on the dock, clamoring for admission to his ship. Russel must admit the first n men in the queue ($0 <= n <= 1000$); the value of n has been left entirely to his discretion. If he takes no refugees on board, he and his (crewless, fully automated) ship will certainly reach the mainland safely. Each refugee he admits will reduce the chances of a safe arrival of the ship at the mainland by .1 percent. (Thus, if he takes only the first man in the queue, the two of them will have a 99.9 percent chance of safe arrival; if he takes everyone, the ship will certainly sink; if he leaves behind only the last many in the queue, there is a 99.9 percent chance the ship will sink.) A very distressing moral problem faces Russel, and I do not know what I should do if I were in his place. But the following statements seem to be reasonable:

Let me discuss what I mean by general versus specific reason in this instance. By analogy, God may have a general reason for sending a certain amount of rain to France, namely, to make it a fertile country. But God might not have any more specific reason for sending just the number of raindrops He does. In fact, God probably could have sent one less rain drop and France would still have been fertile. Still, God had to draw the line somewhere, because his general reason of wanting to make France a fertile country demands it, even if there is no more specific reason for why God sent just this many raindrops and not one fewer. The specific number is arbitrary because (quite probably) it had to be. Likewise, God has a general reason for allowing an arena of suffering and natural interaction — that is, to set the best or only available means to bring people to salvation — and similarly God had to draw the line somewhere. Where God drew the line is probably compatible with His general reason not being undermined even if God had drawn the line at one fewer instance of suffering.

For the sake of illustration, let's say for France to be "fertile" it requires a considerably high number of raindrops, and so God sends 14,700,913 raindrops. Let us also say that for God to set an arena that is the best means for getting people to freely love Him — call that "salvation-fertile" — it requires a considerably high amount of suffering, and so God allows 700,992,213 instances of suffering (this number is totally invented, but that's irrelevant for our purposes). However, just like God could have made France fertile with one less raindrop than he actually sent, surely God could have made our world

Whatever morally acceptable course(s) of action for someone in Russel's situation may be, none of the following is morally acceptable: to take none of the refugees; to take only a handful of them; to leave none of them behind; to leave only a handful of them behind.

It follows from this statement that whatever it is that Russel should do, it will have this consequence: He will have to close the hatch in the face of someone whose admission would not significantly decrease the ship's chances of reaching the mainland safely.

If the defense I proposed ... is true ... then God is in precisely an analogous moral situation. Although he may have miraculously saved all manner of fawns from forest fires, if He is to preserve the lawlike regularity of the world there must come a point at which He will refrain from saving a fawn (or whatever) even though performing this act of mercy would not significantly decrease the lawlike regularly of the world. This 'must' is the must of logical necessity, which constrains even an omnipotent being.

a "salvation-fertile" world with one less instance of suffering. Nevertheless, God had to draw the line somewhere, and so that is what God did. God is justified in doing so because of the general reason God has for allowing suffering — that is, for the purposes of salvation. So, God's general reason for facilitating salvation, along with issues concerning the possibility that there just is no minimum effective amount of suffering that would "do the job," gives reason to not expect a specific reason for every instance of suffering that befalls a person. Some assignments may, in fact, be arbitrary; God could have prevented them without the loss of some greater overall good, but God could not have prevented them all without the loss of some greater overall good. God had to draw the line somewhere, and so He did.[231]

If some suffering befalls a person and it was, in fact, arbitrary, then God, being all just, will have to make things right. If said suffering terminated a person's earthly life, God will have to make things right, not in this life, but in a life hereafter. This gives good reason to suppose that if God exists, then the afterlife follows, in some form or other, not as some theoretical add-on but as an inevitable consequence that we come to understand by gaining the right picture of God. There may be other reasons for supposing human beings survive bodily death, such as the empirical evidence surrounding near-death experiences (something which is not surprising if God exists, but which would be extremely surprising, once one examines carefully the details of near-death experiences, if naturalism is true).

So, an *arena* of certain conditions conducive to our facilitating the right sort of God-and-person-loving character is what God creates. God may leave some or many things up to chance concerning what goes on in this arena, so long as some threshold isn't crossed, at which point God would intervene — and for all we know, God may have done so many times.[232] Nevertheless, perhaps this

---

[231] If someone pushes against this (I think obvious) point about there being cases where no minimum number is available for some effect to be achieved — that is, cases where arbitrariness is demanded — then the theist has every right to say, "Okay, then it must be the case that the number of instances of suffering in this world is just the minimum required for God's overall purpose."

[232] Notice this. Even if we admit there is some threshold of awfulness God would not allow the world to cross into, this is compatible with the world coming right up against that threshold, not just once, but who knows how many times. This means

world, even with all its horrendous evils, is the best God can do while respecting the natures of His created beings and allowing them to be genuinely in charge of their own destinies and shaping the world they inhabit. Having co-creators, even limited ones like us, seems like a genuinely good thing, and almost certainly better to have than not. Perhaps it is the case that God could have not run things according to this general policy and alleviated much, if not all, suffering, but then God would have created a massively chaotic world (think back to C. S. Lewis's point). Taking all of this into consideration, this world, with all its sufferings, along with the characters we form and loving experiences we have, *plus* a hope in an afterlife, is better than some ultimately incoherent hedonic paradise. I certainly think so.

All this so far has been treating the evidential problem of evil by drawing out consequences of the classical theistic paradigm, which renders the suffering and evil of our experience quite unsurprising. Whether suffering and evil are even less surprising if naturalism is true is something we will consider presently.

Response to Metaphysical Problem of Evil

It is one thing to ask whether we should expect God to allow suffering and evil; it is another to ask how God, who is goodness itself, actually *creates* evil. How can God, as perfectly good, positively bring about something that is strictly His contrary, even if that something sets the conditions for greater goods? In other words, how can good actually *produce* evil?

In response, I will emphasize a traditional line of thought that maintains that evil is not really a "thing" in the sense that we can lay our hands on it, like an oven or a cat. Instead, evil always involves some *deficiency* or *lack of being* where it is otherwise due. If that's right, then evil is not something produced; only things are produced. Evil, if anything, is just the result of something left out of creation.

In other words, evil is a *privation*, an unactualized potency that is proper to the perfection of something. Some examples could be blindness, the failure

though God would not have allowed that amount of awfulness plus 1, he would allow that amount of awfulness, which is presumably almost indistinguishable from the awfulness God would not allow. This should invite humility on our part.

to consider the moral rule (itself a lack) in some judgment which thereafter leads to sinful action, or a dog missing one of its legs. What the privation theory of evil holds is that, in the last analysis, evil is just the absence of some due good.[233] There is a hole in being where being otherwise ought to be.

If the privation theory of evil (PTE, hereafter) is correct, then God is off the hook so far as creating evil is concerned, because evil is not a "thing" created.[234] This does not get God off the hook completely, however. While we might not have to account for what created a "hole" in being in the first place, given that a hole has no positive being to be created, we are still warranted in asking why God created beings with holes.

Importantly, the PTE does not claim that evil is completely illusory or anything like that, even if it does mean to say that evil doesn't *exist* in the proper sense like hamsters do. While evil may concern a particular absence, absences of what is otherwise due is just as felt as presence.

Consider what Herbert McCabe has to say about this:

> If I have a hole in my sock, the hole is not anything at all, it is just an absence of wool or cotton or whatever, but it is a perfectly real hole in my sock. It would be absurd to say that holes in socks are unreal and illusory just because the hole isn't made of anything and is purely an absence. Nothing in the wrong place can be just as real and just as important as something in the wrong place. If you inadvertently drive your car over a cliff, you will have nothing to worry about; it is precisely the nothing that you will have to worry about.[235]

---

[233] Of course, the absence that we deem evil may be brought about by an excess in certain respects. "A washing machine may be bad and defective for very positive reasons, like being full of glue, and a man may be bad and defective for very positive reasons, like being full of hatred or lust. But what makes us call this bad is that just as the positive glue stops the washing machine washing, so the positive hated or lust stops the man being human enough." Brian Davies, *The McCabe Reader* (London: T&T Clark, 2016), 92.

[234] Defending the entire privation theory of evil would require a book of its own. Fortunately, two excellent book length defenses have been issued in recent years. See: Oderberg, *Metaphysics* and David Alexander, *Goodness, Good, and Evil* (London: Bloomsbury Academic, 2014).

[235] Davies, *McCabe*, 91.

In summary, the PTE says that evil is a logical (but not real) being.[236] Evil, then, is a due good that is missing. It has no positive aspect of its own but is parasitic upon the good. Stock examples like blindness or holes in socks help illustrate the point, since these absences obviously have effects on the world. But importantly, evil isn't *just* an absence. Instead, evil is an absence *where there should be presence*. A rock lacking sight, for example, isn't an evil, because sight isn't in the nature of a rock. But a person lacking sight once their eyes are mature enough *is* an evil, because something is missing that ought to be there, given that sight is part of what constitutes human nature.

There are many arguments for the PTE, including common sense, but another immediate consideration in its favor is that goodness and badness are special kinds of adjectives.[237] Notice that calling something good is not like calling something red, where the property remains the same across the subjects to which we attribute it. If, for example, you know what it is like for a hammer to be red, then you will know what it is like for a knife to be red. However, if you know what it is like for a hammer to be good (or bad), you will not know from that alone what it is like for a knife to be good (or bad). This is because what we mean by goodness and badness *varies* depending on the nouns they modify. Badness may mean, in the case of a hammer, being too sharp, but that is not what we mean by the badness of a knife, like being too dull. What makes something good in one case may be precisely what makes something else bad in another. To understand what a good thing is, be it a good boxer or a good apple or a good human, we must know something about its nature, and whether an individual instance "lives up to our expectations" for the sort of thing it is and whether it reaches a certain standard. Good boxers land more punches, bad boxers take more punches. But landing or taking more punches has no bearing on whether an apple is good or bad. Being crisp and juicy, however, might.

The point to understand here is that goodness and badness are *objectively relative to natures*, and so our understanding of "good" adjusts according to the subject under consideration. Hence why our understanding of a good apple

---

[236] A logical being is simply a being of reason, which is to say it has objective being in the intellect.

[237] For those interested in the technical distinction, see P. T. Geach, "Good and Evil," *Analysis* 17, no. 2 (1956), 33–42.

provides no understanding of a good boxer. The goodness of an apple depends on features *relevant* to what it means to be an apple, whereas the goodness of a boxer depends on having features relevant to what it means to be a boxer.

Our judgment of something being a bad apple or a bad human is a recognition of those types of things *lacking* certain *relevant features* that we believe they ought to have given what they are: a lack of juiciness for an apple, sharpness for a knife, virtue for a human, and so on. All this should sound familiar given what was covered in the section on making sense of objective morality. The PTE follows from our understanding that goodness and badness adjust in meaning depending on what goodness and badness are attributed to, particularly insofar as we judge something bad when that something *lacks* what is expected of it. We don't call a knife (under ordinary circumstances) bad when it exhibits sharpness; only when it lacks sharpness. We don't call a human being bad when he is full of virtue, but only when he lacks virtue. Badness tracks a lack.

Notice as well that there must always be *some* level of goodness or success before we can judge *any* level of badness or failure. That is, we cannot call an apple bad unless there are already enough good features relevant to being an apple in place to evaluate what the missing features are (crispness, juiciness, and so on). Goodness, in other words, is more fundamental than badness. There is an asymmetry. This asymmetry has an important implication concerning the nature of fundamental reality: if fundamental reality is absolute being or pure actuality, as we have argued, suffering no privations or unactualized intrinsic potencies, then fundamental reality is good all the way through. It could not be bad.[238]

So, accepting the PTE gets God off the hook concerning the charge of why God "created" evil. Evil is not something created. It is something missing in creation.

Naturalism Does Not Predict Suffering and Evil

The major threads of the Thomistic response to the problem of evil are as follows: God creates out of love to unite creation to Himself. He does this by

---

[238] This consequence would make the proposal of the "evil god" challenge, where some have thought that fundamental reality could be a wicked but still supremely powerful entity, impossible.

THE BEST ARGUMENT FOR GOD

creating beings like us, beings that are fallible, free, and which could (and in fact, have) turn from God and embrace sin. God cannot unilaterally override our will to make us love Him if we are resistant — love requires the uniting of two wills.

So, probably the best thing God can do to help human persons avoid the worst outcome (eternal separation with God, which is to say Hell) is to place us in an arena where suffering occurs, so as to bring us to a point of acquiescence or surrender, thus allowing God to begin helping us without coercion. Within this arena, other logically dependent goods become possible as well — courage, forgiveness, empathy, the Incarnation and atonement, and so on. Recall that while positive characteristics may develop through evil and suffering, that is not the main reason for God to permit evil. Bad things are always a real possibility in creating free creatures, and love demands creatures be free. Love is behind everything.

However, for relationships among people and God to be possible — for real love to be possible — the world must not be massively chaotic. God must allow natures to run their course, to interact in various ways, and while God could intervene occasionally, interventions must be the exception, not the rule. God must draw the line somewhere, including how much suffering to allow and to whom that suffering befalls. It is always the case that God could have prevented one more instance of suffering without subverting His general policy, but again, God must draw the line somewhere, and He is justified in doing so. Arbitrariness and the avoidance of a massively chaotic world make sense of mysterious suffering, the suffering that befalls people who may not seem able to benefit from it. God is justified in allowing this to occur because such a general policy is the best or only available means to facilitate the overall good of the human community concerning salvation, and what is more, God will settle all accounts justly in the hereafter.

Now we must ask: is our experience of suffering and evil less surprising if naturalism is true or if God exists? This question matters because, when evaluating whether some data is evidence for this hypothesis or that one, it is the ratio that ultimately matters. Even if the suffering of our experience were surprising given the existence of God, if it is more surprising given the nonexistence of God, then suffering is still evidential weight *for* God.

In one sense, suffering is obviously less surprising if God exists, since suffering depends upon the emergence of conscious entities — as we have already argued, naturalism struggles significantly to explain such entities. If consciousness cannot be explained within the framework of naturalism, then naturalism is knocked out of the explanatory race before suffering can be considered, since the latter requires the former. The same, of course, could be said concerning other features of reality upon which suffering is contingent — for instance, that anything exists at all.

Here, a brief illustration should impress the point: suppose there is an obstacle course with just two competitors. Suppose you know one competitor has already won the race but don't know which one. And suppose you know the following facts about each competitor: from a distance, Competitor 1 (call him Bob) appears relatively thin. From a distance (Competitor 2) call him Jim, appears to have a muscular frame.

From these facts, you make an initial guess as to which competitor won, knowing the final obstacle in the race demanded lifting a heavy boulder and hurling it upon a relatively high pedestal. You probably think Jim, the second, more muscular, competitor, emerged victorious, if only because it seems the first would seriously struggle to lift and hurl significant weight, if he's able to do so at all.

This is how things appear so far. You probably assume that Jim won because he appears better suited to lift the boulder and toss it upon a height. You thereby assign a credence, whatever that is: 75 percent? 90 percent? Certainly more than 50 percent.

I suggest that this analogy maps the initial assessment concerning the data of evil, broadly construed to include all suffering or negative states of affairs and the worldview hypothesis of classical theism and metaphysical naturalism. If we look at the wide range of evil and suffering in our world, it seems that the latter hypothesis might be better suited to explain it. If fundamental reality has no intention for us, no specific aims in mind, then perhaps it is unsurprising that suffering and evil occur. Indifference runs amok. If, however, fundamental reality is pure perfection (which a classical theist like St. Thomas Aquinas takes to include only and all purely positive aspects of being like power, knowledge, and love), then perhaps it is surprising that suffering and evil occur.

Evil is like the boulder. Theism is like Bob. Naturalism is like Jim. Upon superficial inspection, it *might* seem like Jim is more likely to lift the boulder. Upon superficial inspection, it might seem like naturalism is more likely to lead to a world of suffering and evil.

However, suppose we learn more, not just about the competitors, but about the obstacle course race. Suppose upon paying closer attention or by having a closer look or by running experiments or whatever, we come to discover the following additional facts:

First, about the obstacle course race. Prior to the lifting and hurling of the boulder, the competitors must swim and run long distances, complete a long jump, crawl under wire, carry a sandbag uphill, traverse monkey bars, and crawl through a series of mud pits.

Next, we learn the following additional facts about each of the competitors. Bob, while looking slim, is really into weight training. From a distance, he appears scrawny, but up close (and with his shirt off), he is ripped like Bruce Lee. Jim... well... Jim is paralyzed from the waist down, for one thing. Jim is quite overweight, for another. Jim has another issue as well: he's blind.

We can now ask: upon more substantial analysis, which competitor do we believe won the obstacle course race? Our assessment has almost certainly changed. We now think Bob won, and not just probably won, but definitely won. Why? Because even if we believe Bob would struggle to lift and hurl the boulder, we know there is no possible way Jim could have even reached the boulder to attempt it. That means Jim is strictly disqualified — probability zero. Which is sticky.

If there are metaphysical demonstrations for the existence of God, then naturalism is dropped to a zero probability. And if there is no outright contradiction between God and evil, it must be the case that God and evil are compatible, given that both are demonstrably actual. In other words, regardless of how slim the chances are of God creating or permitting a world of suffering and evil (like the one that we experience), it must be that God created or permitted such a world given that (a) such a world is the one we find ourselves in and (b) naturalism could not possibly have done so, being intractably stuck at prior obstacles.

Similar considerations could be said about consciousness or mental content. The *problem* of evil is contingent upon there being conscious beings, but if only theism can account for consciousness — that is, if consciousness reduces naturalism to a zero probability — then we have the same consideration as before. Evidential considerations of evil are thereafter irrelevant.

The point is that there may be one or more explanatory obstacles that the naturalist must but cannot traverse if they want to have any shot at explaining suffering. If naturalism, even before getting to the explanatory target of suffering, is eliminated as a live explanatory option, then suffering is less surprising if theism is true. Naturalism never gets the chance to lead to a world where suffering is possible in the first place. Theism wins.

However — and this is important — if consciousness *does not* reduce naturalism to probability zero, then the game is still on. It then becomes entirely fair for the naturalist to argue that suffering is more likely under naturalism. And suffering itself is not automatically evidence for theism just because certain things that suffering is contingent upon — say, conscious beings — are more likely to occur if theism is true. Why? Because we must take each data point individually, consider its evidential weight, then move it into our background knowledge. Then, onto the other data point, and so on. We cannot pull some previously counted datapoint back out just because some later datapoint logically depends upon it. That logical dependence doesn't give us the right to "double count." In which case, unless consciousness or contingency or something else really does drive naturalism to probability zero, the theist must confront the evidential impact *of suffering itself* — they cannot bundle suffering with other facts that favor theism and think that itself turns *suffering* in favor of theism, when it is really the other facts doing the work, facts that have already been counted.

But for the Sake of Argument: Epiphenomena, Psychophysical Harmony, and Evolution

To make for some interesting argumentation, let's grant that naturalism has not yet been knocked out of the explanatory game; we'll even grant (graciously) that naturalism has arrived at the explanatory target of suffering just as swiftly and easily as theism. Now, from everything argued previously, none of this should be seen as actually the case, but it is *merely* for the sake of argument because even when allowing for the possibility of naturalism to account for everything upon which suffering depends, it can still be maintained that the suffering of our experience is less surprising if theism is true than naturalism. In such a case, the suffering of our experience is evidence for the existence of God. Naturalism does not predict the suffering of our experience unless naturalism is highly specified and complicated to the point of being inherently unbelievable. Naturalism, in its basic form, is just the claim that fundamental reality is run by a principle of indifference: that is, there is no benevolent or malicious entity at the bottom of reality — material, immaterial, or otherwise. There are just natural entities and natural causes.

As a theory, this basic form of naturalism tells us virtually nothing concerning the emergence of conscious beings or, if those beings emerge, whether they will suffer in the general ways that we do.

Of course, to even have the chance to explain suffering, a theory must first clear logically prior explanatory hurdles. Suffering is a problem for conscious beings; if some worldview cannot make sense of the emergence of conscious beings, that worldview is eliminated from the explanatory race prior to the consideration of suffering; this is the case for naturalism, as we have already argued. There really are no good naturalistic philosophies of mind — not of mindless naturalism, anyway, where whatever else mind is, it is a late and local phenomenon. (And, of course, the emergence of "exotic" forms of naturalism, like panpsychism, is itself an admission of this point.) For naturalists, the physical is supposed to precede and be the cause of the mental. Theism predicts that there will be a hard problem of consciousness for naturalists, and there is indeed a hard problem of consciousness for naturalism, an irresolvable one.

But let us set that aside. Because even if one concedes that naturalism can explain and render possible the emergence of conscious beings, it does not predict such conscious beings will suffer as we do. Of course, the initial thought is that the suffering of our experience makes a lot of sense under naturalism, since pain causes us to avoid things and pleasure pursue things and that evolution will select accordingly, *and* since the world is indifferent many people will suffer wantonly and horribly. But all of this is built upon an assumption not only foreign to naturalist philosophy of mind but downright contrary to a naturalistic philosophy of mind, where it is the physical states doing the work, not the mental states. There is, after all, a reason that many naturalists are epiphenomenalists (recall that an epiphenomena is something that is caused but itself causes nothing, which is just what many naturalists take mental phenomena to be): the felt aspect of suffering makes no relevant causal difference to whether we avoid the bite of a mosquito, as it would happen apart from the qualitative dimension of experience. Pain — as in what we *feel* when pinched, stabbed, bitten — is hardly something we would expect if naturalism is true, because it is difficult, if not impossible, to discern just what role the qualitative dimension plays, given source physicalism.

To reiterate, it is not the felt aspect of pain that causes avoidance, according to epiphenomenalism; rather it is the mindless physical interactions underneath. The qualitative dimension has nothing to do with it. It is only by assuming a relation of mind–body/mental–physical that is at home with *theism*, and definitely not at home with naturalism, that one can to some extent generate expectations of why suffering of the sort we experience may not be entirely surprising if naturalism is true. But, of course, nobody should grant such assumptions to naturalism — that would be silly. Worldview comparison must be systematic, and the positions one adopts in one area (say, epiphenomenalism in philosophy of mind) must connect with positions one adopts in another area (explanation of suffering). The immediate point is that naturalism can only to some extent generate expectations of suffering if naturalism disconnects itself from prior commitments and unfairly assumes commitments of which only theism can make sense. At this point everybody should call foul.

This conclusion can be discovered only once the underlying commitments, mechanics, and consequences of a naturalistic perspective are exposed, particularly in how naturalists believe mind and matter (or mental and bodily phenomena) relate. This is in relation to the point that naturalism makes no specific predictions concerning the distribution of suffering. In fact, if naturalism were true, we should expect that suffering would either not occur at all or that the distribution of suffering would be far less or far worse than it is. We would not expect the suffering to be just the sort apparently suited for salvation and soul building; that is, we would not expect the range of suffering to be just the sort that it is, where people become saints.

Why think this? One reason links back to considerations in philosophy of mind, including all the ways physical states could have correlated with mental states if naturalism were true. If, for example, naturalism is true, then there is really no good reason for why our physical states should correlate with our mental states in ways that seem particularly fitting or harmonious, including experiences of suffering. For example, we know by our own experience that bad or damaging physical events are often associated with feeling pain. From a theistic perspective, this obvious harmony between the mental and physical states makes sense. God would ensure such harmony exists, especially if the mental can play a role in determining the physical. From a naturalistic perspective, however, this is quite a surprising, if not outright amazing, correlation.

Naturalism, for all we know, could have had it that we (because of the underlying physical interactions that are ultimately in control of ourselves and the world) always pursued painful states of affairs and avoided pleasurable ones, simply because, by happenstance, painful states were associated with certain functions useful for survival instead of pleasurable ones. Given that it is only the physical states that make the difference, there is no reason the physical functions useful for survival must associate with good feelings or vice versa. Recall that, for the naturalist, the physical precedes and determines the mental, such that it is quite possible that our lives could have been an absolute cosmic farce, that we are stuck pursuing painful states because they are associated with underlying physical functions that are conducive for survival. There is no reason to think this could not have been the case, if naturalism were true. In fact, if naturalism were true, there is good reason to think the ways things could have gone would have been anything *but* harmonious.

Even if matters were not radically disharmonious, where pain and pleasure were somehow perfectly inverted, there could have just been no suffering at all. For example, all physical states could just be accompanied by a rather neutral "buzzing" sensation. In this example, suffering, including morally relevant suffering, would not occur. And between all these options — between all the ways suffering could have been distributed — naturalism seems no more likely to arrive at one or the other.

What I am describing is a phenomenon that philosophers Brian Cutter and Dustin Crummett have called psychophysical harmony:

Roughly, psychophysical harmony consists in the fact that phenomenal states are correlated with physical states and with one another
in strikingly fortunate ways. For example, phenomenal states are
correlated with behavior and functioning that is justified or ratio-
nalized by those very phenomenal states (e.g., pain is correlated
with avoidance behavior), and phenomenal states are correlated
with verbal reports and judgments that are made true by those very
phenomenal states (e.g., we say, "I'm in such-and-such phenomenal
state," and sure enough, we are).[239]

This is a subtle point, so let me expand. Some phenomenal experiences, like pain,
seem intrinsically unpleasant, and in virtue of their felt aspect provide reasons for
avoidance. As it happens, pain is almost always mapped onto physical states that
play the role of tracking bodily damage, escaping harm, and such like — that is,
the pain role. The felt aspect of pain gives reason for avoidance and, surprisingly
(for naturalism, that is), pain maps onto physical states that cause us to avoid or
eliminate certain stimuli. I say surprisingly because, if naturalism is true, there is
no good reason to expect that the phenomenal or felt experience of pain should
harmonize with the physical or functional role associated therewith, particularly
given the primary and causally exclusive role afforded to the physical (again, recall
the points about epiphenomenalism from the previous section on mind).[240]

I suggest that the only reason the idea of psychophysical disharmony seems
ridiculous is because people are thinking in terms of a mind/matter relation that
is itself not consistent with naturalism, where the mental realm is something
late, local, and causally inert. Again, once we peer under the hood of a naturalistic worldview, certain inevitable or highly probable consequences (such as epiphenomenalism) become clear and have dramatic consequences for how to
evaluate other evidence (in our case, the distribution of suffering).

[239] For a full development of the argument from psychophysical harmony to theism:
Brian Cutter and Dustin Crummett, "Psychophysical Harmony: A New Argument
for Theism," *Oxford Studies in Philosophy of Religion* (forthcoming). Importantly, as
well, Cutter and Crummett show that neither physicalism nor functionalist accounts
of mind offer a plausible way out. Such considerations could equally be applied to
how I am using psycho-physical harmony in this context for those wondering if this
case ignores broader perspectives within philosophy of mind.

[240] Neither physicalism nor functionalism offer an escape to this, as Cutter and Crummett argue.

Evolution doesn't provide an answer either, for it would have made no survival difference if the felt aspects were inverted or otherwise disharmonious, as the felt aspects play no causal role from the naturalistic perspective. All that matters is the underlying physical interactions that get our joints into the right place at the right time; whatever felt aspects they're associated with are quite irrelevant. Evolution selects for physical outcomes, not felt experiences. The naturalist is out of any plausible explanatory option here; he is forced to leave it as a matter of rather amazing brute fact that there is so much psychophysical harmony.

God would be interested, of course, in having the felt aspects of experience map on appropriately to certain physical states or situations that should be avoided, like guilt attaching to our body after harming another innocent person, or varying degrees of pain attaching to states of physical damage. From the theistic perspective, this harmony is unsurprising, especially given that the felt aspects of experience can play morally relevant roles for beings that possess purposeful agency (in other words, beings that aren't just driven by underlying physics, as would be the case with naturalism), beings who can respond rationally to feelings, desires, emotions, and intuitions. Psychophysical harmony is valuable in such respects; God would understand this and seek to create a world with such harmony.[241]

THE FINER POINTS

This argument is presented within a dualist framework merely for ease of exposition; the same point could be made for reductionist theories of mind. Even if mental events were only physical events of certain types (for reasons considered in the section on consciousness), we should reject such a thesis as definitely false—it is extremely fortuitous that we have just the mental events that we do; events which map precisely to the physical events underlying

---

[241] Philosopher Jim Madden points out that even the qualitative experience of pain in general, much less its fortuitous correspondence with underlying physical states which seem appropriate, is better expected if God exists, if only because the *experiencing* of pain seems functionally unnecessary or redundant, if naturalism is true, whereas the experience of pain seems to provide important roles for moral character formation, which favors theism. James D. Madden, "The Evolution of Suffering, Epiphenomenalism, and the Phenomena of Life: Evidential Problems for Naturalists," *Religions* 12, no. 9 (2021), 687.

behavior experiences would appear to normatively justify. Surely, it could have been the case that a physical event (some function, say, that entails the felt aspect of pain) was not actually the function that relates the input of getting pricked by a pin with the output of wincing and retracting one's arm. Instead, that function could have been identical instead with a pleasurable feeling or some neutral buzzing sensation.

This is a subtle but important point, so let me further draw it out. Functionalism (though again, one could swap in whatever reductive theory of mind they want) is the thesis that felt aspects are identical to certain functions. Functionalism, of the reductive type, is almost certainly false for the reasons outlined in the section concerning consciousness, among others.[242] But setting that aside, the point for our present purposes is this: functionalism is a general thesis; it is not saying that the felt aspect of pain, for example, is identical to *this* or *that* function in particular, just that pain is identical to *some* function or other. However, possibly (epistemically, if not metaphysically), without gathering data from the actual world, pain could have been identical to this function, that function, or some other function. It is crucial that we don't put information about the actual relation of the felt aspect of pain and physical events into our background knowledge. Of course, saying that all felt aspects are identical to all the functions they appear to be associated with in the actual world would make the probability of that thesis very high, since it (obviously) entails the data, but this comes at the disqualifying cost of so complicating one's theory as to make it virtually unbelievable. Why? Because if we're trying to see which theory better predicts the distribution of suffering experienced, we can't build the specific distribution of suffering (the data to be explained) into our theory. If that's allowed, the theist can play the same game, simply by making his theory something like: God exists *and God wills a universe with exactly the distribution of suffering that we experience.* But then the theist will also have a far more complex (highly specified) theory that by itself is intrinsically very unlikely. The point is one can always make their theory more specific so that it perfectly predicts something, but in doing so render their theory increasingly unlikely, often to the point of making it entirely implausible.

---

[242] For example, John Searl's famous Chinese room argument against functionalist and computation theories of mind. See David Cole, "The Chinese Room Argument," in *The Stanford Encyclopedia of Philosophy* (Summer 2023 Edition), ed. Edward N. Zalta and Uri Nodelman (forthcoming).

To further appreciate this point, we can draw a parallel with fine-tuning and the necessity objection sometimes posed by atheists. The necessity objection states that whatever the initial setup of our physical universe is, including constant values, it is necessary; it just *had* to be this way. However, saying "whatever the constant values happen to be, they are necessary" does not predict or make probable that we will have *the constant values that we do*—namely, values that fall within an exceedingly narrow life-permitting range. For that, one must say instead that the constant values are necessary *and they fall within this very narrow range*, which obviously predicts fine-tuning because it entails fine-tuning. However, this specification comes with the cost of an enormous increase in theoretical complexity, making one's theory intrinsically very unlikely. Here, one is simply "borrowing from the priors" (that is, the probability of one's theory considered apart from the evidence) to increase the likelihood or predictive success of one's theory, and this is definitely not a winning trade.

To make this abstract point concrete, just imagine any extremely convoluted conspiracy theory that would, if true, entail or make highly probable some data we're trying to explain, but is so convoluted and intrinsically improbable in and of itself (considered apart from the evidence) that no one should, nor possibly could, believe it. Once this point is appreciated one should be able to see why the necessity objection to fine-tuning carries no force and why certain reductive theories of mind would do nothing to help naturalism better predict the suffering of our experience than dualistic theories.

Ultimately, I am not interested in running an argument to God from psychophysical harmony, though other philosophers have done so.[243] Rather, I am using the point about psychophysical harmony to show that even if naturalism can account for the emergence of conscious beings, it is not at all clear that those conscious beings are more likely to experience the range of suffering that we observe — a range that, amazingly, seems quite conducive of spiritual goods.

Suffering on naturalism could have been far more, far less, or none at all, even if conscious beings were to emerge. What's more, the *simplest* correlations between felt experiential aspects and underlying physical states would be disharmonious.

[243] Again, see Cutter and Crummett, "Psychophysical."

But obviously such disharmonious experiences would be of zero moral significance, and such an existence would not be the sort of world of saint- or soul-building. That sort of world, no doubt, *would* be evidence for naturalism, but that is precisely not the sort of world we inhabit.

The Broad Range of Suffering and Whether There Actually *Is* Gratuitous Evil

Theism predicts a specific range of suffering and evil that is conducive to human beings becoming saints and finding union with God. Naturalism makes no specific prediction along these lines, as should be obvious given that naturalism is entirely indifferent to suffering (universal indifference being the key feature of naturalism) and that the ways suffering could have gone given naturalism are enormously varied. One will perhaps notice a parallel here between what is being said concerning the range of evil and the argument from physical fine-tuning presented earlier. In fact, that is just how philosopher Trent Dougherty says we should think about it, offering the following "toy model" of the ways suffering could have been distributed:

1. Too frequent and too mild

2. Too frequent and right intensity

3. Too frequent and too intense

4. Right frequency and too mild

5. Right frequency and right intensity

6. Right frequency and too intense

7. Too infrequent and too mild

8. Too infrequent and right intensity

9. Too infrequent and too intense[244]

Quite plausibly, there is something of a "sweet spot" or "sweet range" for how suffering must be distributed if the intended outcome is to be one of spiritual significance — that is, for the sorts of outcomes predicted by the theistic picture concerning the ultimate good of each individual human person.

[244] Dougherty, *Animal Pain*, 121.

As Dougherty points out, even if there is no one "best possible world," there may nevertheless be, and almost certainly is, a best *kind* of world, and that would be a world where the highest values are attainable — namely, the highest virtues, the most preeminent of which is love, which itself is often expressed or exemplified through courage, compassion, empathy, forgiveness, generosity, kindness, trustworthiness, responsibility, mercy, helpfulness, gratitude, and so on.[245]

Because virtues are habits, and because habits are stable dispositions, they take time to acquire (at least for beings like us), and thus demand a particular environment, particularly one suited for the development of the respective virtue. In relation to suffering, this means a world where suffering is neither too intense to overwhelm our psyche most of the time nor too infrequent as to provide too little opportunity to acquire such stable dispositions. Hence, if God is going to create a world, it must be of the type where suffering is of both the right frequency and right intensity; and that, it seems, is just the sort of world we live in, evidenced by the fact that all the above virtues are, in fact, manifested.

Given that naturalism is effectively a "roll of the dice," if these different ranges are possible (and for all we know, they certainly seem possible, especially considering the point about psychophysical harmony or disharmony) and if we land in the range predicted by theism, the problem of suffering can itself provide strong evidentiary confirmation of theism upon substantial analysis.

Things could have been radically different concerning our experiences of suffering if naturalism were true — far more, far less, or none. Theism, however, does predict a particular range of suffering that is conducive for spiritual goods, which by all appearances is just the range of suffering we seem to occupy.

The atheist, of course, will protest this point: *but there are gratuitous evils!* That is, there are evils which are never defeated and cannot be morally justified, even by God. But are there? "Gratuitous" as a label appears to beg the question. At worst, we have *mysterious* evils, evils where we do not clearly or immediately

---

[245] Ibid, 120.

see how they could be defeated or justified.[246] But not seeing the reason for something is not the same as seeing that there is no reason — *not seeing* is not *seeing not*. At worst, we have instances where people have not *appeared* to defeat evil *in this life*. But classical theism, as we have argued, entails an afterlife. The insistence upon gratuitous evils is mere dogmatic foot-stomping and not something that could be definitively or even probably known.[247]

Any truly gratuitous evils are therefore not clear from experience. What *is* clear from experience is this: enormous numbers of people *have* defeated evil in this life, even horrendous evil, and were formed into heroes and saints and lovers of God because of it. That we live in a world with suffering and evil such that saints arise is just what we would expect if God exists, but not at all what we would expect if God does not exist. If we favor what is clear over what is unclear, then there is nothing in our experience that the human soul cannot overcome in principle, even in this life.[248]

Finally, recall that the theist actually does have reason to think that there may be instances of suffering or evil where there is no particular reason for it but rather a general reason, which makes the idea of there being mysterious evils not so mysterious after all. We would expect mysterious evils if God exists, though we would not expect all evils to be mysterious.

---

[246] Theists may further claim that mysterious evils themselves are predicted by theism — at least, that is, the mysterious aspect. After all, God sees the whole, we see only very small parts. Thus, that God may have God-sized reasons for how things play out that do not make sense to us at the time (because of connections only God can see through all creation), is not surprising. So, while we would expect (I contend) to see some reasons for some evils, if classical theism is true, we would not expect to see all reasons for all evils, at least not in this life.

[247] Dougherty argues for this entailment in *The Problem of Animal Pain*.

[248] Theologically, one might think that if we require God's grace for moral perfection then this is incompatible with my hypothesis. However, as Eleonore Stump has proposed, grace and human freedom are not at odds, and a landscape of suffering can be just the sort of thing required to bring the human will to a point of acquiescence such that God can thereby bring a person to justification in accord with their nature. After which, suffering can play a further role, as we cooperate with God's grace, in furthering the virtues, binding us in moral community, attaining further humility, etc. Such theodicy is compatible with the hypothesis above, and, in fact, the hypothesis might give reason to adopt a theodicy like Stump's (including her understanding of libertarian human freedom and God's causality, grace, etc.) than another rival.

For Christians, there is scriptural warrant for this, as Christ Himself teaches that misfortunes that befall people are not necessarily due to their being sinners. It's not the case that all evil or suffering is specific punishment for some individual sin. Recall Luke 13:4: "Or those eighteen on whom the tower in Siloam fell and killed them: do you think that they were worse offenders than all the others who lived in Jerusalem?"

Of course, this is not to suggest *all* instances of suffering are arbitrarily distributed. As Christians (or just classical theists), we should think that is not the case. Many instances of suffering, as I think is experientially obvious, are intended to benefit that individual, for reasons examined earlier. But much suffering may not be like that, which goes some way, if not all the way, toward explaining the suffering of innocents.

This is a consideration worth reiterating: the general conditions for the overall good might demand a certain arbitrariness concerning particular assignments of suffering. But that, of course, does not mean that suffering is *entirely* arbitrary or unjustified, since there is a global purpose that justifies such conditions. Nevertheless, I believe this account requires additional clarification.

The first point is that some overall justifying good (whatever that may be) actually *is* achieved through the permission of such suffering, and we have, of course, already indicated what those goods probably are — namely, the possibility of loving relationship with God, the manifestation of the highest values, and so forth. Moreover, the overall good brought about from God permitting the amount of suffering and evil He does permit may be cumulative in nature, consisting of many, often logically dependent, goods. It doesn't have to be just one thing.

The second clarification — and this is quite important — is that God settles accounts justly for those who suffered horrendous evils *and* for those who committed horrendous evils. Quite obviously, if someone suffered horrendously *and arbitrarily*, their suffering cannot be justified *just* because the general conditions of suffering were conducive *for others*. That particular individual must be provided for as well, if not in this life, then in the next. For this reason, an afterlife is required, which indicates the necessity of Last Judgment, Heaven, Hell, and Purgatory — or something like it. It is here that Christianity has unique resources to overcome the problem of *apparently* gratuitous evils, since Christianity entails the Four Last Things.

If one believes that God exists but thinks His existence is incompatible with gratuitous evil, then one has reason to look in the direction of Christianity, with its economy of salvation, for hope and resolution. In other words, the Christian story of the afterlife is something predicted by classical theism. Overall, however, my claim is not just that the suffering of our experience is equally expected if God exists as if God did not exist. No, suffering is *better* expected if God exists than if He does not.

Upon careful analysis, we seem to fall just within the range of suffering predicted by classical theism, even if the boundaries are a bit fuzzy. Naturalism does not predict this range particularly, even if it is compatible with it. For this reason, the suffering of our experience is evidence for God's existence and not against God's existence.[249]

Summary

Much was covered in this chapter, so let's recap. We began by detailing the various problems of evil and how they present a *prima facie* challenge to theistic belief. Our response to this challenge required a patient unpacking of the classical theistic worldview, including the import of certain Christian teachings, to show that the suffering of our experience is not surprising if God exists, given the ultimate hierarchy of goods concerning human existence, and the complicated interplay of God's governance and human freedom. While our approach may have been different in detail than other theodicies (theodicies being stories for why God allows suffering and evil), I nevertheless have argued that the traditional theodicies are essentially correct: a respect for the natures of the things God creates, particularly fallible human freedom, the avoidance of a massively chaotic world, and the facilitation of greater goods, most especially freely willed union with God.

---

[249] Point of technical clarification: I am not saying the conditions necessary for suffering to occur are what make suffering more expected on theism. If so, that would possibly run afoul of the error of "double counting" and would not show that suffering *itself* is evidence for theism. Rather, I am saying the range and distribution of suffering we actually find in this world is better anticipated by theism than naturalism and thus confirmatory of theism over naturalism.

We then took a slight detour to discuss the metaphysical problem of evil, arguing, again in line with the tradition, that evil is simply a due good gone missing — a hole in being that one otherwise expects to be filled, such as blindness where sight should be. This is relevant since, if correct, evil is not something positively created by God, only permitted.

Our final move was to suggest that the suffering of our experience is far less expected, far more surprising, if God does *not* exist. Surprising as this claim may at first appear, we saw that it is quite unavoidable once one looks closer at the various details of a naturalistic worldview, particularly concerning the relation between mind and matter, or mental and bodily phenomena. Given the most plausible naturalistic accounts within philosophy of mind, all of them render almost completely hopeless the project of explaining the distribution and harmony between our felt experiences and the underlying physical states, which includes all experiences of suffering. The basic claim is that if naturalism were true, the distribution of experienced suffering could have been far less, far more, or none at all (and could have been quite disharmonious to boot), and that we really seem to experience a distribution of suffering that makes available the highest spiritual goods. Once we hashed out the story of why some suffering is mysterious, it became clear that the suffering we experience is far more likely if God exists than if God does not exist. For this reason, the problem of evil is effectively reversed. Often seen as evidence against God, a closer more careful look reveals that even evil is evidence for the existence of God.

Conclusion: Where Does This Leave Us?

HOW STRONG ARE THE arguments in this book? Where do these questions lead us? Is naturalism irrational? Is any religion true?

Many questions remain. Here are some brief responses to each. To the first, I can only speak personally: I would not have presented any of the arguments in this book if I did not believe there was significant force behind them. Of course, my confidence is stronger in some than others — most decisive, I think, are cosmological arguments. But one can see the project as cumulative, with perhaps the most substantial force coming from each of the arguments working in harmony with one another, converging upon a particularly powerful ultimate explanation of things. Taken together, I believe the arguments of this book are decisively strong. Nevertheless, no argument is compelling in the sense that somebody *must* accept it: there is always a way out, always some premise that can be denied. The important question in such instances is this: what are the costs of escape?

What strikes me about theistic reasoning is that the cost of escape is the acceptance of simple absurdity, a radically unintelligible reality. In fact, the fundamental claim of this book is that if one believes the world actually is intelligible — that things make sense, and ultimate explanation can be had — then God exists. Nothing short of that absolutely simple, purely actual first principle (God) can account for the experiences we have.

Does this mean that naturalism is irrational? This is difficult to answer. Some of the philosophers I've cited think so. Then again, other philosophers have said the same about belief in God. But part of this debate depends on what is meant by "being rational." Some philosophers think rationality has to do with making the best use of what you've got, evidentially and experientially. If that's right, then people can probably be rational believing in a considerable number of things, given the situations they may find themselves in and the evidence available to them, even if I personally find their beliefs to be self-evidently false. So maybe it is not irrational to believe naturalism even if naturalism is false. But maybe that is too quick: after all, if belief in God is properly basic, then being a naturalist might involve some epistemic perversity, since there is no really good reason to disbelieve in that basic belief — in that sense, it might be sort of like believing one is a brain in a vat. If this is correct, then perhaps naturalism is irrational. For now, I am happy to leave that question open. After all, I don't think much is ultimately gained by attempting to label certain positions as rational or irrational; rather we should just do the best we can to determine what's true. I have done my best to accomplish that task in this book.

Is any religion true? I think so, yes. But to answer that question would extend far beyond the scope of this project. I made a few minor indications toward the end of the previous section that, I think, should raise interest in the claims of Christianity. There are many others, but again, it is not the aim of this book to argue for Christianity, only classical theism (which, of course, has a longstanding history of being affirmed within Christianity). So here I just make a modest suggestion: if God exists, then some religion compatible with classical theism *might* be true. So, why not look into it? Especially if that religion makes claims of significant importance. Christianity does this, but then again, so do Islam, Judaism, and Hinduism. If I had more pages available to me, I would usher in considerations which I believe favor, quite significantly, Catholicism — not just the accurate predictions that the Catholic Church has made concerning the existence and nature of God, but of course her sheer endurance and the many scientifically scrutinized miracle accounts that serve as strong confirmatory signs. But my space has run out.

My final remark is this: God exists. That is good news no matter what. Reason illumines a foundation to reality that is utterly perfect — as perfect as anything could be. Yet experience tells us many things in this world are imperfect; as we know, suffering abounds. Nevertheless, as our investigation revealed, these two notions are not in conflict. This should give us hope. Why? Because while reason may not be able to tell us each particular reason for the trials and sufferings of this world, reason *can* tell us that there must be supremely good reason for their occurrence. (Revelation, of course, goes further.) Perhaps some people will find that of little personal or pastoral use. I, however, find comfort in this fact — great comfort and great joy.

Appendix: More Objections (and More Responses)

Given the extensive nature of debate concerning the existence of God, not every objection can be considered in a single volume. The best anyone can do is gather what they feel are the best complaints and offer the best response. That I accomplished this, I hope, was reflected in the development of the various arguments covered in this book. Here, I should like to give attention to a few remaining objections, some of them more interesting and forceful than others. I say this because some of these objections are quite poor, but because they are also quite popular, I felt their inclusion was merited. Others are geared more toward the professional philosopher, and thus presented in a less colloquial manner and with less handholding (they also assume greater background knowledge of certain issues).

To clarify, many of these objections relate to the cosmological argument (call these "undermining objections") by attempting to show that the conclusion has not been established, either by attacking premises in the cosmological argument or attempting to undermine the legitimacy of metaphysics as a whole. Others relate to the conclusion (call these "rebutting objections"), arguing that the conclusion is incoherent or entails consequences that are incompatible with our prior commitments. Because the objections are numerous, my response to each must be relatively brief. Still, I will issue enough to diffuse the complaint. Finally, while I will have to introduce additional material (distinctions, metaphysical assumptions) to address certain objections, I will do my best to keep the amount of new material to a minimum.

OBJECTION. God cannot be purely actual because God must have actualized a potency to create this world. This means divine freedom is incompatible with God being purely actual.

RESPONSE. Even if this objection were successful, it would not undercut the cosmological argument for God, but only present a problem for a particular theological commitment. Regardless, the objection fails because it trades on an ambiguity between passive and active potency. Cosmological arguments conclude that God has no *intrinsic passive* potency, meaning God cannot be brought to some higher mode of intrinsic perfection, because God is purely actual subsistent existence itself. However, God has unlimited *active* potency, which refers to God's power to create. This potency is unlimited because God is omnipotent to bring into existence realities *extrinsic to Himself*. Thus, when God creates, all change is extrinsic to Him. Furthermore, it is a fallacy of accident to assume that in producing some effect, the cause itself must be intrinsically different than it would have been otherwise. While this is evident with the things of common experience, we know this is not the case with God, given what the cosmological argument entails. It is essential for a cause to produce an effect in order to be a cause, but it is not essential that the cause changes when doing so (essentially or intrinsically). This means that God could have created this world, some other world, or no world at all, and remained essentially, intrinsically the same. Thus, God is not changed in creating, nor is He forced to create by anything intrinsic or extrinsic to His nature. Once the distinctions above have been made and the fallacy of accident noted, the objection is deflated.

OBJECTION. What caused God?

RESPONSE. To ask what caused God assumes that everything must have a cause, which is not only not an assumption of the cosmological argument but an assumption the cosmological argument rejects. Remember, the first stage of the argument established that not everything could be a caused reality, otherwise nothing would exist. Rather, cosmological arguments — not just this one, but as a general class — proceed from more modest causal principles: anything composed (physically or metaphysically) has a cause, or anything in which there is a real distinction between its essence and existence has a cause, or anything which moves from actuality to potentiality has a cause, or anything which is contingent has a cause, and so on.[250] Thus, God is the ultimate explanation of certain categories that demand an extrinsic cause *precisely because* God, as an absolutely simple, purely actual reality whose essence just is His existence, is not another member within those categories. With this understanding in mind, it then becomes nonsensical to ask who (or what) caused God; such a question is in effect asking, "What caused that which not only does not need a cause but could not in principle have one?" For whatever exists necessarily (in virtue of what it is) and eternally not only does not, but could not, have been caused.

OBJECTION. Perhaps caused realities could have the attribute of existential inertia — that is, they could continue existing once brought into existence unless they encounter some destructive factor — in which case, wouldn't the possibility of existential inertia undercut the need to invoke God as the ultimate, sustaining cause of things?

Mortimer Adler in his book *How to Think About God* explains existential inertia as follows:

> I hold that something akin to the principle of inertia applies in the realm of existence, and leads us to reject the mediaeval view that the continuing existence of individual things needs the continuing action of an efficient cause.[251]

Adler continues in saying that, "The continuing existence of a contingent individual thing is, in part, negatively explained by the absence or inefficacy of counteracting causes. It is also, in part, positively explained by the principle of inertia, extended from the physics of motion to the metaphysics of being."

RESPONSE. Two points. First, the objection of existential inertia is irrelevant to the initial cosmological argument in this book because our argument leaves open the hypothetical scenario that once existence is imparted to something

---

[250] Again, see Feser, *Five Proofs* for examples of how these other cosmological arguments are run.
[251] Adler, *How to Think About God*, 124.

that might continue existing inertially. Either way, we would still need to get back to that which just is pure existence itself to explain how any caused reality (with or without the attribute of existential inertia) came to possess existence in the first place if it does not possess existence inherently.

However, once the cosmological argument is understood *in conjunction* with the metaphysical consequences that follow, we can see how the idea of anything besides God having existential inertia is impossible. Remember, it was argued that there could be only one uncaused reality and that whatever else reality is, it must be a pure act of existence, existing through itself, from which we can infer that everything else that exists is caused in its existence and therefore does not exist in virtue of itself but by some extrinsic factor. The creature is *by nature* not something that exists in virtue of some principle intrinsic to itself (otherwise it would exist of necessity, and just be God). This is equivalent to saying its existence must be imparted to it from something beyond itself. Further, since there can be only one uncaused reality whose essence is its existence, no caused reality can ever convert into an uncaused reality, meaning all caused realities must always receive existence from something extrinsic to themselves. That is, they could never impart existence to themselves (for they would need to already exist to do that, in which case they wouldn't need to impart existence to themselves!) or hold onto existence apart from some underlying sustaining cause continually donating existence to it. Even if they had the attribute of existential inertia, we must also remember that all attributes depend upon substances in which those attributes inhere, in which case existential inertia is useless because it can affect nothing unless the substance is already caused by something extrinsic to itself for however long it exists. Said differently, the attribute depends on the substance and the substance depends on the attribute — a vicious explanatory circle.

OBJECTION. Many of the ancient and medieval philosophers you referenced, such as Aquinas, were wrong about much of science. For example, Aquinas thought the heavenly spheres were eternal, which science has since disproved. Why should we take his arguments for God seriously?

RESPONSE. First, a general point: Just because a person is wrong about something does not mean that he is wrong about everything or even most things. This is just as true now as it would be for thinkers in the past.

What's more, because metaphysics is not treating the same subject matter as science, we should not dismiss what the metaphysician says even if it can be demonstrated that he is wrong scientifically, just as a mathematician can be wrong about scientific facts without us doubting his mathematical reasoning — or vice versa.

Another example: just because Aristotle was off on his biology does not mean Aristotle was off on moral truths in the *Nicomachean Ethics*. Again, these are different subject matters and must be treated independently. Maybe Aristotle was wrong ethically, but that would not follow from his being wrong biologically.

One must be careful not to fall into "chronological condescension" and assume that a position is correct just because it is modern, or that since we know things now that thinkers in the past were mistaken about, *we* cannot now be wrong about something that previous thinkers knew better.

Finally, metaphysics and science (particularly physics) are independent fields of inquiry, with differing methods for hunting truth. Metaphysics often starts from the most general and undeniable aspects of experience, such as contingency, change, and so on, and then deduces some metaphysical principle to make sense of such experiences before using that principle to reach some further conclusion. Nothing in that procedure in any way depends upon the findings of modern science, and so the scientific facts can change without injury to the underlying metaphysics. What's more, modern science must presuppose such basic metaphysical starting points as the act–potency and essence–existence distinctions and such like.

OBJECTION. Why should we take metaphysics seriously at all, or privilege it against science?

RESPONSE. Science presupposes metaphysics. Also, one cannot avoid doing metaphysics but only avoid doing metaphysics well. Thus, it is not a question of *if* somebody is going to do metaphysics, but *how*.

Furthermore, the objection wreaks of scientism, which is the position that only science can produce knowledge (epistemological scientism) and the only real entities are those detectable by the scientific method (ontological scientism).

To reiterate a point made in the introduction: The problem with scientism is that it is either trivial or self-defeating. It is trivial inasmuch as it expands the definition of science to include virtually all subject matters, including philosophy, in which case metaphysics is fair game, or it is self-defeating inasmuch as scientism says our fields of inquiry must be restricted to the hypothetico-deductive method (empirical observation, hypothesis testing, etc.), since the very statement "our fields of inquiry must be restricted to the hypothetico-deductive method" is not something that could ever be established or verified through the hypothetico-deductive method. In short, scientism fails to meet the standard it sets for everything else.

The more reasonable position is to see that science in all its different modes is a powerful and accomplished tool for investigating reality and advancing technology, but nevertheless is restricted in what it can tell us and is not the only tool for understanding. Just because something doesn't count as science (and it is, of course, a notoriously vexed issue of what does) doesn't mean that something isn't a useful subject matter or doesn't contribute meaningfully to human knowledge or experience.

OBJECTION. Why assume that the universe needs a cause and isn't just everlasting/eternal?

RESPONSE. Objections of this sort often mistake the cosmological argument for other, often more popular apologetic arguments, such as the Kalam argument, which argues from the beginning of the universe to a transcendent cause of the universe. While such an objection may be relevant to the Kalam argument, it is irrelevant to the general class of cosmological arguments, and here's why.

First, something does not require a beginning in time to have a cause, even if all things which begin to exist in time do have a cause. It is a logical fallacy to move from "that which begins to exist has a cause" to "because this thing didn't begin to exist, it doesn't have a cause."

This fallacy is known as denying the antecedent and has the following form:

If *P*, then *Q*.

Therefore, if not *P*, then not *Q*.

To see why this reasoning is fallacious, assume the following is true: *If a tornado were hitting this building, this building would be shaking.* Notice that if a tornado weren't hitting this building, we couldn't justifiably infer that the building isn't shaking. Why is that? Simply because effects (in this case shaking) can have multiple causes. Absent a tornado, other things — such as an earthquake — could cause a building to shake. So, just because we deny the antecedent (that a tornado isn't hitting the house) we cannot infer the contradictory of the consequent (that the house isn't shaking).

Same with the causal inference above. Just because something doesn't (temporally) begin to exist, we can't infer that that something doesn't have a cause. For all we know, something may very well have been caused in an everlasting or eternal manner. This is not hard to imagine, after all. For example: even if a bowling ball had been resting on a mattress forever into the past, we can still say that even though there was no beginning to the suppression of the mattress, the suppression of the mattress has *always been caused* by the weight of the bowling ball. Alternatively, imagine an eternally existing sun and moon in which the moon has been eternally illuminated by the sun. That there was no temporal beginning to this event does not permit us to conclude that the event of illumination is uncaused. In fact, it obviously is caused: the sun is causing the illumination of the moon, even if that event never had a beginning in time.

My point holds for existent things. Even if some things have always existed into the past, it does not follow that they haven't been caused. In fact, if such things don't exist in virtue of what they are, then they must have been caused for however long they've existed, even if everlastingly. Such is why the cosmological argument in no way depends upon the universe (or any finite thing) having a temporal beginning, and so the objection is irrelevant.

OBJECTION. Can God create a stone too heavy for Him to lift?

RESPONSE. Various paradoxes have been issued to challenge the coherence of an omnipotent (or omniscient) being. While addressing all these paradoxes would extend beyond what is possible in a single volume, a few general statements can be made to alleviate tension. First, omnipotence is the claim is that God can bring about all possibilities of being — not that God can create nonsense (contradictions). So, whether God can create a stone too heavy for God to lift depends on whether such a creation is possible, and many have suggested an unliftable stone is contradictory just like a square circle is. If that is the case, then the short answer is, "No, God cannot create a stone so heavy that He cannot lift it." That, of course, is no defect on God's part, because God only has all possible powers (of production), not impossible powers. Impossible powers would brandish incoherence in God — the very thing we're arguing against — and signal privation rather than perfection.

OBJECTION. If God exists, there would be no suffering in the world, or at least not as much suffering as there is.

RESPONSE. This objection is treated at length in Chapter 5. But here, a brief summary response may nevertheless be helpful.

The claim is often made that a perfect God is incompatible with the occurrence of evil and suffering. There are a few ways to defuse this objection, but the simplest is this. There is no contradiction in saying that a perfect God has sufficient reason to allow suffering and evil into the world, even if we cannot see what those reasons are. Because no contradiction can be drawn, we must favor the conclusion of a metaphysical argument for God and infer from our demonstration that God *must* have reasons for allowing suffering and evil in virtue of His goodness. Admittedly, this may not be an emotionally satisfying response — especially since suffering and evil impact each of us, often tremendously — but logically/strictly speaking, the problem of evil fails to disprove the existence of God.

By way of suggestion, perhaps God has reasons for valuing the liberty of His creatures even if that increases or guarantees the risk of moral and natural evil. And perhaps God values their fallible liberty because that is in accord with their nature as finite (and therefore naturally imperfect) beings, and a wise God, we might say, governs things according to their mode of existence. Perhaps God can bring about greater goods should finite free creatures fail morally in some respect — compassion, empathy, mercy, forgiveness, the Incarnation and atonement, and so on. The point is not to demonstrate that these are *the* reasons that God allows suffering, but only to demonstrate that there are possible reasons. It is impossible to prove that God couldn't have sufficient reasons, simply because we aren't God and don't know God's mind — only God does.

It should also be noted that if there is an afterlife where every sorrow can be wiped away and where rational beings can participate in the infinite life of God, this could also provide a remedy to the problem of suffering. It would not be enough for the skeptic to just assume that the afterlife either isn't possible or couldn't compensate for the sufferings of this world, for that would be to beg the question and assume what they are trying to prove.

The point? We should privilege what is clear over what is unclear. The cosmological argument and its conclusions are clear: God exists and is perfectly good. It is not clear, but rather speculative and bordering on divine psychologizing, to suggest that God could not have sufficient reason for allowing a world in which evil and suffering are permitted. Given that this is the case, we must follow reason before emotion and assume that the perfectly good existing God does, in fact, have reason — and good reason, at that — for allowing suffering into the created order, even if we cannot see what those reasons are.

OBJECTION. Hasn't quantum mechanics shown that things can occur without a cause?

RESPONSE. That is a common misunderstanding. Rather, certain interpretations of quantum mechanics only claim that effects may be produced indeterministically, given, of course (this is important), the actualized laws of quantum mechanics. And since no causal notion in the preceding argument commits us to deterministic causation, the objection from quantum mechanics is irrelevant.

More generally, physicist Nigel Cundy has this to say regarding the relationship between metaphysical principles of causality (like the sort we've deployed) in relation to specific, scientific descriptions of the physical universe:

> The advantage of Aristotle's concept of act and potency is that it is sufficiently general [so] that it can cope with different physical systems. It does not care whether the process of actualisation is driven by classical forces or the exchange of virtual particles. Instead, it tells us that there must be a background against which these processes takes place.
>
> So when the sceptic summarises by writing, "But Thomists disagree with that, because they see metaphysics as being separate and distinct from physical reality," he is mistaken. Rather, Thomists see metaphysics as underlying physical reality. Metaphysics gives a general framework for what possible universes could be; physics fills in the specific details for this particular universe. Metaphysics tells us that physical theory must assume some sort of background of different states; physics starts by expressing this in a mathematical way.[252]

Further, theists and those who accept that human beings have genuine free will should be heartened by the discovery of indeterministic causation within physical systems, for it provides further independent evidence that an *explanans* (the thing which explains, i.e., the cause) does not entail the *explanandum* (the thing in need of being explained, i.e., the effect), a point that will become relevant in responding to the next objection. It also shows that just because something is not (completely) determined, neither is it (entirely) random (we can get probabilities, after all), opening a third category.

OBJECTION. If God is the cause of everything, then God must cause human action. Therefore, human action cannot be free.

RESPONSE. Even if this objection were successful, it would not refute the argument for God. It would only make the case for theological determinism. That said, the objection is not successful. Here's why.

---

[252] Nigel Cundy, "Is Thomism really refuted by modern science?" The Quantum Thomist (blog), November 22, 2018, at http://www.quantum-thomist.co.uk/my-cgi/blog.cgi?first=44&last=44.

Recall that if something is possible, then it cannot be excluded by (or incompatible with) its necessary conditions for existence. But a free being is possible. Therefore, a free being cannot be excluded by (or incompatible with) God. (Notice: why assume that something being caused is incompatible with that something being free, or that all causation is deterministic?) For example, because someone can only freely eat a hamburger if God causes them to do so, then God's causing them to do so cannot be incompatible with their freely eating a hamburger.

This defense rests predominantly on whether a free being is possible. The simplest support of this premise is just that it is obviously true — that we, qua rational animals, are intuitively free in the libertarian sense, but also that God is free, because God, as pure actuality, cannot be compelled to act by anything beyond Himself.

But we can approach this from another angle. Perhaps the best way to support libertarian freedom is to begin with an explanation of determinism (its negation) and see that the conditions for determinism do not hold under the conception of God developed via the argument above. That is, an absolutely simple and unchanging God.

Argument: If determinism is true, then the effect cannot be different without the prior cause(s) being different. But if divine simplicity is true, then the prior cause(s) are not different, even if the effect is different. Therefore, on divine simplicity, determinism isn't true (or at least not necessarily true).

Justification: Determinism means that there are logically sufficient conditions for some effect E (which are also prior to E) such that if those logically sufficient conditions obtain then E follows inevitably. But we can also infer the opposite: that if E does not obtain then those logically sufficient prior conditions did not obtain (or were at least different in some respect).

For example: (Events A, B, C, D + Laws of Nature) = Your Action E. But if *not* Your Action E, then *not* (Events A, B, C, D + Laws of Nature). Alternatively: God's Internal Decree A = Your Action E. But if *not* Your Action E, then *not* God's Internal Decree A (God is different). However, given an absolutely simple and unchanging God, your action could have been different (or not at all) while God has been absolutely the same. The first example is false because atheistic physicalism is false; and atheistic physicalism is false since God is the ultimate source of everything else in existence. The second example is false because God does not change internally or essentially to create — the change is entirely extrinsic to God (we will cover this in a further objection below), which means God is not *both* prior to and logically sufficient for any created effect. So, since what would be necessary for determinism to be true does not obtain, we can safeguard libertarian free will via divine simplicity.

Simply put, an absolutely simple and unchanging God not only breaks the conditions of determinism but may be the only way of doing so. Thus, if we believe libertarian freedom is a real feature of the world, this may be one further reason to hold to the classical theistic conception of God.

Of course, there is mystery as to how God causes free beings, but we must remember that God is not a cause like finite, limited beings. God is radically transcendent, qualitatively infinite, and unrestricted, which means we must keep in mind the principle of analogy — that God is like us in some ways but infinitely higher.

Finally, the objection against human freedom via God's causality also seems to rest on the assumption that an *explanans* (the thing explaining) must entail the *explanandum* (the thing to be explained), which we have independent reasons to reject, as seen in the chapter on cosmological reasoning and the Principle of Sufficient Reason.

OBJECTION. If God is simple and necessary and unchanging, then God cannot be free to create.

RESPONSE. This objection — like the first objection but pressed from different divine attributes — also rests on overlooking important distinctions — namely that God maintains only a rational relation to creatures, whereas creatures maintain a real relation to God. To see an example of this, consider knowledge itself compared to the object known. If we know that a certain tree exists, our knowledge depends on (has a real relation to) that tree being there. But the tree as an object of being known is made no different by our knowing it; hence, it bears only a rational relation, and not a real relation, to us.[253]

---

[253] For a more detailed exposition of this position, see W. Matthews Grant, "Aquinas, Divine Simplicity, and Divine Freedom," *American Catholic Philosophical Quarterly* 77 (2003), 129–44.

A similar relation is true of God and God's creation. Creatures bear a real relation to God, in virtue of being created by Him. But the effects of God's act are extrinsic to God and do not change God essentially or accidentally, meaning God doesn't have to change (or actualize a passive potency) to create or not create. They do not change God essentially because God would then depend on the effects of His actions, which is absurd, given that God is purely actual and subsistent existence itself. They do not change God accidentally because God has no accidents, since accidents are a form of composition, and God is absolutely simple.[254] All of this is to say that God is not logically sufficient for God's creation, so the charge of modal collapse (everything becoming a necessary reality, because God exists necessarily) is avoided, and the best way to explain a contingent effect produced by a necessary reality is by reference to the necessary reality's (that is, God's) free decision to create and power to do so (active potency).

OBJECTION. If God is simple, necessary, and unchanging, then God cannot gain new knowledge. But He obviously does when He creates. (Additionally, if God does not create, then doesn't God have a piece of contingent knowledge, such as the belief that "there are no horses," and wouldn't that conflict with divine simplicity and immutability?)

RESPONSE. Occasionally, there is a worry that God cannot be immutable because of contingent predication, such as God's knowledge of (or power to create) certain effects, which could have been otherwise. Wouldn't God change if God had created differently, or not at all?

But this objection rests on several fallacies, concerning both the nature of God and what (at least in this case) constitutes knowledge.

Taking them in reverse order, certain aspects of knowledge are often true in virtue of some extrinsic factor. "I am funny to Peter" is a proposition whose truth rests (at least partly) in something extrinsic to me — namely, Peter. And

---

[254] Pruss has argued that if libertarian free will is possible, then we have a potentially analogous model for how an immutable God which could have created otherwise (or not at all) remains absolutely simple and unchanging regardless of what He creates. Alexander Pruss, "On Three Problems of Divine Simplicity," Alexander Pruss (blog), at alexanderpruss.com/papers/On3ProblemsOfDivineSimplicity.html.

so, the truth value of that proposition can change without me changing essentially, for instance by Peter not laughing. Additionally, "I am alone in my room" is made true not just because of my being in my room but because of my relation to something that is *not* there: namely, another person.

Similarly, God can "see" the possibility of a cat on a mat, along with the possibility of God being the cause of a cat on a mat, or not, but what makes God have knowledge *of there being a cat on a mat* is just God's causing there *to be a cat on a mat*; and that, again, is extrinsic to God, and could be or not be without any intrinsic change in God. Same with God knowing Himself as cause of such a creature—what makes that contingent predication true is grounded extrinsically to God, and so constitutes no real change in God. Thus, contingent predication is no threat to divine simplicity once the proper distinctions are drawn.

To the second point, we must remember that God is eternal. As Bernard Lonergan reminds us that, "though the extrinsic denominator is temporal, the contingent predication concerning God can be eternal. For an eternal act is timeless; in it all instants are one and the same instant; and so what is true at any instant is true at every instant. Hence, if at any instant it is true that God understands, affirms, wills the existence of Alexander's horse Bucephalus, then the metaphysical conditions of the truth are the existence of God and the existence of Bucephalus; moreover, though Bucephalus exists only for a short period, still God eternally understands, affirms, and wills Bucephalus to exist for that short period."[255]

Finally, if God did not create, this would not change God intrinsically, because it is in virtue of God's perfect self-knowledge that God knows nothing else could exist distinct from Him *unless* He causes it. That knowledge is invariant and remains the same even if God creates; thus, there is no intrinsic accident in God that would be different had God created. If God then "decides," "chooses," "intends," or "wills" to create some effect E then God "deciding," "choosing," "intending," "willing," and "knowing" E *just is* E's existing with its causal dependence relation on God—all of which, again, is extrinsic and can change without any real change in an absolutely simple, immutable

<hr>

[255] Lonergan, *Insight*, 684–85.

God. This connects with the fact that God's action is 1) basic and immediate (i.e., doesn't run through any intermediate channels) and 2) that the action of the agent is *in the patient*.

How to make sense of this? There are various models, but to give one example, philosopher Alexander Pruss suggests a "theater of perception" model with respect to God's knowing and believing, which he describes this way:

> On the Cartesian model of perception, our sense impressions are on display in something we might call the theater of the mind. We should not suppose, however, that the mind in observing the sense impressions always forms further representations of these sense impressions, for if it always did that, we would have a vicious regress of impressions. Rather, the mind, without having further representations of sense impressions caused in it, directly perceives the sense impressions that are on the mental theater's stage. The sense impressions are explanatorily prior to our perceivings in a constitutive rather than causal way: our act of perceiving saltiness is constituted by an activity of the mind plus a salty sense impression.[256]

Pruss says he is skeptical that the theater of the mind represents an accurate account of our perception but argues it is nevertheless plausible as a model of God's knowledge and that the events of the world do not cause impressions or thoughts in God (and so we avoid needing not posit some intrinsic passive potency) but are only explanatorily prior to divine beliefs in a constitutive way: in other words, God's beliefs about contingent events are constituted by the events they are about together with the activity of God's mind. Pruss's proposal connects to our concern about intrinsic accidents in God in the following way, when he says:

> necessarily, God believes only and all true propositions. Thus, the property of God believing that p, where p is a contingent truth, is a property that God will lack in worlds where p is not true, and hence it is an accidental property. Thus, it cannot be an intrinsic property. Hence, the classical theist has to say that God's beliefs about contingent truths are partially constituted by items external to God. And

---

[256] Pruss, *Infinity, Causation, and Paradox.*

it is particularly elegant to take the facts that the beliefs are about as those items, which then gives us the above model."[257]

In short, God does not change intrinsically whether He creates or does not create, which not only leaves Him free to create but preserves the contingency of creation.

[257] Ibid.

Author Bio

PAT FLYNN IS A writer, philosopher, podcaster, and speaker who lives in Wisconsin with his wife, five children, and a Saint Bernard. He hosts *Philosophy for the People* and *The Pat Flynn Show*. His website is ChroniclesOfStrength.com.

Sophia Institute

SOPHIA INSTITUTE IS A nonprofit institution that seeks to nurture the spiritual, moral, and cultural life of souls and to spread the gospel of Christ in conformity with the authentic teachings of the Roman Catholic Church.

Sophia Institute Press fulfills this mission by offering translations, reprints, and new publications that afford readers a rich source of the enduring wisdom of mankind.

Sophia Institute also operates the popular online resource CatholicExchange.com. *Catholic Exchange* provides world news from a Catholic perspective as well as daily devotionals and articles that will help readers to grow in holiness and live a life consistent with the teachings of the Church.

In 2013, Sophia Institute launched Sophia Institute for Teachers to renew and rebuild Catholic culture through service to Catholic education. With the goal of nurturing the spiritual, moral, and cultural life of souls, and an abiding respect for the role and work of teachers, we strive to provide materials and programs that are at once enlightening to the mind and ennobling to the heart; faithful and complete, as well as useful and practical.

Sophia Institute gratefully recognizes the Solidarity Association for preserving and encouraging the growth of our apostolate over the course of many years. Without their generous and timely support, this book would not be in your hands.

www.SophiaInstitute.com
www.CatholicExchange.com
www.SophiaInstituteforTeachers.org

Sophia Institute Press is a registered trademark of Sophia Institute.
Sophia Institute is a tax-exempt institution as defined by the
Internal Revenue Code, Section 501(c)(3). Tax ID 22-2548708.